Political Scandals

The Consequences of Temporary Gratification

La Trice M. Washington

University Press of America,® Inc.
Lanham • Boulder • New York • Toronto • Plymouth, UK

Library of Congress Control Number: 2014934559
ISBN: 978-0-7618-6363-2 (cloth : alk. paper)—ISBN: 978-0-7618-6364-9 (electronic)

This book is dedicated to God and my family.

To El Shaddai, God Almighty. I am grateful for the way in which you have helped me overcome obstacles place in my path. I can do nothing without you.

To my mother, Shirley W. Jordan. Thanks for teaching me how to believe in myself. You have taught me "hard work pays off."

To my father, Howard Jordan, Sr., thank you for choosing to be my daddy. Although we are biologically connected, the bond we have shared since I was a little girl is undeniable. I appreciate you more than you will ever know.

To my brothers, Lamonn and Howard Jr., growing up together was an adventure! Your love, support, encouragement and camaraderie have thoroughly enriched my life.

Contents

Acknowledgments

The author wishes to thank several people for their contribution to the development of this project. I would like to thank Otterbein University for approving and funding my sabbatical leave project during the fall semester 2013. I would also like to thank Patti Welch for proofreading this manuscript. I want to express my gratitude to Marissa Schnaith and Eshakhia Sobukwe. Finally, I want to extend words of appreciation to my pastor, Dr. Charles E. Booth. Your preaching encouraged and challenged me during a trying season in my life.

Chapter One

Introduction

As a professor of political science, family, friends, colleagues and citizens often approach me in about politics and current events. Many of them inquire and have a special interest in political scandals and government corruption. People seem to be intrigued with trying to understand why elected and appointed political officials appear to be willing to risk everything for temporary gratification or momentary pleasure. Individuals who engage in dialogue with me about political scandals often ask questions that attempt to understand why political personalities and government employees make such horrid decisions. Some ask, "Why did he or she do that?" Others want to know "why did he or she risk their position?" Ultimately, citizens are curious about why a person would jeopardize his or her family life and marriage for temporary pleasure. Many public officials appear to have lost sight of the reality and the effect their behavior will have on their lives and the lives of others once their unethical behavior is publically exposed. Frequently I find myself raising questions like "Did he or she care what the people or electorate would think about his/her decision-making skills or judgment?," Did the official really think no one would find out about his/her inappropriate behavior?," Did he or she really think they would get away with behaving that way?." These are simply a few questions raised when concerned citizens endeavor to understand the scandalous actions public officials engage in behind closed doors that eventually are exposed by the media. These questions point to a much broader issue with which society, employers, educators, pastors, ministers, communities and families must contend with on a regular basis. Scandalous or reckless behavior raises questions about the state of ethics in a community or society.

During the 2011-2012 academic year, I was asked to teach a Freshman Year Seminar that would address issues faculty and administrators think students should learn during their first year at Otterbein University. The course I developed was entitled "Political Scandals: Risking It All For Temporary Gratification." The course was designed to introduce students to a variety of subjects including student scheduling to ensure on-time graduation, ethical and moral expectations of students, and the significance of a liberal arts education. The course was taught during J-Term, a term situated between the Fall Semester and Spring Semester. The beautiful thing about teaching the course was the fact the students voluntarily opted to take the intensive course during winter break. Despite the enormous amount of preparation and work new courses require, I was excited to teach the course because students were interested in taking the course.

The subject matter covered addressed both sex-based and non sex-based political scandals from 2000 through 2011. The political scandals were used as a teaching tool to introduce students to the academic, ethical, and moral expectations the university set forth in the University Student Handbook. Political scandals were used alongside university policies to highlight acceptable and unacceptable behavior and attitudes that are detrimental to student success. At the end of the course, students were challenged to develop a "Blueprint for Collegiate Success." Students were required to construct a plan by which they would be able to complete their academic requirements for their majors while adhering to university standards as it relates to ethically and morally acceptable behavior. Students were also required to develop a tentative academic schedule for their major, minor programs and extracurricular activities. Students enrolled in the course were also required to evaluate and assess their ethical or moral fortitude.

During class sessions, political scandals and the consequences associated with unethical and inappropriate behavior were discussed. Following the discussion of the shortcomings, weaknesses, frailties and proclivities of government officials revealed through sex based and non-sex based scandals, students were given the opportunity to identify ethical and moral issues they contend with on a regular basis that threaten to derail their future. Students were guided in self-reflection exercises in an effort to encourage critical self-assessment of their ethical and moral fiber. Among some of the most identified issues students acknowledged struggling with included: procrastination, lying, willfully breaking dorm rules (i.e., smoking marijuana or drinking in the dorms) and other behaviors prohibited in the University Student Handbook. Among other issues, students were lead in discussions about dishonesty and cheating on campus. The consequences of prohibited behaviors were discussed and many freshman students were surprised when they were presented with the written penalties associated with academic dishonesty. Following the discussions on dishonestly and cheating, a number of students were transparent about behaviors they and their friends engaged in that were unethical and inappropriate. Moreover, a number of students decided to change their friendship circle or the people they normally socialized with heavily because they recognized that they only engaged in risky or inappropriate behavior when they were with people who represented a negative influence in their lives.

PROBLEM STATEMENT

The United States government and the governmental officials elected and appointed to serve the American people are granted significant power to make laws, execute the law and to interpret the law. As such, governmental officials elected to serve in legislative bodies across the nation should be trustworthy individuals capable of keeping their purpose before them. The role and purpose of legislators should serve as a guiding light that provides insight and perspective as they go about their day to day activities navigating their way through a sea of political demands from their constituents, business, and special interests. Likewise, the Chief Executive and the cadre of advisors and employees who serve in the various departments and agencies under the president's leadership should remember they are public servants employed by the citizens of the United States. Finally, many expect judges in the American judiciary to adhere to the very laws they have been entrusted to interpret and pronounce judgment.

However, the United States history is full of scandals involving public officials who have proven themselves unworthy of trust, power and authority to make decisions on behalf of the American people. Political scandals are familiar reminders that humans are creatures who are capable of doing tremendous good and simultaneously capable of ghastly deeds.

When government officials demonstrate poor judgment in their personal or home life questions are raised about his/her integrity, trustworthiness and the ethical code by which he or she conduct themselves and the value placed on those with whom he or she is most intimate. When public officials exercise poor judgment in their professional life (i.e., abuse of power, bribery, corruption, misuse of campaign contributions, favoritism, and perjury) it gnaws away and erodes citizen trust in government officials.

As a professor and student of political science, people often approach me in hopes of discussing political events, new public policies, crises and political scandals. I am often asked my personal and professional opinion about unfolding current events. Once I have offered my analysis of the events issues of the day, I ask those who approached me with questions about the event to share their perspective with me. Undoubtedly, somewhere in the conversation someone would say he or she did not trust the government, politicians or governmental officials. The distrust of government officials is not uncommon especially during an era where there is a proliferation of the

news broadcasts, access to the internet, and social media, which allows a
story to reach millions within a matter of hours or even minutes.

V. O. Key defined public opinion as viewpoints, perspectives and attitudes held by the public. He argues the views or attitudes of the citizenry
have the ability to influence or compel the government to either conform to
or ignore issues. According to Key, when the attitudes expressed by the
general public are popular and pervasive public opinion can lead governments and leaders to adjust and amend decisions in order to appease or
placate the electorate. The expression of public opinion can also influence
the government and political leaders to remain silent on issues or ignore
political and societal issues. Ultimately, the decision making process politicians utilize depends to some degree on support from voters and the cohe-
siveness of the attitude or opinions expressed. Although public opinion is a
valuable tool in American government, not every opinion or perspective
expressed by the public is regarded as public opinion.[1]

Similarly, A. Lawrence Lowell defines the "public" as individuals or
people who are willing to act in accordance with the decision or decisions of
the majority. He identifies several circumstances that are central to the existence of the public. The author postulates there should exist a sense of
homogeneity or uniform agreement of views and the treatment of questions.
Lowell also maintains the public's responses to questions must stimulate
government officials to action or inaction.[2] In addition, Walter Lippman, like
Lowell, concurs that the essential problem with public opinion is participation. Lippman describes the public as spectators or "bystanders"[3] who are

interested in creating the rules by which the political game is carried out.

Francis G. Wilson, another public opinion scholar, maintains public opinion or the expression of the attitudes and views of the public on various
issues is a key part of political life. Wilson believes public opinion adds
value to citizenship by creating a sense of belonging. Furthermore, Wilson
maintains public opinion is significant because it increases the legitimacy
and value of government actions. The author argues when a government
recognizes or acknowledges the attitudes and beliefs held by its citizens,
public opinion has the ability to shape or re-shape the opinions expressed by
others. Moreover, Francis Wilson postulates public opinion is one of the
most basic psychological foundations of the government especially when
political opinions expressed by the people are used to determine government
actions. Furthermore, Wilson conjectures in order for public opinion to guide
the actions of the government and its leaders, the public must believe the
government values its opinion.[4]

In "Concepts of Public Opinion," Wilson says the public is entitled to
their political attitudes, beliefs and opinions. People, who live in a democratic nation, assume their opinions matter and have the ability to influence the
actions of governmental decision makers. Consequently, the expressed opin-

ions of the public becomes an apparatus or instrument of democratic control, which is viewed as the ethical foundation of a government or nation. Hence, Francis Wilson suggests the "development of faith in public opinion coincided with the abandonment of authoritarian notions" of governance in a representative democracy.Nevertheless, he says the function of public opinion as a mechanism for change is minimized when natural biases are prevalently espoused in a nation.[5] ✗

Historically, when Americans have been asked if they trust the government or government officials there is a repeated expression of reservations about whether the United States government and political officials are trustworthy. A Gallup Poll published on November 10, 2013, suggested Americans have very little confidence that the government and political officials will do what is right. In 1993, when asked "How much of the time do you trust the government in Washington to do what is right," 23 percent of people surveyed believed the government could be trusted to do the right thing in comparison to 77 percent who said the government can be trusted to do what is right some of the time or not at all. In 1999, 34 percent of those surveyed believed the government could be trusted to do the right thing while 66 percent believed the government could not be trusted or could be trusted some of the time. Moreover, in 2007, 32 percent of respondents said the government could be trusted to do the right thing the majority of the time, 67 percent of the respondents believed the government would do the right thing some of the time or never. Therefore, public opinion data suggests the American people place little trust in the government and government decision-makers.[6]

The question was asked "How much trust and confidence do you have in our federal government in Washington when it comes to handling International problems?" In May 1972, 20% of those polled indicated they had a great deal of trust in the government's ability to handle international issues while 55% said they had a fair amount of trust in the government's ability to address international problems. Twenty percent of the respondents said they did not place much trust in the government's ability to handle international issues. Two percent of those surveyed responded they had no confidence in the government's ability to handle international problems.[7]

However, when the same question was posed between September 5th through September 8th of 2013, 10% of those polled indicated they had a great deal of trust in the government's ability to handle international issues while 39% said they had a fair amount of trust in the government's ability to address international problems. Thirty-three percent of the respondents did not place much trust in the government's ability to handle international issues. Seventeen percent said they had no confidence in the government's ability to address international problems. Thus, only 49% of those surveyed said they had a fair amount of trust in the United States government's ability to handle international issues and conflict. [8]

When asked in May 1972, "How much trust and confidence do you have in our federal government in Washington when it comes to handling domestic problems?" participants gave the following responses. Eleven percent of those polled indicated they had a great deal of trust in the government's ability to handle domestic issues while 59% said they had a fair amount of trust in the government's ability to address domestic problems. Twenty-six percent of the respondents said they did not place much trust in the government. Only three percent of those surveyed responded they had no confidence in the government's ability to handle domestic problems. [9]

However during the week of September 5, 2013 when Gallup asked people about the degree of trust they had in federal government leaders in Washington, a meager 8% of those polled indicated they had a great deal of trust in the government's ability to handle domestic issues. On the other hand, 34% said they had a fair amount of trust in the government's ability to address domestic problems. Forty percent of the respondents said they did not place much trust in the government's ability to handle domestic issues. Seventeen percent said they had no confidence in the government's ability to address domestic problems. The intensity of the attitudes of respondent's attitudes was identical to the question about confidence in the government's ability to handle international problems. Thus, only 49% of those surveyed said they had a fair amount of trust in the United States government's ability to handle domestic issues and conflict. [10]

Additionally, Gallup conducted a survey wherein they asked people "how much trust do you have at this time in the executive branch headed by the president?" In May 1972, 24% of those polled indicated they had a great deal of trust in the executive branch while 49% said they had a fair amount of confidence in the president's leadership ability. Twenty percent of the respondents said they did not place much trust in the chief executive. Four percent of those surveyed responded they had no confidence in the president's ability to manage the issues plaguing the nation.

In September 2013, Gallup asked the question "how much trust do you have at this time in the executive branch headed by the president?" Between September 5 and September 8, 2013, 18% of those polled indicated they had a great deal of trust in the executive branch while 33% said they had a fair amount of confidence in the president's leadership ability. Twenty-three percent of the respondents said they did not place much trust in the chief executive. Twenty-five percent of those surveyed responded they had no confidence in the president's ability to manage the issues plaguing the American people. [11]

Additionally, Gallup wanted to gain insight into the level of confidence or trust the American people placed in the Congress. In 1972, Americans were asked, "how much trust do you have at this time in the legislative branch?" Thirteen percent of the respondents indicated they had a great deal of trust in Congress while 58% percent said they had a fair amount of confidence in the national legislature. Twenty-two percent of the respondents said they did not place much trust in the national law-making body. Three percent of those surveyed responded they had no confidence in Congress's ability to manage the issues facing the nation. [12]

When respondents were asked about the degree of trust they place in legislative bodies in the U.S., their responses reflected the limited trust citizen's place in lawmakers. Only 6% of the respondents indicated they had a great deal of trust in the national legislature while 58% said they had a fair amount of confidence in Congress. Twenty-eight percent of the respondents said they did not place much trust in the national legislature. Forty-four percent of those surveyed responded they had little confidence in Congress's ability to manage the issues facing the nation compared to 22% of respondents who said they had no confidence or trust in Congress. [13]

Finally, Gallup surveyed people asking them about the degree of trust they had in the American judiciary. In 1972 Americans were asked, "how much trust do you have at this time in the judicial branch?" Seventeen percent of the respondents indicated they had a great deal of trust in Congress while 49% percent said they had a fair amount of confidence in the national legislature. Twenty-four percent of the respondents said they did not place much trust in the national law-making body. Seven percent of those surveyed responded they had no confidence in Congress's ability to manage the issues facing the nation. [14]

In September 2013 when Gallup conducted the survey again between September 5th and September 8th, the level of confidence in the judiciary were very similar. Thirteen percent of the respondents indicated they had a great deal of trust in Congress while 49% said they had a fair amount of confidence in the national legislature; this percentage is identical to the response in 1972. Twenty-eight percent of the respondents said they did not place much trust in the national aw making body. Nine percent of those surveyed responded they had no confidence in Congress's ability to manage the issues facing the nation. [15]

Based on Gallup poll data, the American people do not place much stock in the trustworthiness of the American government (i.e., executive branch, legislative branch and judicial branch). The data suggests there is limited or a lack of confidence in the government and government leaders. One can only presume that the lack of trust in the government is a response to the lethargic, desensitized and corrupt manner in which some leaders conduct themselves in their political career and personal or family life. Public opinion responses as it relates to the public's trust in the government and government officials suggest citizens have limited expectations of the government and decision-makers. As such, one might ask if the American people articulated greater moral and ethical expectations of governmental officials whether the governmental leaders would feel compelled to uphold an ethical code worthy of respect that might lead to increased trust in the government and public officials. If we expect little, we tend to receive or gain little. However, when we have heightened expectations people tend to attempt to fulfill the expectations.

Another issue addressed in the political scandals course was the importance of developing a healthy ethical code. Ethics are important because they are related to influences in our lives that shape the way in which we perceive reality about what is normal and abnormal; our ethics shape how we perceive right and wrong. The word ethics is derived from the Greek word ethos, which means disposition, customs and nature.[16] Ethics deals with the moral principles that governs the conduct or behavior of an individual, a group or community. Ethical focus on "the moral correctness"[17] of behavior in specific areas such as the ethics of psychology, medical ethics, political ethics, science ethics, etc.

Ethics in the western culture is often divided into four dominant schools of thought: (1) virtue ethics, (2) duty ethics (deontological ethics), (3) consequential ethics (utilitarianism), and (4) relativistic ethics. Western philosophy often draws from Aristotle's theories on ethics in which he argues that virtues like love, generosity and justice are dispositions that prompt humans to behave in ways that are beneficial to the individual and the greater society in which he or she exists. Aristotle's Nicomachean Ethics proposes all human behavior possesses some good. Aristotle believed the ultimate good toward which human action is directed is "eudemonia" or happiness which is defined as living well. In order to understand the nature of happiness one must determine the role and function of human beings because an individual's happiness or well living is controlled by his or her understanding of the natural function. Consequently, Aristotle maintained the intellect or rational choice. According to Aristotle, the intellect directs an individual's life and behavior.[18] One's ethical virtue is represented by his or her habitual decision to behave in a decent, honorable or noble manner. Aristotle argues in order for actions to be honorable or virtuous they must be deliberate and the individual must be well aware of what he or she is doing. Moreover, the individual engages in virtuous or honorable behavior because he or she understands it is the noble, righteous or honorable thing to do. Finally, Aristotle stresses the importance of human beings intellectual ability is the greatest capacity human beings possess as it relates to a life of contemplation of the highest goods. He believes an individual's greatest happiness or ability to live well lies in the utility of the intellect. According to Aristotle, contemplation is virtually divine in nature and can only be achieved to the degree that there is something divine or Godly that lies within men and women.[19]

Immanuel Kant in "Good Will, Duty and the Categorical Imperative," acknowledges humans are creatures with "desires and appetites."[20] Despite human desires and appetites, Kantianism places greater value and priority on rationality, which enables humans to distinguish right from wrong or appropriate behavior from inappropriate behavior. Thus, Immanuel Kant argues people have the ability to "exercise their wills"[21] and the ability to harness their desires by choosing to engage in "right action."[22] As such, Kant stressed the behavior of "moral persons."[23] He believed the upstanding behavior of "moral persons"[24] would positively influence the behavior of unethical persons in a society. He stressed the ethical conduct of "moral persons[25] " and believed all human beings should embrace their conduct. Thus, Kant argues universal principles establish categorical imperatives, which demands people behave in a particular manner. Categorical imperatives are "moral"[26] imperatives. They are unequivocal in nature and represent absolutes. Ultimately, categorical imperatives presupposes the "absolute worth of all rational beings as ends in themselves."[27] Finally, categorical imperatives serve as formulas for identifying or defining behaviors that deemed necessary or inherently good based on reason and rationality.[28]

Unlike Kant and Aristotle, John Stuart Mill argues in favor of utilitarian ethics. He argues everything humans engage in is geared toward happiness. In his work Utilitarianism, Mill declares, "happiness is the sole end of human action, and the promotion of it the test by which to judge of all human conduct."[29] He also makes it clear that the test is its promotion of happiness "to the greatest extent possible."[30] According to Mill, human beings are motivated by pleasure and happiness. He highlights the desirability of pleasure and happiness. He argues pleasure is more desirable than pain. Thus, Mill argues people will do that which brings them greatest pleasure. Likewise, he presupposes human beings will avoid pain.[31] He distinguishes the difference between desirable things. He argues human behavior is guided by those things that "promote happiness to the greater extent."[32] According to John Stuart Mill, human beings decide whether a particular action or a series of actions should be carried out based on the degree to which humans derive pleasure from the pattern of behavior. Based on Mill's writings, a happy individual is satisfied or content with the condition of his or her life the majority of the time. Moreover, Mill presupposes that a happy individual experiences pain or misery infrequently.[33]

There are two schools of thought or perspectives associated with utilitarianism. Act utilitarianism is primarily concerned with the behavior or actions that contribute to increased levels of happiness while simultaneously experiences diminishing the level of pain an individual experiences throughout the course of his or her life. People who subscribe to act utilitarianism are more apt to exhibit inconsistencies in their actions. According to J. J. C. Smart, act utilitarians determine the correctness or incorrectness of actions based on the

outcomes or consequences associated with the behaviors.[34] The second perspective is rule utilitarianism. Rule utilitarianism stresses the importance of
adhering to rules or guidelines that lead increase pleasure and decrease
pain.[35] Thus, an individual guided by rule utilitarians believe it is best for
everyone to follow rules established by a community or society. Rule utilitarians maintain life is comprised of consistently increased levels of happiness
or contentment when humans follow rules that are created to diminish dis-
comfort, pain and hardship.

Many Americans are familiar with Kant's categorical imperative, Aristotle's Nicomachean Ethics and utilitarianism as posited by John Stuart Mill.
The purpose of the previous discussion of the three dominant ethics theories
is to provide context by which political scandals can be used as precautionary
tales of the loss, embarrassment, humiliation and devastation caused by behaviors and actions government officials undoubtedly believed would lead to
increased happiness and pleasure. The political scandals presented in this
research, paint a portrait of what happens when people are heavily driven by
temporary pleasure of lascivious sexual affairs, abuse of power, accepting
bribes, and the like. Political scandals point to the lingering effects of being
motivated by temporary gratification that have the propensity to ruin the
reputations and lives of the perpetrators and those in relationship with them.
Political scandals can teach us about the residual effects inappropriate or
unethical behavior can have on our families, friends, colleagues and the
people we serve in the workplace.

Hence, there is a practical value associated with ethics and developing an
ethical code because our ideas of right and wrong are crucial in the development of the boundaries or lack of boundaries people allow to govern their
lives. Perhaps a major problem associated with ethical training is those
charged with training students and employees about what is appropriate or
normal behavior in a specific discipline, field or industry after inappropriate
and unethical behavior has become concretized in the individual. Rice and
Dreilinger maintain those receiving ethical training whether they are students
or employees "want guidelines - not rules - and I want them to say: Here's
how we do business around here."[36]

Despite strides made by trainers and businesses that attempt to prevent
unethical behavior on the part of employees, the difficulty lies in teaching
institutional, industry, or professional expectations on the job. Ethics instruc-
tors, trainers and industries must engage in deconstructing inappropriate perspectives, attitudes and behavioral practices employees have used to guide
their actions. A number of scenarios people confront in the workplace are
discussed in "Rights and Wrongs of Ethics Training" by Dan Rice and Craig
Dreilinger. One example of an ethical issue the authors highlight is a scenario
of an employee who made a significant mistake and one of his or her peers
was blamed for the error. The innocent individual's career would not likely

to be ruined. However, telling the truth would likely damage how he/she are perceived or harm his/her career. What should the employee who committed the mistake do? Should the person(s) responsible for the mistake take responsibility for the error? Should they take responsibility for their actions? Should the person responsible for the error save face and remain silent?[37]

Another example Rice and Dreilinger offer is what an employee should do when they stumble across information that suggests a colleague has included qualifications on his or her resume they did not possess before being hired. Although he or she lacked the qualifications prior to being hired, he or she has repeatedly demonstrated an ability to manage the position. Should you share the information with others in the company? With whom do you share the information?[38] Although many trainers and companies try to provide insight about their ethical expectations of employees' inappropriate behavior persists to the degree initiatives are developed to curb unethical behavior in the workplace. Similarly, academic institutions spend time developing faculty and student manuals that list their expectations of members of the academic community. Nevertheless, inappropriate, unethical and sometimes illegal behavior persists on college campuses throughout the country. No matter who we are, no matter the positions we hold or the environment in which we work or study that which we choose to do speaks volumes about our character. Likewise, when we choose not to engage in inappropriate and unethical behavior, attests to our ethics, integrity and the value placed on truth. Ultimately, every human being is fallible. We are prone to make mistakes and to exhibit lapses in judgment. It is important to remember our integrity is not judged based on our ability to be perfect. Our integrity is rooted in how we address the mistakes we make. Our integrity is judged on whether we acknowledge our mistakes. Our integrity is judged based on whether we learn from our mistakes or continue to perpetuate the pattern of thought that led to the error. If left unchecked or uncorrected, the inappropriate disposition and behaviors can lead to the demise of the perpetrator.

In conclusion, each human being has at least one weakness, flaw or proclivity that has the propensity to ruin their life and detrimentally affect the lives of others. Despite human imperfections and human frailties, elected officials and public servants are expected to remember the oath and responsibilities they are expected to fulfill on behalf of the people they serve. It is crucial elected and appointed officials avoid becoming morally insulated. When leaders or workers become morally insulated they conclude the only role they serve in the workplace is to "simply do the job"[39] they were hired to do. However, "Self-Interest and Political Integrity," written by Joel Fleishman, suggests political officials and public servants should conduct themselves in an ethical manner when they "know what is right."[40] Fleishman maintains integrity requires an individual to possess "a genuine, wholehearted disposition to do the right and just thing in all circumstances and to shape"[41] his or her behavior based on that knowledge.

As such, this author maintains there is an intrinsic value in political scandals that goes beyond the sensational conversations we have in the workplace, on the bus, or in the coffee shop about the failures of political officials or public personalities. Political scandals are useful because they provide real life scenarios by which we can begin a dialogue about ethics, ethical decision-making processes, and the outcomes associated with adopting an unethical or corrupt approach to the way we conduct ourselves in both our personal and professional lives. It is in this vein that I have embarked upon writing about and identifying the cost associated with unethical behaviors exhibited by those elected or appointed to political office in the United States.

HYPOTHESIS

yes

The consequences associated with non-sex based scandals carry greater penalties than sex-based scandals because the unethical or inappropriate use of power is committed against the citizens.

RESEARCH QUESTIONS

This study addresses the following research questions: (1) What impact do political scandals have on the people's trust in government officials, (2) What are the consequences associated with sex based scandals committed by government officials, (3) What are the consequences associated with non-sex based scandals committed by public officials, (4) Which category of scandals (sex based or non-sex based) carry greater penalties and consequences? and (5) What lessons can be learned from political scandals?

METHODOLOGY

This study utilizes a descriptive analysis or the qualitative approach to examine sex based and non-sex based political scandals from 2000 through 2011. This study aims to identify which category of scandals (sex based or non-sex based) tend to yield the greatest consequences.

In an effort to examine national political scandals, this research utilizes both secondary and primary sources. Primary sources used in this study include public opinion polls on the impact governmental scandals have on the people's trust in the government as well as legal documents. Secondary sources consulted include scholarly literature in ethics, and newspaper articles on political scandals from 2000 through 2011.

STATEMENT OF PURPOSE

The purpose of this study is to provide a means by which educators, administrators, families, communities and society can begin to discuss the importance of ethical and moral behavior as it relates to the well-being of the individual and society. Through the study of political scandals and the consequences of unethical or inappropriate behavior, it is the author's belief political scandals and the public fallout associated with unethical behavior can be used as cautionary tales of what happens to people who intentionally exhibit unethical behavior in their professional and personal lives.

RESEARCH GOALS

The researcher has several goals for this research. The primary goal is to provide a treatment or discussion of 21st century political scandals in hopes of determining which category (sex based or non-sex based) of scandals carry with them the greater consequences. Additionally, this writer hopes to develop a document or tool that diminishes the sensationalism of political scandals in hopes of illuminating what happens when human beings cease to set or respect boundaries within their personal and professional lives. Finally, the author seeks to develop a tool or book that can be utilized and incorporated into secondary and post-secondary curriculum to address ethical issues faced in schools, on college campuses and in the workplace to begin dialogue about the long-term effects unethical and corrupt behavior can have on an individual's life.

LIMITATION OF STUDY

This study examines political scandals of 2000-2011 for the expressed purpose of determining which category of scandals (sex based and non-sex based) tend to carry weightier penalties. It is not the author's intent to determine which scandals were the most grievous or calamitous. The intent of this research is to determine whether sex based or non-sex based scandals carry greater consequences to develop a resource that provides an avenue for educators, administrators, supervisors, communities, and families to discuss the consequences related to personal and professional ethical failures.

SIGNIFICANCE OF STUDY

The primary focus of this study is to investigate the consequences associated with political scandals of 2000-2011. This research is significant because it attempts to use governmental or political scandals in a less sensational manner. The aim of this research is to provide educators, administrators, and the public a resource or tool that helps demonstrate through the experiences of others what happens when we fail to self-assess our ethical and moral fiber.

This work also presents a discourse on ethics. It is the author's belief this study will serve as an important document for students of social science, particularly political science. This research will also serve as an important document for teachers, students, businesses and the general public because it highlights the importance of a healthy ethical code. Finally, this research identifies consequences associated with inappropriate and unethical behavior in the public sector.

NOTES

1. V. O. Key, *Public Opinion and Democracy* (New York: Alfred Knopf, 1961), 13-14.

2. A. Lawrence Lowell, *Public Opinion and Popular Government*, (New York: Longmans Green and Company, 1930).

3. Walter Lippman, *The Phantom Public* (New York: Harcourt Brace, 1925), 52.

4. Francis Wilson, "Concepts of Public Opinion," The American Political Science Review, vol. 27, no. 3 (June 1933): 371-372.

5. Ibid, 384.

6. "Trust in Government," Gallup Poll [database online] available from www.gallup.com/poll/5392/trust-government.aspx; Internet; accessed November 10, 2013, 1.

7. Ibid.

8. Ibid, 2.

9. Ibid.

10. Ibid, 3.

11. Ibid, 3.

12. Ibid, 5.

13. Ibid, 4.

14. Ibid.

15. Ibid, 4.

16. "Definition of Ethics," Oxford Dictionaries [database online] available from http://www.oxforddictionaries.com/us/definition/american_english/ethos ; Internet; accessed November 3, 2013, 1.

17. Ibid.

18. Aristotle, Harris Rackham, ed., *The Nicomachean Ethics (Great Britain: Wordsworth Editions, Ltd., 1996).*

19. Ibid.

20. Immanuel Kant, "Good Will, Duty, and the Categorical Imperative," in Christina Hoff Sommers, ed., Right and Wrong: Basic Readings in Ethics, (San Diego: Harcourt Brace Jovanovich Publishers, 1986), 8.

21. Ibid.

22. Ibid.

23. Ibid.

24. Ibid.

25. Ibid.

26. Ibid, 9.

27. Ibid.

28. Ibid, 14.

29. John Stuart Mill, Utilitarianism, Oskar Piest ed., (Indianapolis: The Bobbs-Merrill Company, Inc., 1957), 49.

30. Ibid, 48.

31. Ibid, 44-45.

32. Ibid, 48.

33. Ibid.

34. J. J. C. Smart, "Utilitarianism," in Right and Wrong: Basic Readings in Ethics, ed. Christina Hoff Sommers (San Diego: Harcourt Brace Jovanovich, 1986), 81.

35. Ibid.

36. Dan Rice and Craig Dreilinger, *"Rights and Wrongs of Ethics Training,"* *Training and Development Journal*, May 1990, accessed July 15, 2013, 1.

37. Dan Rice and Craig Dreilinger, "Rights and Wrongs of Ethics Training," *Training and Development Journal*, May 1990, accessed July 15, 2013, 1.

38. Ibid.

39. William Felice, *How Do I Save My Honor?* (Maryland: Rowman & Littlefield Publishers, Inc., 2009), 12-13.

40. Joel Fleishman, "Self-Interest and Political Integrity," in Joel Fleishman, Lance Liebman, and Mark Moore, eds., Public Duties: The Moral Obligation of Government Officials (Cambridge: Harvard University Press, 1981), 53-54.

41. Ibid.

Chapter Two

Sex-Based Political Scandals
of the 21st Century

This chapter focuses on sex-based scandals that made national news between 2000 and 2011. This section of the study chronicles twenty-two (22) sex-based scandals. A number of elected officials, appointed officials and public servants are highlighted in this chapter. The primary focus is on the individual who engaged in inappropriate sexual activity or relationships. Additionally, some attention is given to the individual with whom governmental officials or public servants engaged in extramarital affairs and other behavior deemed inappropriate or unethical. This chapter includes sex-based scandals that involved David Wu, Anthony Weiner, Samuel Kent, General David Petraeus, John Ensign, John Edwards, Mark Foley, Randall Tobias, DC Madam Deborah Jeane Palfrey, Chris Lee and Gary Condit and other notable government officials.

The goal of this chapter is to (1) discuss sex-based scandals, (2) identify the consequences associated with the decisions elected and public officials made to engage in extramarital and illicit "sexcapades," and (3) identify the impact the scandal had on the government official, their families and others implicated in sex scandal.

DAVID WU

In May 2011, United States Representative David Wu (D-OR), a member who was serving his seventh term in the House of Representatives,[1] was accused of making unwanted sexual advances towards an eighteen (18) year old woman. The young woman was the daughter of one of the Representative's close friends who contributed to Wu's political campaign. The young woman left a voicemail that was heard by Representative David Wu's aides. Aides described the message as "a panicked voicemail from a young woman accusing Wu of aggressive and unwanted sexual behavior."[2] The scandal became public on July 22, 2011. When confronted about the allegations David Wu said he did have a sexual encounter with the young woman. However, the former legislator maintained that the sex was consensual.[3] This was not the first time David Wu found himself under scrutiny for strange or inappropriate behavior. The former Member of Congress had been under scrutiny behavior his staff described as "bizarre behavior"[4] like emailing his staff photos of himself dressed in a tiger costume around Halloween.[5] Oregon State Representative Brad Witt, a Democrat representing Clatskanie, said when interviewed by New York Daily News, "If this accusation proves to be true, it is time for David Wu to resign and get the help he needs."[6] Four days after the media reported the allegations made by his friend and campaign donor's daughter, Mr. Wu announced his resignation. His resignation was announced shortly after United States Senators Ron Wyden and Jeff Merkley and State Representative Witt urged him to resign from office.[7] Wyden and Merkley issued a joint statement in which they maintained, "The accusations against David Wu are jarring and exceptionally serious."[8] The senators argued Wu's constituents needed an effective leader. They wrote, "This is a critical time for our state and our nation and Oregonians need every member of their Congressional delegation to be effective. While no one takes pleasure in asking a colleague to resign, we believe he can no longer be an effective representative for our shared constituents and should, in the best interest of Oregon, step down."[9] Furthermore, David Wu received advice from Representative John Larson, then the Chair of the House Democratic Caucus, a Democrat from Connecticut. Larson advised Wu to "do what's in the best interest of your young family, and yourself and then the institution, in that order."[10]

David Wu was born in Taiwan and moved to the United States with his parents in 1961. After graduating from high school, he graduated from Stanford University in 1977 with a Bachelor's degree. Wu went on to attend Harvard Medical School but had a desire to pursue a career in law. He graduated from Yale University with a Juris Doctor degree in 1982. Before being elected to the United States House of Representatives as the first Chinese American elected to Congress, David Wu practiced law in Oregon. At the time the allegations made headline news, Wu was separated from his wife with whom he has two young children.[11]

No one really knows what was behind David Wu's "bizarre" antics. However, there has been speculation about whether his inappropriate behavior was linked to drug use. Mr. Wu has acknowledged use of painkillers. Shortly after resigning from Congress, he was "being treated for an unspecified mental health condition." He and his wife were unable to resolve issues that led to the failure of their marriage. [12]

ANTHONY WEINER

On Wednesday, May 28, 2011, seven term Representative Anthony Weiner (D-NY) found himself in the middle of a national scandal related to an image he posted to his Twitter account. Wiener apparently intended to send the image to a 21-year-old college student who resided in Seattle, Washington who did not follow him on Twitter. The image was a picture of Weiner featuring "a bulge" in his underwear. In a day and age of Facebook, Twitter and texting, one must wonder why public figures, politicians, and celebrities post extremely personal images and disseminate them for public consumption. Somehow, the Representative managed to post the image to twitter for the world to see. It reminds me of the words of my elders who would say things like "what's done in the dark will come to the light" or "what is hidden will one day be seen."

In this millennium, we have become all too well familiar with the damage that can occur when an image taken for private purposes somehow finds itself in the hands of the nation by way of the media. This is precisely what happened in the Wiener scandal. Representative Wiener had to face the music in the court of public opinion for showing "his Wiener."

When confronted about the picture, Mr. Weiner used the typical strategy of denial [13] often employed by politicians and many people who are caught in extramarital affairs or "sex-capades." He denied it. When it became obvious that denying posting the image on Twitter was not effective, Representative Weiner continued to insist he had nothing to do with the picture. Furthermore, he argued that any connection made between him and the college student was purely coincidental. The 21-year-old female to whom Representative Wiener intended to send the image told reporters she and the member of Congress were not in a relationship. She went as far as to suggest the photo must have been posted to Weiner's Facebook account by a hacker. [14]

Despite attempts to absolve himself of culpability in the scandal, Anthony Weiner eventually realized his lies were not helping the matter. On June 11, 2011, he requested a leave of absence to seek treatment [15] for what he called a sex addiction.

On June 16, 2011, Representative Weiner held a brief press conference to address the matter. As he approached the podium, "a small group of hecklers hollered vulgar questions at him and called him a "pervert." [16] Anthony Weiner apologized to the crowd that gathered for his press conference. He said, "I am here today to again apologize for the personal mistakes I have made and the embarrassment I have caused." [17] He continued, "I am announcing my resignation from Congress so my colleagues can get back to work, my neighbors can choose a new representative and most important so that my wife and I can continue to heal from the damage I have caused."[18] Weiner referenced his wife, Huma Abedin, in his resignation speech, but Ms. Abedin, rumored to be pregnant at the time,[19] did not attend the press conference with her husband.[20]

Weiner's resignation was a breath of fresh air for democratic members of Congress who were increasingly uncomfortable with details about Representative Weiner's online interactions with women. After announcing his resignation by way of a press conference, Anthony Weiner placed a call to Representative Steve Israel (D-NY), who served as chair of the Democratic Congressional Campaign Committee, to inform him of his decision to resign from office. Upon hearing the news, Mr. Israel handed the telephone to Representative Nancy Pelosi, who was serving as House Democratic Leader, in order for Anthony Weiner to share his decision with her as well. Representative Pelosi (D-CA) had been very outspoken about Weiner's behavior. Pelosi had gone as far as to urge Weiner to resign from the U.S. House of Representatives.

Additionally, Anthony Weiner acknowledged having engaged in inappropriate communications with six (6) women over a six-year period. He explained the relationships were not physical in nature. Moreover, Weiner announced his plans to seek treatment for a sex addiction to the media.[21]

More recently, Anthony Weiner re-emerged and is campaigning for Mayor of New York City.[22] Apparently, his marriage survived his Twitter antics and online relationships with other women during his marriage. Weiner's wife, Huma Abedin, is expected to campaign with him as he attempts his political come back.[23] There is no word as to whether the two of them will bring their baby boy along as Weiner campaigns for mayor. The cost associated with Anthony Weiner's actions led to the end of his congressional career, temporary damage to his then new marriage, and the public embarrassment that comes with being exposed or over-exposed to the public. The public will have to wait and see if the residents of New York City are willing to overlook his past mistakes and entrust him with the position of mayor.

After leading the pack in the New York City Mayoral Election, Weiner found himself facing the cameras again about new revelations that he continued sending lewd images and sexually explicit text messages after his resignation from the United States Congress. On July 23, 2013, Weiner along with his wife, Huma Abedin, held a press conference to address questions related to explicit text messages he sent to a woman during the time he was in rehab for a sex addiction. He and his wife, Huma Abedin, addressed the media. Anthony Weiner admitted he continued texting explicit images to women other than his wife. Having previously acknowledging he had continued to send lewd images of himself to women while attempting save his marriage,

Anthony Weiner told the press, "I said that other texts and photos were likely to come out, and today they have."[24] Ms. Abedin stood beside her husband and told reporters her husband "made horrible mistakes both before he resigned from Congress and after."[25] According to Abedin, they discussed his past including additional text messages that might surface. Furthermore, she explained her decision to forgive her husband and to continue with the marriage despite her husband's indiscretions. Abedin said, "it was not an easy choice."[26]

Despite his wife's statement of forgiveness, Weiner's campaign was severely affected by his continued inappropriate sexual behavior. Prior to the second "sexting" episode, Weiner was projected to be the favorite in the New York City Mayoral Election. Consequently, support for his campaign has decreased dramatically.[27] Once the frontrunner, Weiner is now trailing his opponents in fourth place. Weiner's "mistakes" or lapses in judgment raised questions about his ability to make good decisions. His habitual behavior caused voters to wonder whether he can be trusted to make good decisions on behalf of the city of New York.[28] Despite the media scrutiny and demands for him to withdraw from the primary election, Anthony Weiner continued to run for mayor of New York City. Ultimately, the voters sent a strong message to the repeatedly disgraced former congressional representative when he was defeated in his bid for the Democratic Party nomination for mayor only garnering "4.9 percent of the vote."[29] During his concession speech, Weiner told the press, "I have to say we had the best ideas, but sadly, I was the imperfect messenger."[30]

CHRIS LEE

Representative Christopher Lee (R-NY) found himself in the headlines of national news in February 2011 when the media became aware that he sent emails and photographs of himself shirtless to a woman on Craigslist.[31] Representative Lee was in his second term representing the people who resided in suburban Buffalo, New York.[32] Despite being married, Lee claimed to be "divorced"[33] in his response to a dating ad posted by a 34-year-old African American woman. According to the craigslist ad, the woman was interested in meeting a man who was "financially & emotionally secure"[34] and who did not look like a toad.[35] In his response to the ad, the U.S. Representative claimed he was a "39 year old lobbyist."[36] Moreover, he said he was "a fit fun classy guy." In reality, Lee was a 46-year-old married man with a young child.[37]

Mr. Lee's shirtless photos and emails were initially posted on "Gawker" a newspaper/blog that focusses on well-known figures and celebrities.[38] Upon receiving a series of emails from Christopher Lee, Yesha Callahan, the object of Mr. Lee's flirtatious gestures, gave the email communications and photo to Gawker. According to news reports, Ms. Callahan posted a dating ad as a joke. Once she googled his name she realized he was not single nor was he a lobbyist. She found out he was a member of Congress serving in the United States House of Representatives.[39]

When approached about the pictures the media, Lee's initial response was familiar to Anthony Weiner and every other person caught in wrongdoing. He maintained his email account must have been hacked.[40] The representative failed to provide evidence to support his claim that he was a victim of someone's cruel actions. Although the photograph shows Lee holding his cell phone in the picture, Lee continued to deny sending the image to the woman on Craigslist. A few hours after the story broke, Congressman Christopher Lee admitted he sent the emails and photos of himself on Craigslist in his resignation speech acknowledging he "made profound mistakes."[41] He also asked for forgiveness from his family, staff and constituents. The member of Congress went on to say "It has been a tremendous honor to serve the people of Western New York."[42] Moreover, Mr. Lee stated "I regret the harm my actions have caused my family, my staff and my constituents. I deeply and sincerely apologize to them all. I have made profound mistakes and I promise to work as hard as I can to seek their forgiveness."[43] Finally, he added, "The challenges we face in Western New York and across the country are too serious for me to allow this distraction to continue, and so I am announcing that I have resigned my seat in Congress effective immediately."[44] Mr. Lee did not allow the scandal to linger; he quickly resigned from Congress within a few hours of the scandal breaking on national news. This led many people to believe there was more to the story. Several of his congressional colleagues referred to him as being a part of the "party circuit."[45] Consequently, former U.S. Representative Christopher Lee paid the price associated with emailing photos of oneself to a woman other than his wife over the web. It is not known if Mr. Lee had ever been unfaithful to his wife, but one thing is clear he was caught trying to connect with a woman who placed a "dating ad" on Craigslist on January 14, 2011. His inappropriate behavior cost him his congressional seat and political career. Christopher Lee's behavior also led to his becoming the butt of jokes about "mid-life crises" men.

MARK SOUDER

On Monday, May 17, 2010, Mark Souder (R-IN) announced resignation from the United States House of Representatives. The fifty-nine year old legislator was married with three children and two grandchildren.[46] Mr. Souder was serving his eighth term representing the third congressional district of Indiana when his affair with one of his district office female aides was publicly exposed.[47]

In February 2011, the Indiana New Center began to investigate whether there was any truth to rumors that Representative Souder was engaged in an adulterous affair.[48] Three months later, the national media would expose his dirty laundry out before the world. Mr. Souder acknowledged his affair with Tracy Jackson. In a press conference, the representative from Indiana declared he had "sinned against God, my wife and my family by having a mutual relationship with a part-time member of my staff."[49] Very few details are known about Souder's liaisons with Ms. Jackson.

Representative Souder did not wait for members of Congress, particularly members of the House Ethics Committee, to urge him to resign his position. He was well aware of the damage his affair posed to himself, his family, and the Republican Party. In his initial response, it appeared that Mark Souder would assume complete responsibility for his adulterous behavior. When he resigned from Congress, Souder remarked, "I wish I could have been a better example."[50] However, Representative Souder switched gears and placed blame on the political environment in which he worked saying, "In this poisonous environment of Washington, D.C., any personal failing is seized upon, twisted, for political gain. He did not offer more details on the affair during his resignation announcement but simply said he was resigning because he did not want to "put my family through the painful drawn-out process."[51] Moreover, Representative Souder continued saying, "We are a committed family but the error is mine and I should bear the responsibility."[52] Souder also said, "It has been all consuming for me to do this job well.... I do not have any sort of normal life—for family, for friends, for church, for community.... But I am so ashamed to have hurt those I love. I am very sorry to have let so many friends down."[53] Mr. Souder expressed his gratitude for his family and God stating "Not only am I thankful for a loving family but for a loving God."[54] Consequently, Ms. Jackson resigned her position of legislative aide shortly after Mr. Souder announced he was leaving Congress.[55]

Souder's extramarital affair caused him to be viewed as a hypocrite because he campaigned on a platform of "family values" in 1994. Six months before his extramarital affair making headline news, Representative Mark Souder and Tracy Jackson, filmed a video in which they discuss the "virtues of abstinence" and his advocacy efforts in support of abstinence education. In the video, he discusses the virtues of abstinence and the importance of abstinence education.[56]

In exchange for the temporary gratification he found cheating on his wife, Mark Souder had to hand over his congressional career and political aspirations. He jeopardized his marriage and family life for momentary excitement.

In the end, he was left to return to his family in an attempt to salvage his marriage and an attempt to regain the trust of his family.

ERIC MASSA

When U.S. Representative Eric Massa, a first term Democrat from the state of New York, found himself at the center of a sex scandal involving a male staffer, announced his decision not to run for another term.[57] On March 3, 2010, the Congressman said his decision was based on his physicians telling him he could not "run at 100 miles an hour"[58] leading people to conclude his medical condition was compromised by the fast pace or intensity associated with lawmaking. Hence, people initially thought his decision to bow out of politics was related to his battle with "non-Hodgkins lymphoma."[59]

Shortly after his announcement, Eric Massa found himself at the center of a sex scandal when a number of aides told a POLITICO reporter the House Ethics Committee had received information suggesting the married Representative from New York,[60] "groped male staffers and behaved improperly with interns."[61] The allegations were related to a complaint made to the House Ethics Committee on February 8, 2010, by a Ronald Hikel, Massa's "former chief of staff and legislative director"[62] on behalf of a junior male staffer who said Eric Massa made unwanted advances towards him. The Ethics investigation ended on March 11, 2010.[63]

Congressman Steny Hoyer's office released a statement announcing he was made aware of allegations against Congressman Massa in early February. Hoyer's press release maintained allegations of misconduct where brought to his attention by one of Massa's staffers. Representative Steny Hoyer instructed his staff to give Representative Massa and his staff 48 hours to report the matter to the House Ethics Committee. Representative Massa's staff reported the allegations of sexual misconduct to the committee. Mr. Hoyer would do so. Within 48 hours, Mr. Hoyer received confirmation from both the Ethics Committee staff and Mr. Massa's staff that the Ethics Committee had been contacted for the purpose of reviewing allegations made against him. Shortly thereafter, the House Ethics Committee began its investigation into whether Congressman Massa engaged in lewd behavior with the page. Hoyer did not know whether the accusations made against Eric Massa were true. Nevertheless, Hoyer believed the allegations warranted an investigation to "determine the facts."[64]

When the allegations were shared with the public by the media, Mr. Massa announced his resignation on March 5, 2010.[65] When confronted about the allegations, Massa's first response was "No, no, no, no, I did nothing sexual."[66] When he appeared on the Glenn Beck Show, Eric Massa was asked about his behavior. He acknowledged he should not have groped his employee, but said the "groping incident"[67] had been "taken out of context."[68] He also told the Glen Beck show, the former member of Congress, said he had been advised "to move out of the house he was living in"[69] with several single staffers. Eric Massa acknowledged he sometimes "tickled his staffers and Navy friends."[70] Some news accounts refer to his "wrestling" with staffers at his 50th birthday party.[71] Insofar as he accepted responsibility, Massa said, "If somebody on my staff was offended... I own that. That's why I resigned."[72] Despite being married with several children, Mr. Mass did not seem to see anything inappropriate or scandalous about "tickling" and "wrestling" with men including those who were on his payroll. Ultimately, he vacated his Congressional seat amiss much speculation about the motivations for ticking his employees and living with a group of single men in a house his wife was not allowed to visit. Nevertheless, the consequences associated with his bad behavior left him with a short-lived political career and being the butt of many inappropriate jokes. There is no evidence that his wife divorced him nor any mention about how his children perceived the matter. Ultimately, another elected official shamed himself, his family, friends and supporters.

TOM GANLEY

Tom Ganley was a Republican candidate campaigning in northwestern Ohio for United States Congress. He was sued by a woman who alleged the GOP candidate propositioned and groped her after she volunteered with his congressional campaign. According to the Cleveland Plain Dealer newspaper, the "39 year-old married mother of four,"[73] said the GOP candidate said, "he wanted to dominate her, parade her on a leash and have sex with her in front of his "play-friends."[74] Furthermore, she accused Mr. Ganley of "grabbing her from behind, wrapping his arms around her and kissing her."[75] The alleged victim maintained she resisted his advances, but he continued "reaching in her pants."[76] News reports suggested both Ganley and his alleged victim attempted to reach a settlement but were unable to reach an agreement. When negotiations proved worthless, Ganley's accuser decided to file a lawsuit. Mr. Ganley's attorney, Steve Dever, referred to the lawsuit as an attempt to extort money from the GOP candidate. Additionally, attorney Dever claimed the charges were "politically motivated."[77]

When news of the allegations made national news, the "millionaire used car salesman"[78] was said to have been "Sued by customers from fraudulent and deceptive practices. It was even reported that Ganley received two failing grades from the Better Business Bureau and had received more than "160 complaints"[79] over a three year period. As if the sex scandal was not bad enough, Huffington Post reported Mr. Ganley's dealerships were "facing lawsuits for racial, gender and age discrimination."[80]

A few weeks later, Ganley found himself in the midst of a second allegation of "sexual misconduct."[81] This time the GOP candidate was alleged to have been sexually inappropriate with a "50 year-old Broadview Heights woman"[82] who alleged he "grabbed her"[83] in 2005 when she visited his car dealership. The woman failed to report the incident to the police and failed to file a police report regarding the alleged misconduct that occurred five years prior. The second alleged victim did file a police report when she became aware that "another woman had also made similar allegations"[84] against Mr. Ganley. The congressional hopeful, denied the allegations made by the 39 and 50 year-old women."[85]

Despite denying all the allegations and charges made against him, Tom Ganley was indicted by the Cuyahoga County Prosecutors office on March 15, 2011. He was indicted on one count of kidnapping, three counts of gross sexual imposition, one count of abduction, one count of soliciting and one count of menacing by stalking.[86] The GOP candidate maintained his innocence and pled not guilty to the charges. On July 16, 2011, Cuyahoga County Prosecutors office dropped the charges filed against Ganley when his accuser refused to participate in the trial as a witness.[87] He lost his campaign despite spending millions of his own money. Nevertheless, Tom Ganley's hopes of becoming a member of Congress were dashed when he lost is congressional bid for office in November 2010. One can only presume the negative media coverage coupled with the Better Business Bureau complaints filed by customers of his car dealership harmed his campaign and decreased his ability to win. Although, his hopes for a career in politics were derailed, his marriage to his wife Lois remained intact.

SAMUEL B. KENT

In May 2007, Texas United States Federal District Judge Samuel Kent was accused of sexual harassment and sexual misconduct by two female employees who worked at the district courthouse.[88] Mrs. Cathy McBroom and Ms. Williams alleged the judge repeatedly touched them in an inappropriate manner.[89] Mrs. McBroom replaced Ms. Williams who accepted a position working at the federal courthouse located in Houston, Texas. Mrs. McBroom was married with three children at the time she was harassed by the judge.[90] She maintained Judge Kent "touched her inappropriately in mid-2003."[91] She said she "told her supervisor that the judge lured her into an office used as an exercise room and groped her."[92] According to news reports, Cathy McBroom reported the incident to her supervisor. Her supervisor informed her that she could lose her job if she filed a complaint against the judge. Due to a lack of support in the workplace exhibited by her female supervisor, McBroom requested a job transfer. She also filed an official complaint against the judge for "judicial misconduct."[93] According to Cathy McBroom, the judge "summoned"[94] her to his "chamber's on Friday, March 23, 2007."[95] McBroom said Kent "asked for a hug"[96] when she entered his office. According to news reports, Cathy McBroom told the judge she did not think hugging him was appropriate. Nevertheless, she approached him reluctantly. McBroom said the judge "grabbed"[97] her and "pulled up her blouse and her bra."[98] Moreover, she alleged Judge Kent began to "put his mouth on her."[99] Mrs. McBroom also stated the judge "forced her head down toward his crotch."[100] He did not stop there. McBroom maintained Kent continued to tell her in graphic terms "what he wanted to do to her."[101] Eventually, there was the sound of footsteps in the hallway. Hearing the footsteps, McBroom said the judge "loosened his grip."[102] As she began to exit the room, she maintained the judge complimented her work "then made suggestions about engaging in a sexual act"[103] with her.

Ms. Williams, the second woman who alleged Kent harassed her, said he repeatedly "asked her for 'hugs'"[104] and made "lewd remarks"[105] to her. She said the judge told her he was willing to "service me when my husband was being treated for prostate cancer."[106] Kent allegedly told the woman "sexual dirty jokes"[107] and made rude comments about other people. Ms. Williams never told anyone, not even her husband, out of fear of retaliation. She explained how she and Cathy McBroom were concerned about being dismissed from their jobs due to the power Judge Kent exhibited in the workplace. Williams said she felt more secure discussing what happened to her because she no longer worked for the Kent.[108]

In August 2008, Judge Kent was indicted on three counts of abusive sexual contact and attempted aggravated sexual abuse."[109] Despite denying allegations of sexual misconduct, Kent maintained all acts between him and the women were "consensual."[110] He later pleaded "guilty" to one count of obstruction of justice for lying to investigators about his behavior. He admitted to harassing the women. As a part of the plea bargain, the court dismissed the sexual misconduct charges against Kent.[111] As a consequence of his judicial misconduct, Kent received 33 months in prison for harassment and obstruction of justice.[112]

On June 19, 2009, the United States House Judiciary Committee voted unanimously to impeach Judge Samuel B. Kent. The impeachment charges included obstruction of justice, sexual assault, providing false statements to federal investigators. Mr. Kent became the fourteenth federal judge in American history to be impeached by the United States House of Representatives. The thirteenth judge to be impeached was removed from the bench in 1989. Members of the U.S. Senate had also introduced legislation to impeach the judge. Members of the Senate did not have an opportunity to debate and vote on the measure to impeach Judge Kent because he resigned from the Circuit Court on June 30, 2008.[113] The cost associated with the former judges sexual misconduct ultimately led to his incarceration.

JOHN ENSIGN

U.S. Senator John Ensign (R-NV) was 51 years of age when he admitted engaging in an extramarital affair with the spouse of a close family friend. Previously a veterinarian by training, Ensign was considered to be on the fast track within the Republican Party at the time of his affair.[114]

Mr. Ensign was first elected to the U.S. Senate in 2000 and reelected to his second term in 2006. Moreover, he was elected chair of the Republican Policy Committee in 2008. Although Ensign never identified the woman by name (Cindy Hampton), he did acknowledge the fact that her husband (Doug Hampton) was one of his employees. Cindy Hampton was employed as one of Ensign's campaign staffers. According to news reports, the affair began in December 2007. The "extra-marital affair" lasted approximately 9 months. Both Doug and Cindy Hampton resigned their positions in May 2008.[115]

The legislator told the media, "Last year, I had an affair," the Republican senator said outside his office in Las Vegas. "I violated the vows of marriage. It's absolutely the worst thing I've done in my life."[116] Ensign did not attempt to deny the allegations; rather he accepted "full responsibility for my actions."[117] When referring to the impact on his family, he stated, "I know I have deeply hurt and disappointed my wife, Darlene, my children, my family, friends, my staff and those who believed in me. And to all of them, especially my wife, I'm truly sorry."[118]

Ensign's office issued a statement on behalf of the senator's wife regarding the affair. Darlene Ensign's public response was "Since we found out last year, we have worked through the situation and we have come to a reconciliation. This has been difficult on both families. With the help of our family and close friends, our marriage has become stronger. I love my husband."[119]

In December 2011, the U.S. Senate Ethics Committee deemed its findings severe enough to refer its case against Ensign to the Department of Justice for obstruction of justice charges for making false statements to federal investigators. The U.S. Senate Ethics Committee became aware Ensign's parents gave Doug and Cindy Hampton $96,000. After engaging in an affair with Doug Hampton's wife, Senator Ensign used his influence to assist Doug Hampton a position as a lobbyist. As a result of the evidence, the Senate Ethics Committee referred its findings to the Federal Election Commission (FEC) for consideration regarding potential campaign finance violations and possible misuse of campaign funds. Although, the timing of the sizable payment and new job are questionable, the Department of Justice investigation was halted. No reason was given as to why the justice department decided not to continue its investigation or to bring charges of bribery and misconduct. Displeased with the Department of Justice decision to end its investigation, the U.S. Senate Ethics Committee resumed its investigation into Ensign's actions.[120] Initially Ensign attempted to move beyond the sex scandal. He decided against resigning and continued to run for a third term while attempting to regain the trust of his political supports. The senator eventually had to acknowledge the affect his sexual indiscretion was having on his Senate campaign. Consequently, Ensign announced to the public he was no longer going to continue his Senate campaign. The reason he gave for not seeking reelection was the campaign had become extremely ugly.[121] Although, Ensign denied breaking the law, he resigned from the United States Senate on April 21, 2011.[122] He also told reporters he resigned because he did not want to continue to subject his family to public scrutiny.[123]

The price John Ensign paid for having an extra-marital affair with one of his top aides included forfeiting his leadership position within the Republican Party and his Senate seat. He also lost the trust of his constituents likely including his wife and family. He had to walk the "walk of shame," politicians experience when they find themselves embroiled in when their "sexcapades" are exposed to the public. John Ensign and his family had to pay $54,000 to the Federal Election Commission (FEC) for breaching campaign finance regulations.[124] Nevertheless, Ensign's infidelity did not result in a divorce. He and his wife are still married. Mr. Ensign returned to Nevada and resumed his medical career as a veterinarian.[125]

JOHN EDWARDS

John Edwards, former Democratic vice-presidential and presidential candidate, found himself having to address his extramarital affair with Rielle Hunter. The first broke when the National Enquirer ran the story of accusing him of having an extramarital affair in October 2007. Despite being true, Edwards, Hunter and his campaign staff vehemently denied the relationship.[126] Nevertheless, the gossip news outlet continued to run the story until mainstream media outlets began to investigate allegations of Edwards' infidelity.[127] There was even speculation about a sex tape Edwards and Hunter allegedly made during their sexual liaisons.[128]

Many were astonished when *The National Enquirer* revealed, in December 2007, Rielle Hunter was pregnant with the secret "love child" of John Edwards. Johns Edwards had been married to his wife, Mary Elizabeth, since 1977. They met while attending law school at the University of North Carolina in Chapel Hill.[129] The couple had two children together.[130] The revelation was supported by statements made by a female friend of Ms. Hunter. Hunt-

er's friend told the media "Rielle told me she had a secret affair with Edwards. When she found out she was pregnant, she said he was the father."[131]
When asked who the father of her unborn child was, Hunter responded, "The
fact that I am expecting a child is my personal and private business. This has
no relationship to nor does it involve John Edwards in any way."[132] She
named "Andrew Young"[133] as the father of her child.

After numerous national news outlets began to run the story of Edwards'
affair and naming him as the father of Rielle Hunter's child, he finally told
the truth. According to news reports, John Edwards first met Hunter in 2006.
They met in a bar in New York City. Shortly after their first meeting, Edwards hired Rielle Hunter to develop and maintain a website for his campaign. According to news reports, Hunter received a salary of "$114,000"[134]
although she lacked technical training and knowledge of website construc-
tion. Her salary was paid by Mr. Edward's political action committee (PAC).
According to the former presidential candidate, he began having an affair
with Rielle Hunter shortly after hiring her as a part of his campaign staff. He
also admitted she regularly traveled with him around the world[135] while his
wife remained home to parent their children.

The denials of infidelity would begin to shatter in front of Edwards' own
eyes. On July 22, 2008, Edwards exited an elevator in the Beverly Hilton
Hotel around 3 a.m. He was immediately greeted by a National Enquirer
reporter and six photographers. When the reporter asked him about the affair
and alleged pregnancy, Edwards ran away from the reporters and hid in the
hotel restroom.[136] A few weeks after the humiliating experience of seeking
refuge in a men's restroom in a five star hotel, the only thing left for John
Edwards to do was tell the complete truth. That is exactly what the former
presidential hopeful did on August 8, 2008. After two years of denying the
affair, John Edwards admitted having a sexual relationship with Rielle Hunter. In an interview with Bob Woodruff of ABC News, Edwards said he did
have an affair with the "42 year old campaign employee."[137] Despite acknowledging the affair, he denied paying her money to be quiet about the
affair. Edwards also continued to deny being the father of her unborn
child.[138] Despite acknowledging the affair, when asked if he was in love with
Ms. Hunter, John Edwards remarked, "I've been in love with one woman for
31 years. She is the finest human being I have ever known."[139]

John Edwards recounting how he told his wife and family about his
infidelity. He said his wife was "furious."[140] Elizabeth Edwards wrote in her
statement responding to the affair, "Our family has been through a lot. Some
caused by nature, some caused by human weakness, and some—most recently—caused by the desire for sensationalism and profit without any regard for
the human consequences. None of this has been easy. But we have stood with
one another through them all. Although John Edwards believes he should
stand alone and take the consequences of his action now, when the door

closes behind him, he has family waiting for him."[141] Edwards admitted to going to see Rielle Hunter to convince her "not to tell the public what happened."[142] Moreover, when Hunter told Edwards she was pregnant with his child, he pleaded with her to abort the pregnancy.[143]

The National Enquirer correctly broke the Edwards' sex-scandal. Not only did Edwards engage in an adulterous affair, he fathered a child with his mistress. The consequences for his indiscretion and the subsequent lies told to cover up the affair cost Mr. Edwards greatly. Edwards lost his political career and his aspirations of becoming president of the United States were dashed. He lost the trust of many political constituents. Elizabeth, his wife of more than 31 years, separated from him. However, she never divorced him. In the end, John Edwards had to watch his wife and the mother of his children fight cancer for a second time. Elizabeth Edwards eventually succumbed to the disease. She died in her home surrounded by her children, her family and estranged husband.

John Edwards was indicted by a grand jury in Raleigh, North Carolina in 2011, on six counts of campaign finance law violations.[144] Mr. Edwards has gone on to live a very private life. In June 2013, when asked about the indictment, Edwards said, "While I do not believe I did anything illegal or ever thought I was doing anything illegal, I did an awful, awful lot that was wrong. And there is no one else responsible for my sins."[145] Perhaps, he just did not understand the fact that it is illegal to hire your mistress to do work she is not remotely qualified to do and pay with campaign funds. On June 5, 2013, John Edwards announced his plans to "open a law firm."[146]

VITO FOSSELLA

Vito Fossella (R-NY) was arrested on May 1, 2008, for drunk driving when he was pulled over in Alexandria. Shortly after being arrested, the Member of Congress was "bailed out of jail by a woman who was reported to have been his mistress, a woman with whom he fathered a child.[147]

Following his arrest, the legislator, who represented Staten Island and a portion of Brooklyn,[148] found himself in a media whirlwind caused by DWI arrest and the revelation he was engaged in an "extra-marital affair" and had a daughter with his mistress Laura Fay.[149]

At the time of his arrest, the Representative told officers, he was on his way to "visit his sick daughter."[150] Initially, people thought the child with whom he spoke was one of the children Fossella fathered with his wife. Under further examination, it became clear that he was referring to a 3 year old female child he fathered with his mistress Laura Fay.[151]

On May 2, 2008, the Washington Post covered U.S. Representative Vito Fossella's press conference in which he publicly apologized to his wife, his

children and those constituents who elected him for driving drunk after cele-
brating with residents from New York who traveled to the District of Columbia to celebrate with NFL 2008 Super Bowl champions the New York
Giant's who had been invited to the White House by President George W.
Bush.[152] At the time of his arrest, Fossella's blood alcohol level was "0.17
percent."[153]

During his press conference, the member of Congress acknowledged his
error in judgment.[154] Mr. Fossella also said, he continued, "This was a mistake I will never make again."[155] Initially, Fossella said he would continue to
serve the constituents who elected him to serve them in Congress. Although,
he refrained from discussion the details surrounding his arrest. His immediate focus appeared to be his wife and children. Mr. Fossella told reporters,
"Politics right now is the last thing on my mind. Right now, it's the embarrassment I caused my family, my friends and the people of this community."[156]

There were questions about whether his wife, Mary Pat, would divorce
him. However, Ms. Fay told the Daily News in an interview she was under
the impression that the representative was "separated from his wife."[157] After
a couple of weeks of scrutiny by the media, Mr. Fossella decided against
running for another term in Congress saying his primary focus was "healing
wounds"[158] he inflicted upon his wife and family by his adulterous actions.

Despite calls for his resignation and an investigation into whether Fossella used campaign contributions to finance his travels with Fay, he managed
to keep his political career on path.[159] However, in October 2008, Fossella
was convicted of drunk driving and later sentenced to 5 days in jail for the
offense.[160] The legislator had planned to appeal the case. However, in April
2009, Mr. Fossella decided to plead "guilty" to the DWI charges due to his
involvement in another drunk driving incident.[161] The incident caused the
death of a Los Angeles pitcher who Fossella struck while driving under the
influence of alcohol. On May 20, 2008, less than a month after causing the
death of three people, one of which was a Los Angeles pitcher, Fossella
announced his decision to retire from Congress.[162]

TIM MAHONEY

On October 13, 2008, Democratic Florida Congressman Tim Mahoney found
himself in the middle of his own sex scandal after being elected following
former U.S. Representative Mark Foley whose legislative career abruptly.
Foley was accused of sending "suggestive e-mail and text messages."[163]
Mahoney had an affair with Patricia Allen, a 50-year-old woman he met
during his congressional campaign in 2006. Representative Mahoney's sexual affair was exposed several weeks before the 2008 congressional elections.

Twenty-four hours after his affair made national news, Mahoney with his wife in tow, addressed questions about whether he attempted to cover up his extramarital affair by paying his former mistress $121,000.[164] The payment was a part of a mediation settlement reached in March 2008 between Mahoney and Allen.[165] Tim Mahoney also allegedly promised to help Allen get a job with an annual salary of $50,000 a year for a two-year period.[166] Whether she resigned or was fired remains unclear, however, Mahoney effectively managed to avoid going to court for sexual harassment by reaching a settlement agreement with Allen.

Representative Mahoney acknowledged his wrongdoing in a press conference. He told reporters he took "full responsibility"[167] for his behavior. He continued by saying he was sorry for the "pain I have caused" my family. Furthermore, Mahoney said, "I'm sorry that these allegations have caused embarrassment and heartache."[168]

The news of the Mahoney sex scandal hit the national media circuit on October 13, 2008. Originally, Mahoney staffers maintained Patricia Allen resigned her congressional position. They also maintained Mahoney did not pay her $121,000 when she left the staff. The irony in the scandal can be found in Mahoney's 2006 campaign platform, which promised increased ethics and trustworthy leadership after campaigning to replace former U.S. Representative Mark Foley.[169]

United States Representative Nancy Pelosi strongly urged the House Ethics Committee and the Federal Bureau of Investigation (FBI) to investigate Tim Mahoney's behavior for possible campaign finance violations. Mahoney accepted responsibility for the extramarital affair but insisted he never paid Allen money to be quiet about their relationship. In an ABC News report, Mr. Mahoney maintained he did not violate campaign finance regulations. Moreover, he declared, "I will be completely vindicated."[170] Despite all the allegations, Representative Mahoney continued to campaign for reelection until additional allegations surfaced about him helping another woman with whom he had an affair obtain a federal grant in the amount $3.4 million.[171] On October 15, 2008, Tim Mahoney finally admitted having multiple extramarital affairs.[172] Mahoney stressed he used personal funds to assist Allen financially. Mahoney continued to run for reelection in November 2008. Mahoney was defeated in the 2008 congressional election[173] likely due at least in part to his extramarital affairs and allegations of misconduct in the handling of campaign contributions. Not only did Mahoney lose his reelection bid, his wife filed for divorce and sought equitable division of property and assets accumulated during their marriage.[174]

RANDALL L. TOBIAS &
"D.C. MADAM" DEBORAH JEANE PALFREY

On April 28, 2007, Deputy Secretary of State Randall Tobias announced his resignation because he was linked to an "escort service" based in Washington, D.C. Mr. Tobias had a series of responsibilities he was entrusted with by the Bush Administration. Among his responsibilities was combat prostitution on a global scale. Brian Ross, a correspondent for ABC News, discovered Deborah Jeane Palfrey's escort client list. Mr. Tobias' name was on the list as having frequently used Palfrey's services. Ms. Palfrey, known as the "DC Madame, had been maintaining an elite escort service in the District of Columbia for a number of years.[175]

Tobias acknowledged using Palfrey's services. However, he admittedly denied paying for sex. He maintained he only used the service to have women give him home massages. Nevertheless, within 24 hours after admitting his wrongdoing, Randall Tobias resigned. He also agreed to testify in court in the DC Madame case.[176]

Deborah Jeane Palfrey was charged with running an escort service/prostitution service in the District of Columbia for more than ten years. Shortly after the scandal made national news, Ms. Palfrey gave the "client list" to media outlets to secure money for her legal defense. According to Deborah Jeane Palfrey, "it wasn't prostitution, it was fantasy sex, legal sex."[177] ABC news correspondent Brian Ross said Ms. Palfrey wanted to call her clients to testify in her case to testify that the services her service provided were "fantasy"[178] services.

Palfrey's "client list" included "thousands of names and tens of thousands of telephone contact numbers.[179] Among those who frequented the escort/prostitution service were of Pentagon officials, lobbyists, prominent attorneys, and White House officials. The women in her employ were educated professional women. Many of Palfrey's escorts or prostitutes were military officers, scientist, university professors, and legal secretaries.[180]

Despite being offered a plea bargain, the DC Madam rejected the plea deal which would have required her to serve 4 months in jail.[181] The government prosecuted Palfrey for running a prostitution ring. She was found guilty on all counts on April 15, 2008. Deborah Jeane Palfrey never served a day of her sentence because her body was found on May 1, 2008. Her death was ruled a suicide.[182]

This sex scandal bore a few casualties. Randall Tobias forfeited his position as Deputy Secretary of State and became the butt of jokes for being exposed for engaging in prostitution—the very thing he was charged to attempt to eradicate. The names of other prominent officials who frequented the escort service were identified as well. Ultimately, the inability to face the consequences of her actions, led Deborah Jeane Palfrey to take her own life.[183] According to news reports, Palfrey committed suicide by hanging.[184] This scandal reminds us that there are times when we have the ability to influence the lives of others. Although, everyone involved was an adult, we must evaluate our actions and the influence we have on others to determine whether our influence is positive or negative. Ms. Palfrey decided to open an escort/prostitute service to meet the sexual needs of prominent men. She recruited highly educated women to attract an upscale clientele. Palfrey continued to maintain and grow her client list over a period of more than a decade. In reality, each adult involved had access and the ability to influence another individual to participate in the escort service as a prostitute or as a "John." Influence in and of itself is not a bad thing—how we utilize the influence we have over others is crucial. In some shape or form, we leave a positive or negative imprint upon the lives of others based upon our choices and influence. Tobias' second marriage remained intact despite the sex-scandal. His current wife is a concert pianist in Indiana.[185]

DAVID VITTER

On July 10, 2007, the media revealed another prominent name associated with the DC Madam sex scandal. U.S. Senator David Vitter (R-LA), a staunch conservative, was also identified as having been a client of the "DC Madam," Deborah Jeane Palfrey, who was known for running a high-priced prostitution service in Washington, DC. Vitter only addressed the scandal one time describing his actions as "a very serious sin"[186] for which he said he confessed to God and his wife. David Vitter told the public he and his wife, Wendy, were seeking "marriage counseling."[187]

Like former Secretary of State Tobias, Senator Vitter, admitted to being a client of Palfrey's escort service.[188] However, Vitter acknowledged he engaged in sexual affairs with Palfrey escorts. The then 46 year old Rhodes Scholar, was first elected to the United States Senate in 1999. David Vitter was allowed to use campaign contributions to pay for legal representation associated with the DC Madam sex scandal.[189] The government did not file charges against Senator Vitter nor did the government call upon him to testify during the trial of the DC Madam.

David Vitter admitted his involvement in the DC Madam sex scandal. There was no talk of resigning on his part nor that of the Republican Party. He ran for a second Senate term in 2010. Senator Vitter currently serves on the Committee on Environment and Public Works, Committee on Banking, the Housing and Urban Affairs, Committee on Armed Services, and the Committee on Small Business and Entrepreneurship. He is also a member of several Senate subcommittees including: the Subcommittee on Clean Air and Nuclear Safety,

The Subcommittee on Transportation Safety, Infrastructure Security, and Water Quality. Finally, David Vitter is the ranking member of the Subcommittee on Transportation and Infrastructure.[190]

LARRY CRAIG

On June 11, 2007, United States Republican Senator Larry Craig of Idaho was arrested for "lewd conduct"[191] in a bathroom at the Minneapolis-St. Paul International Airport. Craig was allegedly in a bathroom stall when he tried to use his foot to touch the foot of the man in the adjacent stall. The man whose foot Craig was trying to touch turned out to be a law enforcement officer. The police officer whose foot Craig was trying to touch interpreted the gesture as a homosexual advance.[192]

Senator Craig initially pleaded guilty to the misdemeanor charge. However, once the media made his arrest public 8 weeks later, the Senator expressed regret about pleading guilty to the charges. Despite his guilty plea, Craig insisted his behavior was misconstrued by the police officer. According to Karsnia, the officer who was in the other stall, the Senator was trying to find someone with whom he could to engage in "lewd" behavior.

Karsnia explained, he could see the legislators "feet and ankles"[193] from his seated position. The officer said, Craig would periodically tap his foot to get his attention while moving his foot into the other stall. According to Karsnia the foot tapping was "a signal used by persons wishing to engage in lewd conduct."[194] The officer said he moved his foot up and down.[195] The officer explained they were not in the restroom alone at the time. Despite the presence of other men in the restroom, the Senator continued to move his right foot into the other stall until his foot reached the officer's foot.[196]

In a statement released by his staff, the legislator said, "Let me be clear: I am not gay and never have been."[197] He explained "I overreacted in Minneapolis."[198] Craig also said, "I should not have kept the arrest to myself, and should have told my family and friends about it."[199]

Craig later attempted to change his guilty plea to not guilty. He also announced he had no intention to resign from the United States Senate despite the urging of a few of his colleagues. His attempt to modify his plea was denied by the court. Moreover, the American Civil Liberties Union (ACLU) supported his continued efforts to change his plea to "not guilty." His and the ACLU's efforts failed.[200]

On September 1, 2007, Craig announced his resignation saying, he appreciated the support of the Governor and other public officials who stood with him at the time of his resignation announcement. Craig explained "he was proud of his record."[201] He said he would not continue serving while attempting to explore his legal options. He said his resignation was effective

September 1, 2007.[202] Despite having announced his resignation, the Senator changed his mind and decided to resign in 2008 at the conclusion of his Senate term.[203]

However, on October 4, 2007, after learning his request to change his plea from guilty to not guilty was denied, Craig withdrew his resignation and announced he would continue to serve his constituents until the end of his term in 2008. The U.S. Senator said, he was "extremely disappointed with the ruling" [204] and declared he was innocent of the charges."[205] He issued a statement saying, "I will continue to serve Idaho in the United States Senate, and there are several reasons for that. As I continued to work for Idaho over the past three weeks here in the Senate, I have seen that it is possible for me to work here effectively." However, Craig said he would retire and not seek reelection when his term expires in 2008. On February 12, 2008, The United States Senate Ethics Committee found Senator Craig's behavior "improper."[206] Despite the disapproval of his colleagues, The Idaho Senator said, "I will continue to serve the people of Idaho."[207]

Craig was also reprimanded by the Ethics Committee for using campaign funds to pay for legal fees associated with his case. The Committee maintained Craig was guilty of inappropriately using $213,000 of his campaign funds despite knowing he should have requested permission before doing so.[208]

After completing his senate term, Craig continued legal maneuvers in federal court to get charges of campaign finance violations dismissed. In March 2008, a federal judge declined Craig's motion to dismiss the charges due to failure to demonstrate he was traveling on official Senate business at the time of his arrested in a Minneapolis airport in 2007. U.S. District Court Judge Amy Berman Jackson disagreed, saying, his actions in the airport bathroom were not related to his legislative duties.[209] As a consequence of his bathroom antics and use of campaign funds to pay legal fees, Craig thwarted any hopes he may have had to run for a second U.S. Senate term. Former Senator Craig is retired and occasionally engages in public speaking engagements.[210] He is married and has three adopted children.[211]

MARK FOLEY

The United States House of Representatives voted on September 29, 2006, to investigate allegations that Congressman Mark Foley (R-FL) sent "explicit emails and instant messages"[212] to male pages working in the House of Representatives. Foley was a member of the Republican Party leadership and sponsored anti-pornography legislation and co-chaired a committee charged with protecting "missing and exploited children."[213] The legislator was alleged to have requested a picture from a sixteen year old page.[214] Another former page told the media Foley had sex with him; Foley never admitted to having a sexual encounter with a page.[215] Mark Foley admitted sending the messages but referred to them as common practice."[216] Foley told the media his office kept photos of pages for future requests for letters of recommendations for college.[217]

Foley's staff admitted the congressman sent the e-mails. However, congressional staffers described the content of the emails as "completely innocent." Foley's staff said the congressman was innocent of wrongdoing, but was "too friendly and too engaging" with pages. The inappropriate emails were sent by Representative Foley from his personal email account,[218] which raised questions about whether his communication with the former page was official congressional business. In fact, the former congressional page was unnerved by the lewd emails. Foley's staffer told the media, "This freaked me out."[219]

Mark Foley's Chief of Staff, Elizabeth, told reporters the e-mail exchange began when the teen asked the congressman for a letter of recommendation. The explanation sounds reasonable. However, the teen never worked for Representative Foley. Foley's Chief of Staff maintained the scandal was a part of an "ugly smear campaign,"[220] on the part of Democrats who wanted to damage the legislator's reputation and political career.[221]

In one message, Mark Foley wrote, "did you have fun at your conference...what do you want for your birthday coming up...what stuff do you like to do." In another email, the congressman inquired about how the teen was weathering the hurricane. In the same email, Foley asked the teenager to send him a picture. The teen shared the email with Foley staff writing, "sick sick sick sick sick."[222]

Despite his insistence that he was innocent, U.S. Representative Mark Foley announced his resignation less than twenty-four hours after the scandal broke and the House Ethics Committee announced its decision to investigate the teen's allegations against Foley. Moreover, Foley was informed that ABC News had copies of more explicit emails and instant messages he sent to other male congressional pages.[223] The congressman's resignation was likely prompted by knowledge that the gravity of his predatory actions would become public.

Shortly after resigning, the former congressman checked into an alcohol treatment facility.[224] Moreover, Foley told the media he was molested as a child by a Catholic priest.[225] The former Catholic priest, Anthony Mercieca, admitted to having had a sexual relationship with Foley when he was in his teens.[226] Finally, the former member of Congress admitted he was homosexual in 2007.[227] Rumors about his sexual orientation had been since "the early 1970s."[228]

In 2009, the state of Florida announced it would not pursue charges against Mark Foley[229] According to court officials, there was "insufficient evidence to pursue criminal charges."[230] Ultimately, Foley's political career was not ruined by a smear campaign on the part of the opposition party, but rather Foley's political career was ruined because he attempted to seduce former congressional pages.

BRIAN J. DOYLE

On April 5, 2006, Department of Homeland Security Press Secretary Brian Doyle (R) was arrested for attempting to seduce a teenage girl. Mr. Doyle thought he was exchanging emails with a 14-year-old girl. Doyle was communicating with an undercover Polk County police officer who was "conducting a computer crimes detective."[231] Doyle allegedly sent graphic sexual material to someone he thought was a teenage girl.[232] The fifty-five year old Doyle "graphically explained to a 14-year-old girl what he would like to do to her and what he would like her to do to him."[233] Oddly enough, The Homeland Security employee told the "young girl," his real name, age, and telephone contact information.[234] Mr. Doyle was arrested and charged with "23 charges"[235] with a Polk County police officer who posed as a child in a sting operation.[236] He was charged with using the internet to transmit inappropriate sexual material to a minor. Shortly after being arrested, Mr. Doyle confessed he preferred "young girls."[237] Although he was single, Doyle was in a fourteen year relationship at the time of his arrest.

After learning of Brian Doyle's arrest, The Department of Homeland Security issued a statement saying, "We take these allegations very seriously and we will cooperate fully with this ongoing investigation."[238] The federal government employee was suspended for his actions for engaging in inappropriate conduct with a minor and using the internet to send her pornographic material.[239] Brian Doyle pleaded "no contest to seven counts of using a computer to seduce a child and 16 counts of transmitting harmful material to a minor,"[240] which could have landed the former Department of Homeland Secretary employee in federal prison for up to 115 years.[241] Doyle was 56 years old when he received his punishment for sending pornographic material to a young girl. Doyle received a plea agreement, which reduced the jail sentence to five years and ten years probation. The plea deal also requires Doyle to pay fines assessed by the court. Lastly, the agreement required the former government press secretary to "register as a sex offender."[242] Mr. Doyle was released from prison in 2011.

JACK RYAN

In the summer of 2004, Jack Ryan's (R-IL) race for U.S. Senate began to unraveled when allegations made by his wife, Jeri Ryan, in their divorce proceedings were made public.[243] The Ryans were married in 1991. The forty-four year old wealthy investment banker was married to his wife for seven years. Jeri Ryan filed for divorce in 1998 citing "irreconcilable differences."[244]

As if the sex scandal was not enough, Jack Ryan's wife, Jeri, was a well known for playing the role of "Seven" on Star Trek: Voyager. Jeri Ryan filed for divorce claiming her husband "pressured her to have sex at swinger's clubs in New York, Paris and New Orleans while other patrons watched."[245] The divorce petition maintained Mr. Ryan forced his wife to engage in public sex with strangers. Jeri Lynn Ryan told court officials, the clubs were exclusive sex clubs. She said she refused to go into one of the clubs because it had mattresses in cubicles. Jeri Ryan described another club as having cages, whips and an apparatus hanging from the ceiling. She said her husband asked her to have sex with him while another couple watched. According to court records, Jeri stated Jack Ryan repeatedly asked her to engage in sexual activity with him in the presence of onlookers. Eventually, the Ryans left the sex club. She told the court her husband apologized to her and "it was out of his system."[246]

Jack Ryan told the media he was faithful to his wife. He did acknowledge planning trips for them, but insisted the trips "did not include the type of activities she describes."[247] Despite maintaining his innocence, Mr. Ryan announced he was ending his campaign for the Illinois Senate seat. In his speech, Ryan saying, "It's clear to me that a vigorous debate on the issues most likely could not take place if I remain in the race." Ryan went on to say, "What would take place, rather, is a brutal, scorched-earth campaign—the kind of campaign that has turned off so many voters, the kind of politics I refuse to play."[248] Finally, Ryan told the audience, he was withdrawing from the Senate race.[249]

Despite the public fallout from the scandal discovered through the Ryan's divorce proceedings, Jeri Lynn Ryan issued a statement saying, Ryan was a good person and a good parent. According to court records, Mrs. Ryan received approximately "$20 million in Goldman Sachs stock."[250] The wealthy former investment banker was able to keep "$40 million" of his Goldman Sachs investments.[251] Jack Ryan became another "wanna-be" politician whose political aspirations became a casualty of a sex scandal.

DON SHERWOOD

In October 2006, Congressman Don Sherwood (R-PA) found himself embattled in a sex scandal that involved alleged physical abuse. Ms. Ore, Sherwood's mistress claimed he "choked her."[252] Police had been called to the Congressman's apartment for a domestic violence incident. Charges were not filed against the member of Sherwood, a four-term member. At the time the scandal made national news, Representative Sherwood was in was in the middle of a congressional reelection. Prior to the scandal breaking, his reelection was practically guaranteed.

The U.S. Representative acknowledged having an extramarital affair and told reporters he regretting cheating on his wife in a campaign advertisement. He also said his behavior alienated him from his family saying, "the affair nearly cost him the love of his wife and his daughters."[253] Although he acknowledged the sexual relationship with Ms. Cynthia Ore, Sherwood adamantly denied abusing his mistress.[254] He attempted to appeal to constituents saying, "While I'm truly sorry for disappointing you, I never wavered from my commitment to reduce taxes, create jobs and bring home our fair share."[255] He asked for their forgiveness telling them "Should you forgive me, you can count on me to keep on fighting hard for you and your family."[256]

The representative was not charged with domestic violence, Ms. Ore sued Representative Sherwood for "repeatedly choking"[257] her. Sherwood apologized for the affair but denied abusing Ore. Don Sherwood and Ms. Ore reached a settlement agreement. The amount of the settlement was not disclosed to the public.

Chris Carney, the Democratic challenger who ran against Sherwood remarked, "Don Sherwood really hasn't represented our values or our interests in Washington, people are ready for a change."[258] Carney, moved to Pennsylvania when he accepted an "assistant professorship position at the University of Pennsylvania"[259] to teach American Government and U.S. Foreign Policy.[260]

In his efforts to defeat Sherwood, Carney ran a campaign ad that featured a voter commenting on Congressman Sherwood's adulterous behavior. The voter remarked, "This incident with Don Sherwood just cuts right at the core values of our district." Carney's campaign ad also displayed the words "repeatedly choking"[261] and trying to"strangle the plaintiff"[262] which were taken from the lawsuit filed against Congressman Sherwood.

President George W. Bush attempted to minimize the damage by campaigning with Sherwood at a luncheon. He told Sherwood's supporters, "I'm pleased to be here with Don Sherwood. He has got a record of accomplishment."[263] Despite receiving campaign assistance from the president, news of Sherwood's extramarital affair and alleged physical abuse effectively derailed Sherwood's reelection efforts. The incumbent Congressman was defeated in the 2004 congressional election. Not only did the extramarital affair and physical abuse scandal shake Sherwood's political career, it heavily impacted his family life as well.

DAVID DREIER

Conservative Republican Congressman David Dreier found himself facing
media scrutiny about his homosexual relationship with Brad Smith, his Chief
of Staff. The California member of Congress also lived with Smith. Dreier's
Chief of Staff was also paid "$156,600 salary before benefits."[264] Smith's
salary was extremely high unusually high," especially when compared to
other chief of staff salaries of members of his rank. Smith's salary was
comparable to the salary of the Speaker's Chief of Staff and other powerful
members of the United States House of Representatives.[265]

Dreier was known for his service on the House Rules Committee. Moreover, the self-proclaimed conservative member had earned a reputation for
consistently voting against gay rights legislation.[266] Dreier voted against
"Don't Ask. Don't Tell,"[267] legislation and legislative measures that would
permit homosexuals to adopt children. He also voted against legislation that
advocated giving homosexuals "protected status" in hate crime policy. Moreover, Dreier voted against the "Don't Ask. Don't Tell," legislation.

In the end, Dreier became a casualty of his own doing. His anti-gay stance
and homosexual lifestyle infuriated members of the homosexual community
and his constituents. The fifty-nine year old member from California announced he would not seek reelection on February 29, 2012.[268] The former
representative has gone from a position of power to virtual anonymity. Dreier
currently works for a commission where he is responsible for promoting
retreats.[269]

ED SCHROCK

Legislator Ed Schrock found himself in the middle of a sex scandal in 2004.
Schrock was married with one child at the time questions about his sexuality
were raised when he was "outed" for being homosexual by Michael Rogers
creator of blogACTIVE.[270] Rogers' website publishes names of homosexual
lawmakers who are not supportive of gay rights. Mr. Rogers told the media
he was angry with the legislator. Like David Dreier, Congressman Schrock
consistently voted against gay rights legislation.[271] Dreier voted against legislation that would give marriage rights to homosexuals.[272] Rogers posted an
audio link, allegedly of Schrock on a gay sex line looking for someone to
engage in homosexual acts.[273]

Schrock's chief of staff Tom Gordy issued a statement about the accusations made by gay activist Michael Rogers. Gordy argued the rumors and
accusations were "unsubstantiated."[274] Gordy also told reporters Schrock
would continue with is reelection campaign.[275]

When Mark McKinney, Virginia Beach Republican Committee Chairman, was asked about Schrock's departure from Congress, he said, "It's a shame that he had to resign because of a Web site that is trying to push a point of view . . . but . . . I have to believe that this was the reason he stepped down."[276]

Despite claiming the allegations about his sexuality were false, the two-term member of Congress suspended his reelection campaign. On August 30, 2004. He did not give a reason for his decision to retire from his position. He did indicate there were "allegations" made against him, which caused him to reconsider his ability to serve his congressional district in Virginia.[277] Ed Schrock now lives a very private life in Virginia with his family.

GARY CONDIT

Prior to 2004, Representative Gary Condit's congressional seat was considered a "safe seat."[278] The Democratic member of Congress from California had managed to avoid negative media coverage.[279] The quiet, relatively unknown member made national and international news when his extramarital affair with Chandra Levy, a 23-year-old intern who worked in his Washington office, was exposed following her disappearance in May 2001.[280] Levy disappeared while "exercising in Rock Creek Park in Washington, D.C."[281] She was reported missing by her parents when she failed to return home after completing her internship.

Despite the sex scandal and questions about whether he was involved in Levy's disappearance, Condit continued to pursue his party's nomination for California's 18th congressional district for the seventh time. However, amid questions about his extramarital exploits, the media began digging into Representative Condit's sex life. Condit's constituents were surprised when information surfaced suggesting he was a "serial"[282] adulterer. Consequently, Gary Condit's political reputation dramatically suffered when news of the affair and her death made national and international headlines.[283]

The member of Congress consistently denied being involved in Ms. Levy's disappearance.[284] Nevertheless, his political career was compromised because of his extramarital affair with the young intern who met with an untimely death.[285] Ms. Levy's "skeletal remains"[286] were eventually discovered in Rock Creek Park on May 22, 2002, more than one year after she disappeared.[287]

Representative Condit likely never imagined he would find himself at the center of a sex scandal, especially considering comments he made about William Jefferson Clinton's affair with a young White House intern named Monica Lewinsky.[288] However, life has a strange way of highlighting hypocrisy.

In September 2001, a prison informant told law enforcement officials he befriended a 20-year-old Salvadorian man named Ingmar Guandique who said he killed Ms. Levy. Police admitted they spoke with Guandique about Ms. Levy in July 2001. However, in September the suspect was shown a photograph of Chandra Levy. In 2001, Ingmar Guandique told investigators "he had seen her in the park"[289] when he was questioned by the police about Levy's disappearance. Eventually, Guandique was arrested and charged with Levy's murder.[290] In November 2011, Ingmar Guandique was convicted of first-degree murder for killing Washington intern Chandra Levy.[291] Despite Guandique's conviction for the murder of Levy, her parents continue to question whether police caught her murderer.[292]

In an interview with NBC, Bert Fields, the Condit's family attorney, told reporters, "At least Gary Condit can find some measure of closure to this nightmare."[293] Fields further explained, "It's a complete vindication, but that comes a little late."[294]

In November 2011, Gary Condit's son, Chad, told the media his father was irreparably harmed by the intern's disappearance and murder. Chad Condit told Good Morning America viewers, "I don't know that it will ever entirely be behind him."[295] Moreover, the former legislator's son said, "He didn't deserve what had happened and we have been dealing with it for ten years. It is just unfortunate. It has worn on my Mom and Dad."[296]

Gary Condit paid a hefty price for his infidelity. The admitted adulterer was defeated in his congressional reelection bid. The former member of Congress is 60 years old and lives in Phoenix, Arizona. He and his wife Jean, spend their time with their son and grandchildren. Condit lives a quiet life away from the media spotlight. He currently works in real estate.[297]

GENERAL DAVID PETRAEUS

General David Petraeus retired from the United States Army on August 31, 2011. One week after retiring from the military, Petreaus was appointed director of the U.S. Central Intelligence Agency (CIA) on September 6, 2011. Shortly after receiving his appointment to lead the CIA, David Petreaus was under attack for having an adulterous affair with a graduate of West Point named Paula Broadwell. Both Petreaus and Broadwell were married when they got involved in an adulterous affair.[298]

The relationship between David Petraeus and Paula Broadwell drew attention from the FBI when someone noticed a series of emails from Broadwell to a woman named Jill Kelley. Broadwell sent Kelley emails telling her to keep her distance from Petreaus. Broadwell apparently thought Ms. Kelley was romantically involved with the general. Ms. Kelley reported the "harassing" emails. It was later revealed Paula Broadwell sent the messages. Thus,

Mrs. Broadwell's jealous antics set in motion a series of actions that would eventually expose her extramarital affair with the married four-star general.[299]

Ms. Broadwell chronicled the general's rise to power in "All In"[300] a book she wrote about the four star-general's life and education. Oddly enough, Petreaus' rise to political power was short-lived. In early January 2013, only a few months after assuming the leadership role with the CIA, Petreaus became the focus of a Federal Bureau of Investigations (FBI) probe. Consequently, General David Petreaus announced his resignation on January 30, 2013, after the FBI investigation exposed his extramarital affair with his biographer. Questions were also raised about whether Ms. Broadwell had access to "classified information."[301]

Revelations about Petreaus' "sex-ploits' further caused the government to question General John Allen's relationship and email communications with Jill Kelley. Allen was a top ranked military official who led troops in Afghanistan. Due to questions raised by the U.S. Department of Defense about Allen's relationship with Jill Kelley and questions about whether he shared classified information with her through email, Allen's nomination for Supreme Allied Chief of NATO was suspended by the Obama administration.[302]

A few months after his resignation, the retired four star general and ex-CIA director told a group of veterans in Los Angeles, "I join you keenly aware that I am regarded in a different light now than I was a year ago when (University of Southern California brass) invited me to speak at this event."[303] Patreaus acknowledged he exhibited "extremely poor judgment."[304] The former CIA director also said, "Such behavior is unacceptable, both as a husband and as the leader of an organization such as ours."[305]

Ultimately, the adulterous affair with Mrs. Paula Broadwell cost the former CIA director his political career and tarnished his reputation as a leader. His marriage to his wife, Holly, remains intact. Petreaus had to deal with his "furious" wife who let him brave the media scrutiny alone.[306] Broadwell's family had to deal with the media scrutiny caused by her actions. She and her husband, Scott, are still married and raising their children together.[307] The Petreaus scandal caused residual damage to others associated with him. The sex scandal also hurt the political career of four star general John Allen. General Allen failed to receive the nomination to post with NATO. He retired from the United States Army in February 2013.[308] It remains to be seen as to whether Petreaus' career can be revived. Only time will tell.

CONCLUSION

The aforementioned sex-based scandals brought some level of embarrassment to the personal and professional lives of those involved in adulterous, illicit sexual relationships or activities. As a consequence of having their lustful and sexual activities exposed to the general public, each public official suffered some degree of disapproval or backlash for his/her inappropriate behavior. Some officials involved in sex scandals lost their political career. Among those whose political careers ended due to an inability to gain control over their sexual urges which led to their resigning from office were David Wu, Anthony Weiner, John Ensign, Randall Tobias, David Vitter, Larry Craig, Chris Lee, Mark Souder, Tom Ganley, and Samuel B. Kent. Samuel Kent, Vitto Fosella, and David Vitter were indicted, tried, convicted in a court of law and sentenced to prison for their illegal actions. Some were fined for their inappropriate behavior. A large number of elected or public officials resigned from political office. Among those who resigned from office after their sex scandal was revealed to the public were David Wu, Anthony Weiner, Chris Lee, Mark Souder, Eric Massa, Samuel Kent, John Ensign, Larry Craig, Mark Foley and General David Petraeus. Some officials like John Edwards experienced strained family relationships due to their inability to control or manage their sexual appetite. As a consequence of his behavior, a court of law required Brian Doyle to register as a sex offender on the National Sex Offender Registry. Both David Wu and Mark Foley entered rehabilitation centers for treatment to attempt to put their splintered or shattered lives back together. In conclusion, every elected official or government official involved or implicated in the sex scandals addressed in this chapter tainted his/her professional and personal lives because they were unable to control his/her sexual urges.

NOTES

1. Paul Stanley, "David Wu Faced Pressure to Resign After Sex Scandal," *Christian Post* [database online] available from http://www.christianpost.com/news/david-wu-faced-pressure-to-resign-after-sex-scandal ; Internet; accessed December 14, 2011.

2. Paul Stanley, "Democrat Congressman David Wu Embroiled in Sex Scandal," *Christian Post* [database online] available from http://www.christianpost.com/news/congressman-david-wu-at-center-of-dc-scandal ; Internet; accessed December 14, 2011.

3. Charles Pope, "Sources: Young Woman Accuses Oregon Rep. David Wu of Aggressive, Unwanted Sexual Encounter," *The Oregonian* [database online] available from http://www.oregonlive.com/politics/index.ssf/2011/07/ rep_david_wu_accussed_of_aggres.html; Internet; accessed December 14, 2013, and Paul Stanley, "Democratic Congressman David Wu Embroiled in Sex Scandal," *Christian Post* [database online] available from http://www.christianpost.com/news/congressman-david-wu-at-center-of-dc-scandal ; Internet; accessed December 14, 2011.

4. Paul Stanley, "Democrat Congressman David Wu Embroiled in Sex Scandal," *Christian Post* [database online] available from http://www.christianpost.com/news/congressman-david-wu-at-center-of-dc-scandal; Internet; accessed December 14, 2011.

5. Stephanie Condon, "David Wu Announces Resignation Amid Sex Scandal," *CBS News* [database online] available from http://www.cbsnews.com/2101-503544_162-20083560 .html?tag+contentMain;contentBoo ; Internet; accessed December 14, 2011.

6. Paul Stanley, "Democrat Congressman David Wu Embroiled in Sex Scandal," *Christian Post* [database online] available from http://www.christianpost.com/news/congressman-david-wu-at-center-of-dc-scandal ; Internet; accessed December 14, 2011.

7. Charles Pope and Janie Har, "Rep. David Wu Announces He Will Resign After Accusations of Sexual Misconduct," *The Oregonian* [database online] available from http://www.oregonlive.com/politics/index.ssf/2011/07/rep_david_wu_resigns.html and http://www.cnn.com/video/#/video/politics/2011/07/31/rs.david.wu.resignation.cnn; Internet; accessed December 14, 2013, and Paul Stanley, "Democrat Congressman David Wu Embroiled in Sex Scandal." *Christian Post* [database online] available from http://www.christianpost.com/congressman-david-wu-at-center-of-dc-scandal ; Internet; accessed December 14, 2011.

8. Paul Stanley, "David Wu Faced Pressure to Resign After Sex Scandal," *Christian Post* [database online] available from http://www.christianpost.com/news/david-wu-faced-pressure-to-resign-after-sex-scandal ; Internet; accessed December 14, 2011.

9. Paul Stanley, "David Wu Faced Pressure to Resign After Sex Scandal," *Christian Post* [database online] available from http:/www.christianpost.com/news/david-wu-faced-pressure-to-resign-after-sex-scandal ; Internet; accessed December 14, 2011.

10. Ibid.

11. Paul Stanley, "Democrat Congressman David Wu Embroiled in Sex Scandal," *Christian Post* [database online] available from http://www.christianpost.com/news/congressman-david-wu-at-center-of-dc-sex-scandal; Internet; accessed December 14, 2011.

12. Paul Stanley, Democrat Congressman David Wu Embroiled in Sex Scandal," *Christian Post* [database online] available from http://www.christianpost.com/news/congressman-david-wu-at-enter-of-dc-sex-scandal ; Internet; accessed December 14, 2011.

13. Joyce Chen, "Anthony Weiner is The Latest Politician To Don Notorious 'Sex Scandal Face," *Zimbio* [database online] available from http://www.zimbio.com/Huma+Abedin/ articles/ajw9rblwLK1/Anthony+Weiner+latest ; Internet; accessed December 14, 2011, 1

14. "Weinergate: Congressman Claims "Facebook Hacked" As Lewd Photo Hits Twitter,'" BigGovernment.com [database online] available from http://www.biggovernment.com/ publius/2011/05/28/weinergate-congressman-claims-facebook-hacked-as-lewd-photo-hits-twitter, May 28, 2011; Internet; accessed December 18, 2011.

15. "Anthony Weiner to Seek Treatment," *Huffington Post* [database online] available from www.huffingtonpost.com/2011/06/11/anthony-weiner-treatment_n_875422.html , June 11, 2011; Internet; accessed July 8, 2013.

16. Michael Barbaro, Matt Flegeheimer and Ashley Parker, "Weiner Resigns in Chaotic Final Scene," *The New York Times* [database online] available from http://www.nytimes.com/ 2011/06/17/nyregion/anthony-d-weiner-tells-friends-he-will-resign.html?pagewanted=all& _r=0 ; Internet; accessed December 14, 2011, 1.

17. Micahel Babaro, Matt Flegenheimer and Ashley Parker, "Weiner Resigns in Chaotic Final Scene," *The New York Times* [database online] available from http://www.nytimes.com/ 2011/06/17/nyregion/anthony-d-weiner-tells-friends-he-will-resign.html?pagewanted=all& _r=0 ; Internet; accessed December 14, 2011, 1 and "Weiner Admits Tweet," CNN News [database online] available from http://www.cnn.com/video/#/video/bestoftv/ 2011/06/16/ exp.sot.weiner.admits.tweet.cnn; Internet; accessed December 18, 2011, and "Weiner Re-signs," *CNN News* [database online] available from http://www.cnn.com/ video/#/video/be-stoftv/2011/06/16/exp.weiner.resigns.com ; Internet; accessed December 18, 2011.

18. Micahel Babaro, Matt Flegenheimer and Ashley Parker, "Weiner Resigns in Chaotic Final Scene," *The New York Times* [database online] available from http://www.nytimes.com/ 2011/06/17/nyregion/anthony-d-weiner-tells-friends-he-will-resign.html?pagewanted=all& _r=0 ; Internet; accessed December 14, 2011, 1.

19. Joyce Chen, "Anthony Weiner is Latest Politician To Don Notorious 'Sex Scandal Face,'" *Zimbio* [database online] available from http://www.zimbio.com/Huma+Abedin/articles/ ajw9rblwLKq/Anthony+Weiner; Internet; accessed December 14, 2011, 2.

20. Micahel Babaro, Matt Flegenheimer and Ashley Parker, "Weiner Resigns in Chaotic Final Scene," *The New York Times* [database online] available from http://www.nytimes.com/ 2011/06/17/nyregion/anthony-d-weiner-tells-friends-he-will-resign.html?pagewanted=all& _r=0 ; Internet; accessed December 14, 2011, 1.

21. Ibid, 3.

22. "Weiner Featured in Exhibition in New York Museum of Sex," *ABC News* [database online] available from abcnewsgo.com/Health/wirestory/anthony-weiner-featured-museum-sex-exhibit-19603620#unsuphafeme; Internet; July 8, 2013.

23. Emily Ngo, "Huma Abedin to Join Husband Anthony Weiner's Campaign for NYC Mayor," *Huffington Post* (New York) [database online] available from www.huffingtonpost.com/ 2013/06/17/huma-albedin-to-join-husband-anthony-weiner 's-campaign-for-nyc-myor_n_3451562; Internet; accessed July 8, 2013.

24. Jonathan Lemire, "I Have Forgiven Him: Huma Abedin Defends Embattled Husband Anthony Weiner As Pressure Mounts To Quit New York Mayoral Race," *National Post* [database online] available from http://www.nationalpost.com/m/wp/news/world/ blog.html?b=news.nationalpost.com/2013/07/24/i-have-forgiven-him-huma-abedin-defends-embattled-husband-anthony-weiner-as-pressure-mounts-to-quit-new-york-mayoral-race ; Internet; accessed July 31, 2013, 1.

25. Ibid.

26. Jonathan Lemire, "I Have Forgiven Him: Huma Abedin Defends Embattled Husband Anthony Weiner As Pressure Mounts To Quit New York Mayoral Race," *National Post* [database online] available from http://www.nationalpost.com/m/wp/news/world/ blog.html?b=news.nationalpost.com/2013/07/24/i-have-forgiven-him-huma-abedin-defends-embattled-husband-anthony-weiner-as-pressure-mounts-to-quit-new-york-mayoral-race ; Internet; accessed July 31, 2013, 1.

27. Abby Phillip, "Weiner Falls Hard in Latest Poll," *ABC News* [database online] available from http://abcnews.go.com/m/blogEntry?id=19808987&ref=https%3A%2F%2F www.google.com%2F ; Internet; accessed July 31, 2013, 1, and "Weiner Should Drop Out, NYC Likely Dem Voters Tell Quinnipiac University Poll; Quinn Leads, With De Blasio, Thompson Tied For Second,"Quinnipiac University [database online] available http:// www.quinnipiac.edu/institutes-and-centers/polling-institute/new-york-city/release-de-tail?ReleaseID=1929 ; Internet; accessed July 31, 2013, 1.

28. Michael Howard Saul, "Weiner Drops To Fourth In Poll," *Wall Street Journal* [database online] available from http://online.wsj.com/article SB1000142412788732435470457863 6532483079010?mg=reno64-wsj,%20July%2030,%202013.html?dsk=y ; Internet; accessed July 31, 2013, 1.

29. Tara Palmeri and Josh Saul, "Weiner Flips Out In Defeat," *New York Post* [database online] available from http://nypost.com/2013/09/11/sext-gal-crashes-weiners-party/ ; Internet; accessed September 25, 2013, 1.

30. Ibid.

31. Brian Montopoli, "GOP Congressman Christopher Lee Resigns Over Craigslist Scandal," *CBS News* [database online] available from http://www.cbsnews.com2012-503544_162-20031264.html ; Internet; accessed December 14, 2011, 1.

32. Ibid, 2.

33. Brian Montopoli, "GOP Congressman Christopher Lee Resigns Over Craigslist Scandal," *CBS News* [database online] available from http://www.cbsnews.com2012-503544_162-20031264.html ; Internet; accessed December 14, 2011, 1.

34. Ibid.

35. Ibid.

36. Ibid.

37. Ibid, 2.

38. Maureen O'Connor, "Married GOP Congressman Sent Sexy Pictures to Craigslist Babe," *Gawker* [database online] available from http:gawker.com/5755071/married-gop-congressman-sent-secy-pictures-to-craiglist-babe ; Internet; accessed December 18, 2011.

39. "Woman Behind Congressman Chris Lee's Craigslist Fallout Speaks Out," *ABC News* [database online] available from abcnews.go.com/Politics/congressman-christopher-lees-craigslist-woman-yesha-callahan-speaks/story?id=12890665#.UdwYWBafemE; Internet; accessed December 18, 2013.

40. Brian Montopoli, "GOP Congressman Christopher Lee Resigns Over Craigslist Scandal," *CBS News* [database online] available from http://www.cbsnews.com/2101-503544_162-20031264.html ; Internet; accessed December 14, 2011, 1.

41. Brian Montopoli, "GOP Congressman Christopher Lee Resigns Over Craigslist Scandal," *CBS News* [database online] available from http:www.cbsnews.com/2101-5303544_162-20031264.html ; Internet; accessed December 14, 2011, 1, and Maureen O'Connor, "Congressman Chris Lee Resigns Following Gawker Revelation," *Gawker* [database online] available from http://gawker.com/575677/craiglist-congressman-resigns ; Internet; accessed December 14, 2011 and "Craigslist Congressman Resigns," *CNN News* [database online] available from http://www.cnn.com/video/data/2.0/video/bestoftv/2011/02/09/exp.jk.christopher.lee.resigns.chh.html ; Internet; accessed July 9, 2013.

42. Brian Montopoli, "GOP Congressman Christopher Lee Resigns Over Craigslist Scandal," *CBS News* [database online] available from http://cbsnews.com/2101-5303544_162-20031264.html ; Internet; accessed December 14, 2011, 1.

43. Ibid.

44. Ibid.

45. "Woman Behind Congressman Chris Lee's Craigslist Fallout Speaks Out," *ABC News* [database online] available from http://abcnews.go.com/Politics/congressman-christopher-lees-craigslist-woman-yesha-callahan-speaks/story?id=12890665#.UdwYWBafemE; Internet; accessed December 14, 2011.

46. "Indiana Congressman Resigns After Admitting Affair," *CNN* [database online] available from http://news.blogs.cnn.com/2010/05/18/gop-aid-indiana-rep-mark-souder-to resign/?iref=allsearch; Internet; accessed December 10, 2011.

47. Chad Pergram, "Indiana Rep. Mark Souder Resigns After Affair With Staffer," *Fox News* [database online] available from http://www.foxnews.com/politics/2010/05/18 ; Internet; accessed December 10, 2011, 1.

48. "Questions About Souder Affair Surfaced in February," *Indiana News Center* [database online] available from http://www.indiananewscenter.com/news/local/94158474 ; Internet; accessed December 18, 2011, 1.

49. Chad Pergram "Indiana Rep. Mark Souder Resigns After Affair With Staffer," *Fox News* [database online] available from http://foxnews.com/politics/2010/05/18 ; Internet; accessed December 14, 2011, 1.

50. Ibid.

51. Ibid.

52. Ibid.

53. Ibid.

54. Ibid.

55. Scott Sarvay, "Tracy Jackson Resigns From Congressional Staff," *INC NOW* [database online] available from http://www.indiananewscenter.com/news/local/94293449.html ; Internet; accessed December 12, 2010.

56. "Tracy Jackson: Alleged MISTRESS of Rep. Mark Souder," *Huffington Post* [database online] available from http://huffingtonpost.com/2010/05/18/tracy-jackson-mark-souder_n_580144.html ; Internet; accessed December 12, 2011.

57. John Bresnahan and Josh Kraushaar, "Hoyer Knew of Massa Allegations," *Politico* [database online] available from http://www.politico.com/news/stories/0310/33864.htm l; Internet; accessed December 12, 2011, 1.

58. Ibid.

59. Susan Crabtree and Jordan Fabian, "Massa Scandal Expodes," *The Hill* [database online] available from http://thehill.com/homenews/house/85829-massa-scandal-explodes-?tmpl=component; Internet; accessed December 14, 2011, 1

60. John Bresnahan and Josh Kraushaar, "Hoyer Knew of Messa Allegations," *Politico* [database online] available from http://www.politico.com/news/stories/0310/33864.html ; Internet; accessed December 14, 2011, 1.

61. Susan Crabtree and Jordan Fabian, "Massa Scandal Explodes," *The Hill* [database online] available from http://thehill.com/homenews/house/8529-massa-scandal-explodes-?tmpl=component ; Internet; March 9, 2010, 1.

62. John Breshahan and Josh Fabian, "Hoyer Knew of Messa Allegations," Politico [database online] available from http://www.politico.com/news/stories/0310/33864.html ; Internet; accessed December 14, 2011, 1.

63. "House Leader: Ethics Panel Ends Massa Probe," *Fox News* [database online] available from http://www.foxnews.com/politics/2010/03/10 ; Internet; accessed December 15, 2011, 1.

64. John Breshahan and Josh Kraushaar, "Hoyer Knew of Massa Allegations," *Politico* [database online] available from http:politico.com/news/stories/0310/33864.html ; Internet; accessed December 15, 2011, 1.

65. John Bresnahan and Glenn Thrush, "Rep. Eric Massa To Resign," *Politico* [database online] available from http://politico.com/news/stories/0320/34001.html ; Internet; accessed December 14, 2011, 1.

66. Susan Crabtree and Jordan Fabian, "Massa Scandal Explodes," *The Hill* [database online] available from http://thehill.com/homenews/house/85829-massa-scandal-explodes-?tmpl=component ; Internet; accessed December 14, 2011, 1.

67. Ibid.

68. Ibid.

69. Susan Crabtree and Jordan Fabian, "Massa Scandal Explodes," *The Hill* [database online] available from http://thehill.com/homenews/house/85829-massa-scandal-explodes-?tmpl=component ; Internet; accessed December 14, 2011, 2 and "Exclusive: Eric Massa on Glenn Beck," *Fox News* [database online] available from http://www.foxnews.com/story/0.2933.588685.00.html ; Internet; accessed December 14, 2011.

70. Susan Crabtree and Jordan Fabian, "Massa Scandal Explodes," *The Hill* [database online] available from http://thehill.com/homenews/house/85829-massa-scandal-explodes-?tmpl=component ; Internet; accessed December 14, 2011, 2

71. "House Leader: Ethics Panel Ends Mass Probe," *Fox News* [database online] available from http://foxnews.com/politics/2010/03/10/ethics-panel-ends-massa-probe-house-leader-says/ ; Internet; accessed December 12, 2011.

72. Ibid, 2.

73. Nick Wing, "Tom Ganley Accused of Sexually Assaulting Woman He Met At Tea Party Rally," *Huffington Post* [database online] available from http://www.huffingtonpost.com/2010/10/01/tom-ganley-sexual-assualt_n_746858.html?v ; Internet; accessed December 14, 2011, 2 and Chris Russel, "Woman Sues Ohio Candidate for Congress Alleging Harassment," *The Columbus Dispatch* [database online] available from www.dispatch.com/content/stories/local/ 2010/10/01/woman-sues-ohio-candidate-alleges-groping.html; Internet; accessed December 15, 2011.

74. Nick Wing, "Tom Ganley Accused of Sexually Assaulting Woman He Met At Tea Party Rally," *Huffington Post* [database online] available from http://www.huffingtonpost.com/2010/10/01/tom-ganley-sexual assault_n_746858.html?v; Internet; accessed December 14, 2011, 2.

75. Ibid.

76. Ibid.

77. Ibid.

78. Nick Wing, "Tom Ganley Accused of Sexually Assaulting Woman He Met At Tea Party Rally," *Huffington Post* [database online] available from http://www.huffingtonpost.com/2010/10/01/ tom-ganley-sexual-assualt_n_746858.html?v ; Internet; accessed December 14, 2011, 2.

79. Ibid.

80. Ibid, 2.

81. James McCarty and Mark Naymik, "Tom Ganley Blames Opponent, Democrats After Second Woman Accuses Him of Sexual Misconduct," Cleveland.com [database online] available from http://blog.cleveland.com/metro//print.html ; Internet; accessed December14, 2011, 1.

82. Ibid, 1.

83. Ibid.

84. Ibid.

85. James McCarty and Mark Naymik, "Tom Ganley Blames Opponent, Democrats After Second Women Accuses Him of Sexual Misconduct," Cleveland.com [database online] available from http://blog.cleveland.com/metro//print.html ; Internet; accessed December 14, 2011, 1.

86. Jen Steer, "Auto Dealer Tom Ganley Indicted on Sex, Kidnapping Charges," *News Net* [database online] available from http:www/newsnet5.com/dpp/news/local_news/cleveland_metro/ auto-dealer- tom-ganley-indicted-on-sex-kidnapping -charges; Internet; accessed December 15, 2011.

87. Mike Waterhouse, "Criminal Charges Dropped Against Tom Ganley After Alleged Victim Won't Continue With Trial," *News Net* [database online] available from http://www.newsnet5.com/dpp/news/local_news/cleveland_metro/criminal-charges-dropped-against-tom-ganley-after-alleged-victim-wont-continue-with-trial ; Internet; accessed July 10, 2013, 1.

88. Lise Olsen, "Details Emerge in Judge Kent Scandal," *Houston Chronicle* [database online] available from http://www.chron.com/news/houston-texas/article/Details-emerge-in-judge-Kent-scandal ; Internet; accessed December 14, 2011, 1 and Scott Michaels, "Federal Judge Probed on Harassment Allegations," *ABC News* [database online] available from http://abcnews.go.com/ The Law/story?id=3996717&page=1 ; Internet; accessed June 10, 2011, 1.

89. Lise Olsen, "Details Emerge in Judge Kent Scandal," *Houston Chronicle* [database online] available from http://www.chron.com/news/houston-texas/article/Details-emerge-in-Judge-Kent-scandal; Internet; accessed December 14, 2011, 1- 3.

90. Ibid, 2.

91. Ibid, 1.

92. Ibid.

93. Ibid, 2.

94. Ibid.

95. Ibid.

96. Ibid.

97. Ibid, 2.

98. Ibid.

99. Ibid.

100. Ibid.

101. Ibid.

102. Ibid.

103. Ibid.

104. Ibid, 3.

105. Ibid, 3.

106. Ibid, 3.

107. Ibid, 3.

108. Ibid, 3.

109. Theresa Cook and Gina Sunseri, "Federal Judge Indicted in Sex Abuse Case," *ABC News* [database online] available from://abcnews.go.com/TheLawFedCrimes/story?id=5681319&page=1 ; Internet; accessed July, 10, 2011, 1 and Theresa Cook and Gina Sunseri, "Not Guilty Plea in Judges Sex Abuse Case," *ABC News* [database online] available from http://www.abcnews.go.com/TheLaw/FedCrimes/story?id=5716176&page=1 ; Internet; accessed July, 10, 2013, 1.

110. "Judge Cops Plea To Elude Sex Crime Trial," *CBS News* [database online] available from http://www.cbsnews.com/stories/2009/02/23/national/main4821904.shtml?tag=mncol ;1st;1 ; Internet; accessed July 10, 2011, 1.

111. Ibid, 1.

112. "Judge Cops Plea To Elude Sex Crime Trial," *CBS News* [database online] available from   http://www.cbsnews.com/stories/2009/02/23/national/main4821904.shtml?tag=mncol ;1st;1 ; Internet; accessed December 14, 2011, 1.

113. "Senate Ends Impeachment of Jailed Judge Following Resignation," *Fox News* [database online] available from http://www.foxnews.com/politics/2009/07/22/senate-ends-impeachment-jailed-judge-following-resignation ; Internet; accessed July 10, 2011, 1 and S.A. Miller, "Impeached Judge Samuel B. Kent Tenders His Resignation," *The Washington Times* [database online] available from http://www.washingtontimes.com/news/2009/jun/27/impeached-judge-tenders-his-resignation ; Internet; accessed July 10, 2011, 1.

114. John Lofflin, "John Ensign Returns to Veterinary Practice," *U.S. Department of Veterans Affairs* [database online] available from http://veterinarynews.dvm360.com/dvm/Law+and+Ethics/John-Ensign-returns-to-veterinary-practice/ArticleStandard/Article/detail/781653 ; accessed July 12, 2013, 1 and Jane Morrison, "Senate Missteps No Longer Dog Veterinarian John Ensign," *Las Vegas Review Journal* [database online] available from http://www.reviewjournal.com/jane-ann-morrison/senate-missteps-no-longer-dog-veterinarian-john-ensign ; Internet; accessed July 12, 2013, 1.

115. "Nevada Sen. Ensign Admits Affair," *CNN News* [database online] available from http://www.cnn.com/2009/POLITICS/06/16/ensign.affair/index.ntml?iref=allsearch ; Internet; accessed June 16, 2013, 1.

116. Ibid.

117. Ibid, 1.

118. Ibid, 1.

119. Ibid.

120. Trish Turner, "Ensign Affair Referred o DOJ & FEC - - Torrid Affair Detailed," *Fox News* [database online] available from http://politics.blogs.foxnews.com/2011/05/12/ensign-affair-referred-doj-fec-torrid-affair-detailed ; accessed July 12, 2013, 1 and "Ethics Panel Urges Probe Ensign," ABC News [database online] available from.http://abcnews.go.com/Politics/ ethics-panel-urges-probe-ensign/storyid=13593947; Internet; accessed December 15, 2011.

121. Trish Turner, "Ensign Affair Referred o DOJ & FEC - - Torrid Affair Detailed," *Fox News* [database online] available from http://politics.blogs.foxnews.com/2011/05/12/ensign-affair-referred-doj-fec-torrid-affair-detailed ; accessed July 12, 2013, 1.

122. "John Ensigns Affair Prompts Resignation," *ABC News* [database online] available from http://abcnews.go.com/GMA/video/john-ensigns-affair-prompts-resignation-13595686 ; Internet; accessed July 12, 2013, 1.

123. Trish Turner, "Ensign Affair Referred to DOJ & FEC - - Torrid Affair Detailed," *Fox News* [database online] available from http://politics.blogs.foxnews.com/2011/05/12/ensign-affair-referred-doj-fec-torrid-affair-detailed ; Internet; accessed July 12, 2013, 1.

124. John Bresnahan, "FEC Fines John Ensign's family $54,000," *Politico* [database online] available   from   http://www.politico.com/story/2013/05/fec-fines-ensign-family-54000-91575.html ; Internet; accessed July 12, 2013, 1.

125. John Lofflin, "John Ensign Returns to Veterinary Practice," *Veterinary News* [database online] available from http://veterinarynews.dvm360.com/dvm/Law+and+Ethics/John-Ensign-returns-to-veterinary-practice/ArticleStandard/Article/detail/781653 ; Internet; accessed July 12, 2013, 1 and Jane Morrison, "Senate Missteps No Longer Dog Veterinarian John Ensign," *Las Vegas Review Journal* [database online] available from http://www.reviewjournal.com/jane-ann-morrison/senate-missteps-no-longer-dog-veterinarian-john-ensign ; Internet; accessed July 12, 2013, 1.

126. Rhonda Schwartz, Brian Ross and Chris Francescani, "Edwards Admits Sexual Affair; Lied as Presidential Candidate," *ABC News* [database online] available from http://abcnews.go.com/Blotter/story?id=5441195 ; Internet; accessed June 15, 2013, 1.

127. "Update: John Edwards Love Child Scandal!," *National Enquirer* [database online] available   from   http://www.nationalenquirer.com/celebrity/update-john-edwards-love-child-scandal ; Internet; accessed December 14, 2011, 1.

128. James Hill, Teri Whitcraft, Nadine Schubailat and Lauren Sher, "John Edwards Made Sex Tape, Abortion Plea, Aide Says," *ABC News* [database online] available from http://

abcnews.go.com/2020/John_Edwards_Scandal/john-edwards-made-sex-tape-abortion-plea-aide says; Internet; accessed December 14, 2011, 1.

129. Sheri Stritof and Bob Stritof, "John and Elizabeth Edwards Marriage Profile," *About Marriage* [database online] available from http://marriage.about.com/od/celebritymarriages/ p/ johnedwards.htm ; Internet; accessed July 12, 2013.

130. Ibid.

131. "Update: John Edwards Love Child Scandal!," *National Enquirer* [database online] available from http://www.nationalenquirer.com/celebrity/update-john-edwards-love-child-scandal ; Internet; accessed December 14, 2011, 1.

132. Rhonda Schwartz, Brian Ross and Chris Francescani, "Edwards Admits Sexual Affair; Lied as Presidential Candidate," *ABC News* [database online] available from http://abc-news.go.com/Blotter/story?id=5441195 ; Internet; accessed June 15, 2013, 1.

133. Ibid.

134. Ibid.

135. Ibid.

136. David Perel, "John Edwards Hiding in the Bathroom," *Newsweek* [database online] available from htttp://2010.newsweek.com/top-10/sex-scandal-details/john-edwards-hiding-in-the-bathroom; Internet; accessed December 14, 2011, 2.

137. Rhonda Schwartz, Brian Ross and Chris Francescani, "Edwards Admits Sexual Affair; Lied as Presidential Candidate," *ABC News* [database online] available from http://abc-news.go.com/Blotter/story?id=5441195 ; Internet; accessed June 15, 2013, 1.

138. Ibid.

139. Ibid.

140. Ibid.

141. Ibid.

142. Ibid.

143. James Hill, Teri Whitcraft, Nadine Schubailat and Lauren Sher, "John Edwards Made Sex Tape, Abortion Plea, Aide Says," *ABC News* [database online] available from http:// abcnews.go.com/2020/John_Edwards_Scandal/john-edwards-made-sex-tape-abortion-plea-aide says; Internet; accessed December 14, 2011, 1.

144. "Indictment Shows Six Charges Against Edwards," *The New York Times* [database online] available from http://www.nytimes.com/interactive/2011/06/04/us/politics/04edwards-text.html?ref=johnedwards&_r=0 ; Internet; accessed July 12, 2013, 1.

145. "John Edwards Looking To Open New Law Firm," *CNN Politics Political Ticker* [data-base online] available from http://politicalticker.blogs.cnn.com/2013/06/05/john-edwards-look-ing-to-open-new-law-firm/ ; Internet; accessed July 12, 2013, 1.

146. Ibid.

147. Trish Turner, "Watchdog Group Calls For Ethics Review of Fossella," *Fox News* [data-base online] available from http://www.foxnews.com/story/0,2933,356632,00.html ; Internet; accessed December 14, 2013, 1.

148. "New York Congressman Apologizes for Drunk Driving Arrest," *Fox News* [database online] available from http://www.foxnews.com/story/2008/05/02/new-york-congressman-apologizes-for-drunk-driving-arrest/ ; Internet; accessed on December 15, 2011, 1.

149. Ibid.

150. Jo Anne Way, "Sex Scandal Photos: Laura Fay and Vito Fossella Affair Exposed," *The National Ledger* [database online] available from http://www.nationalledger.com/pop-culture-news/sex-scandal-photos-laura-fay--109931.stml ; Internet; accessed December 14, 2011, 1.

151. Jo Anne Way, "Sex Scandal Photos: Laura Fay and Vito Fossella Affair Exposed," *The National Ledger* [database online] available from http://www.nationalledger.com/pop-culture-news/sex-scandal-photos-laura-fay--109931.stml ; Internet; accessed December 14, 2011, 1 and Devlin Barrett, "NY Congressman Admits Child From Affair, " *Fox News* [database online] available from http://www.foxnews.com/wires/2008May08/0,4670,CongressmanAf-fair,00.html ; Internet; accessed December 15, 2011, 1.

152. "New York Congressman Apologizes for Drunk Driving Arrest," *Fox News* [database online] available from http://www.foxnews.com/story/2008/05/02/new-york-congressman-apologizes-for-drunk-driving-arrest/ ; Internet; accessed on December 11, 2011, 1.

153. Ibid.

154. Ibid.

155. Ibid.

156. Ibid.

157. "How Vito Lied," Daily News [database online] available from http://www.gothamist.com/ 2008/05/10/vito_fossella_r.php ; Internet; accessed December 14, 2011, 1 and "Family Affair," *New York Post* [database online] available from http://gothamist.com/2008/05/10/vito_fosella.r.php ; Internet; accessed December 14, 2011, 1.

158. Devlin Barrett, "NY Congressman Fossella Won't Seek Re-Election," *Fox News* [database online] available from http://www.foxnews.com/wires/ 2008May20/ 0,4670,CongressmanAffair,00.html ; Internet; accessed December 15, 2011, 1.

159. "Rep. Fossella Faces Calls to Resign After Admitting Secret Child," *Fox News* [database online] available from http://www.foxnews.com/story/2008/05/10/rep-fossella-faces-calls-to-resign-after-admitting-secret-child/#ixzz2Z8VenphWhttp://www.foxnews.com/ story/ 0,2933,354869,00.html ; Internet; accessed December 14, 2011, 1 and Trish Turner, "Watchdog Group Calls For Ethics Review of Fossella," *Fox News* [database online] available from http://www.foxnews.com/story/0,2933,356632,00.html ; Internet; accessed December 14, 2013, 1.

160. "Rep. Fossella Sentenced to 5 Days for Drunk Driving," *Fox News* [database online] available from http://www.foxnews.com/wires/2008Oct17/0,4670,CongressmanDWI,00.html; Internet; accessed December 14, 2011, 1.

161. "Former NY Rep. Pleads Guilty to DUI," *Fox News* [database online] available from http://www.foxnews.com/wires/2009Apr13/0,4670,FossellaPlea,00.html ; Internet; accessed December 14, 2011, 1.

162. Jen Chung, "Fossella's Plea Partly Prompted By Ball Player's Death," *Gothamist* [database online] available from http://gothamist.com/2009/04/14/ fossellas_plea_partly_prompted_by_b.php ; Internet; accessed December 10, 2011, 1.

163. Hector Florin, "Mahoney's Florida District Has Sex Scandal Deja Vu," *TIME* [database online] available from http://www.time.com/time/printout/0,88161851084,00.html ; Internet; accessed December 14, 2011, 1.

164. The dispute was settled through mediation in March 2008. Mahoney settled with Allen for $61,000. He also agreed to pay the legal fees of $60,000 associated with her claim.

165. "Congressman's $121,000 Payoff to Alleged Mistress," *ABC News* [database online] available from http://abcnews.go.com/Blotter/story?id=5997043&page=1 ; Internet; accessed December 14, 2011, 1.

166. Emma Schwatz, Rhonda Schwartz and Vic Walter, "Congressman's $121,000 Payoff to Alleged Mistress," *ABC News* [database online] available from http://www.abcnews.go.com/Blotter/Politics/story?id=5997043&page=1 ; Internet; accessed December 14, 2011, 1 and Hector Florin, "Mahoney's Florida District Has Sex Scandal Deja Vu," *TIME* [database online] available from http://www.time.com/time/printout/0,88161851084,00.html ; Internet; accessed December 14, 2011, 1.

167. Emma Schwartz, "Rep. Mahoney Takes 'Full Responsibility' But Doesn't Admit Affair," *ABC News* [database online] available from http://abcnews.go.com/Blotter/ Politics/story?id=6030518&page=1 ; Internet; accessed December 13, 2011, 1.

168. Hector Florin, "Mahoney's Florida District Has Sex Scandal Deja Vu," *TIME* [database online] available from http://www.time.com/time/printout/0,88161851084,00.html ; Internet; accessed December 14, 2011, 1.

169. Amanda Ruggeri, "Sex Scandal Fails Florida Democrat in Former Mark Foley District," *U.S. News and World Report* [database online] available from http://www.usnews.com/ news/campaign-2008/articles/2008/11/04/sex-scandal-fells-florida-democrat-in-former-mark-foley-district ; Internet; accessed December 17, 2011, 1.

170. Emma Schwartz, "Pelosi Calls for Investigation Into Mahoney," *ABC News* [database online] available from http://abcnews.go.com/ Blotter/ story?id=6025230&page=1#.UeSRSBafemE; Internet; accessed December 20, 2011, 1 and Emma Schwartz, "FBI Reported to Begin Probe of Florida Congressman," *ABC News* [database online] available from

http://abcnews.go.com/Blotter/Politics/story?id=6034123&page=1 ; Internet; accessed December 20, 2011, 1.

171. Emma Schwartz, "Did Mahoney Help Second Alleged Mistress Win Federal Grant?," *ABC News* [database online] available from http://abcnews.go.com/Blotter/ story?id=6040580&page=1 ; Internet; accessed December14, 2011, 1.

172. Emma Schwartz and Vic Walter, "Congressman Mahoney Admits to Multiple Affairs," *ABC News* [database online] available from http://abcnews.go.com/Blotter/ Politics/story?id=6058992&page=1 ; Internet; accessed December 20, 2011, 1.

173. Amanda Ruggeri, "Sex Scandal Fails Florida Democrat in Former Mark Foley District," *U.S. News and World Report* [database online] available from http://www.usnews.com/ news/campaign-2008/articles/2008/11/04/sex-scandal-fells-florida-democrat-in-former-mark-foley-district; Internet; accessed December 17, 2011.

174. Kit Bradshaw and Tyler Treadway, "Rep. Tim Mahoney's Wife File for Divorce, Seeks Assets," TCPALM [database online] available from http://www.tcpalm.com/news/2008/oct/20/ mahoney/ ; Internet; accessed December 14, 2011, 1.

175. "Senior Official Linked to Call Girl Ring," *ABC News* [database online] available from http://abcnews.go.com/WNT/video?id=3096548 ; Internet; accessed July 16, 2013.

176. "Senior Official Linked to Call Girl Ring," *ABC News* [database online] available from http://abcnews.go.com/WNT/video?id=3096548 ; Internet; accessed July 16, 2013.

177. Ibid.

178. Ibid.

179. Ibid.

180. "Senior Official Linked to Call Girl Ring," *ABC News* [database online] available from http://abcnews.go.com/WNT/video?id=3096548 ; Internet; accessed July 16, 2013.

181. Ibid.

182. "Police Close 'DC Madam Investigation, Confirmed She Died By Suicide," *Fox News* [database online] available from http://www.foxnews.com/story/0,2933,445538,00.html ; Internet; accessed July 16, 2013, 1.

183. Ibid.

184. "Florida Police: Woman Known As DC Madam Commits Suicide in Apparent Hanging," *Fox News* [database online] available from http://www.foxnews.com/story/2008/05/01/ florida-police-woman-known-as-dc-madam-commits-suicide-in-apparent-hanging/ ; Internet; accessed July 16, 2013, 1.

185. "Farewell, Randall Tobias, the Man Who Turned His Wife's Suicide into a Sales Pitch for Prozac," Information Liberation [database online] available from http:// www.informationliberation.com/?id=21807 , May 2, 2007, accessed July 16, 2013, 1.

186. "Senator Caught In "D.C. Madam" Scandal," *CBS News* [database online] available from http://www.cbsnews.com/2102-201_162-3037338.html?tag=contentMain;contentBody ; Internet; accessed December 14, 2011, 1 and "Hustler Says It Revealed Senator's Link To Escort Service," *CNN* [database online] available from http://www.cnn.com/2007/POLITICS/ 07/10/vitter.madam/index.html?iref=allsearch ; Internet; accessed July 13, 2013, 1.

187. "Senator Caught In "D.C. Madam" Scandal," *CBS News* [database online] available from http://www.cbsnews.com/2102-201_162-3037338.html?tag=contentMain;contentBody ; Internet; accessed December 14, 2011, 1.

188. "Vitter Admits Mistake and Takes Full Responsibility," *CNN* [database online] available from http://www.cnn.com/video/#/video/politics/2007/07/10/callebs.vitter.dc.madam .cnn ; Internet; accessed July 16, 2013, 1.

189. "Senator Tied To Sex Ring allowed To Use Campaign Money For Legal Fees," *Fox News* [database online] available from http://www.foxnews.com/story/0,2933,407743,00.html ; Internet; accessed December 14, 2011, 1.

190. "About David Vitter," *U.S. Senate* [database online] available from http:// www.vitter.senate.gov/about-david ; Internet; accessed July 16, 2013, 1.

191. John McArdle, "Craig Arrested, Pleads Guilty Following Incident in Airport Restroom," *Roll Call* [database online] available from http://www.rollcall.com/news/-19763-1.html ; Internet; accessed December 15, 2011, 1.

192. Ibid.

193. Ibid.
194. Ibid.
195. Ibid.
196. Ibid.
197. Ibid.
198. Ibid.
199. Ibid.
200. "ACLU Backs Sen. Craig, Argues Sex in Public Bathroom Stalls is Private," *Fox News* [database online] available from http://www.foxnews.com/story/0,2933,323094,00.html #ixzz2ZKQ9NRFP and http://www.foxnews.com/story/0,2933,323094,00.html ; Internet; accessed December 14, 2013, 1.
201. "Senator Larry Craig Resigns," *ABC News* [database online] available from http://abcnews.go.com/US/video?id=3549735 ; Internet; accessed December 5, 2011.
202. Ibid.
203. "Craig Decides to Stay on as GOP Senator," *ABC News* [database online] available from http://abcnews.go.com/blogs/politics/2007/10/judge-craigs-gu/ ; Internet; accessed December 5, 2011, 1.
204. "Craig Decides to Stay on as GOP Senator," *ABC News* [database online] available from http://abcnews.go.com/blogs/politics/2007/10/judge-craigs-gu/ ; Internet; accessed December 5, 2011, 1.
205. Ibid.
206. "Senate Ethics Committee Finds Senator Craig Acted Improperly in Airport Sex Sting," *Fox News* [database online] available from http://www.foxnews.com/story/2008/02/14/senate-ethics-committee-sen-larry-craig-acted-improperly-in-airport-sex-sting/#ixzz2ZKWxfR00 ; Internet; accessed July 11, 2013, 1.
207. Ibid.
208. Ibid.
209. "Ex Senator Larry Craig Loses Last Court Battle Over Bathroom Sex Sting," *The Raw Story* [database online] available from http://www.rawstory.com/rs/2013/03/29/ex-sen-larry-craig-loses-last-court-battle-over-bathroom-sex-sting/ ; Internet; accessed July 17, 2013, 1.
210. "Former U.S. Sen. Larry Craig Addresses University of Idaho Graduates," *Oregon Live* [database online] available from http://www.oregonlive.com/pacific-northwest-news/index.ssf/2013/05/former_us_sen_larry_craig_addr.html ; Internet; accessed July 17, 2013, 1.
211. Russell Goldman, "Senator's Wife Finds Herself at Center of Storm," *ABC News* [database online] available from http://abcnews.go.com/Politics/story?id=3538964&page=1#.UebtoxafemE; Internet; accessed July 12, 2013, 1.
212. "Sixteen-Year-Old Who Worked as Capitol Hill Page Concerned About E-mail Exchange with Congressman," *ABC News* [database online] available from http://abcnews.go.com/blogs/headlines/2006/09/sixteenyearold_/ ; Internet; accessed July 16, 2013, 1.
213. "Congressman Quits In Disgrace," *ABC News* [database online] available from http://abcnews.go.com/WNT/video?id=2509590 ; Internet; accessed July 17, 2013.
214. "Sixteen-Year-Old Who Worked as Capitol Hill Page Concerned About E-mail Exchange with Congressman," *ABC News* [database online] available from http://abcnews.go.com/blogs/headlines/2006/09/sixteenyearold_/ ; Internet; accessed July 16, 2013, 1.
215. "Hannity: Mark Foley Breaks His Silence," *Fox News* [database online] available from http://www.foxnews.com/on-air/hannity/transcript/hannity-mark-foley-breaks-his-silence ; Internet; accessed July 10, 2011, 1.
216. "Sixteen-Year-Old Who Worked as Capitol Hill Page Concerned About E-mail Exchange with Congressman," *ABC News* [database online] available from http://abcnews.go.com/ blogs/headlines/2006/09/sixteenyearold_/ ; Internet; accessed July 16, 2013, 1.
217. Ibid.
218. Ibid.
219. Ibid.
220. Ibid.
221. Ibid.
222. Ibid.

223. "House Votes For Probe of Foley Email Episode," *CNN* [database online] available from http://www.cnn.com/2006/WORLD/europe/09/29/friday/index.html?iref=allsearch ; Internet; accessed December 14, 2013, 1 and "Former Rep. Mark Foley Leaves DC in Hurry After E-Mail Scandal," *Fox News* [database online] available from http://www.foxnews.com/story/0,2933,216839,00.html ; Internet; accessed December 10, 2011, 1, and "Congressman Quits In Disgrace," *ABC News* [database online] available from http://abcnews.go.com/WNT/video?id=2509590 ; Internet; accessed July 17, 2013.

224. Anne-Marie Dorning, "Running To Rehab," *ABC News* [database online] available from http://abcnews.go.com/Politics/story?id=2518173&page=1 ; Internet; accessed July 17, 2013, 1.

225. "Sixteen-Year-Old Who Worked as Capitol Hill Page Concerned About E-mail Exchange with Congressman," *ABC News* [database online] available from http://abcnews.go.com/blogs/headlines/2006/09/sixteenyearold_/ ; Internet; accessed July 16, 2013, 1.

226. "Priest Confesses: Had A 'Relationship' With Teenage Mark Foley," *ABC News* [database online] available from http://abcnews.go.com/blogs/headlines/2006/10/priest_confesse/ ; Internet; accessed December 12, 2011, 1.

227. "Sixteen-Year-Old Who Worked as Capitol Hill Page Concerned About E-mail Exchange with Congressman," *ABC News* [database online] available from http://abcnews.go.com/ blogs/headlines/2006/09/sixteenyearold_/ ; Internet; accessed July 16, 2013, 1 and "Hannity: Mark Foley Breaks His Silence," *Fox News* [database online] available from http://www.foxnews.com/on-air/hannity/transcript/hannity-mark-foley-breaks-his-silence ; Internet; accessed July 10, 2011.

228. Gail Sheehy and Judy Bachrach, "Don't Ask... Don't Email," *Vanity Fair* [database online] available from http://www.vanityfair.com/politics/features/2007/01/foley200701 ; Internet; accessed July 15, 2011, 1.

229. Vic Walter and Justin Rood, "No State Charges In Foley Case," *ABC News* [database online] available from http://abcnews.go.com/Blotter/story?id=5840934&page=1 ; Internet; accessed December 10, 2011, 1.

230. Ibid.

231. "DHS Official Accused Of Sending Porn To A Minor," *ABC News* [database online] available from http://abcnews.go.com/US/story?id=1806674 ; Internet; accessed December 15, 2011, 1.

232. Ibid.

233. Ibid.

234. Ibid.

235. Ibid.

236. Ibid.

237. Ibid.

238. Ibid.

239. "Feds Suspend Official Facing Child Sex Charges," *CNN* [database online] available from http://www.cnn.com/2006/LAW/04/05/homeland.arrest/index.html?iref=allsearch ; Internet; accessed December 15, 2011, 1.

240. Vic Walter and Krista Kjellman, "DHS Official Makes Plea Deal In Online Sex Scandal," *ABC News* [database online] available from http://abcnews.go.com/blogs/ headlines/2006/09/dhs_official_ma/ ; Internet; accessed December 15, 2011, 1.

241. Ibid.

242. Vic Walter and Krista Kjellman, "DHS Official Makes Plea Deal In Online Sex Scandal," *ABC News* [database online] available from http://abcnews.go.com/blogs/headlines/2006/09/dhs_official_ma/ ; Internet; accessed December 15, 2011, 1 and Dana Willhoit, "5 Years in Prison For Porn E-Mails," *The Ledger* [database online] available from http://www.theledger.com ; Internet; accessed December 15, 2011, 1.

243. "Ryan Drops Out Of Senate Race In Illinois," *CNN* [database online] available from http://www.cnn.com/2004/ALLPOLITICS/06/25/il.ryan/ ; Internet; accessed July 18, 2013, 1 and "Ex-Wife Of GOP Candidate Alleged Sex-Club Forays," CNN [database online] available from http://www.cnn.com/2004/ALLPOLITICS/06/22/ryan.divorce/ ; Internet; accessed July 18, 2013, 1.

244. "Senate Race Sex Scandal," *The Smoking Gun* [database online] available from http://www.thesmokinggun.com/documents/crime/senate-race-sex-scandal ; Internet; accessed December 14, 211, 1.

245. David Montgomery, The Sex Scandal From Outer Space," *The Washington Post* [database online] available from http://www.washingtonpost.com/wp-dyn/articles/A6778-2004Jun25_2.html ; Internet; accessed July 18, 2013, 2.

246. David Montgomery, "The Sex Scandal From Outer Space," *The Washington Post* [database online] available from http://www.washingtonpost.com/wp-dyn/articles/A6778-2004Jun25_2.html ; Internet; accessed July 18, 2013, 2 and "Ex-Wife Of GOP Candidate Alleged Sex-Club Forays," *CNN* [database online] available from http://www.cnn.com/2004/ALLPOLITICS/06/22/ryan.divorce/ ; Internet; accessed July 18, 2013, 1.

247. Ibid., 2.

248. "Ryan Drops Out Of Senate Race In Illinois," *CNN* [database online] available from http://www.cnn.com/2004/ALLPOLITICS/06/25/il.ryan/ ; accessed July 19, 2004, 1.

249. Ibid.

250. "Senate Race Sex Scandal," *The Smoking Gun* [database online] available from "http://www.thesmokinggun.com/documents/crime/senate-race-sex-scandal ; Internet; accessed December 14, 211, 1.

251. Ibid.

252. "Congressman Apologizes For Affair in TV Ad," *NBC News* [database online] available from http://www.nbcnews.com/id/15132240/ns/politics/t/congressman-apologizes-affair-tv-ad/ ; Internet; accessed July 20, 2013, 1.

253. "Congressman Apologizes For Affair in TV Ad," *NBC News* [database online] available from http://www.nbcnews.com/id/15132240/ns/politics/t/congressman-apologizes-affair-tv-ad/ ; Internet; accessed July 20, 2013, 1.

254. Ibid.

255. Ibid.

256. Ibid.

257. Ibid.

258. "Don Sherwood Tries To Shake Scandal in Pennsylvania," Fox News [database online] available from http://www.foxnews.com/story/0,2933,199050,00.html ; Internet; accessed July 20, 2013, 1.

259. "Don Sherwood Tries To Shake Scandal in Pennsylvania," Fox News [database online] available from http://www.foxnews.com/story/0,2933,199050,00.html ; Internet; accessed July 20, 2013, 1.

260. Ibid.

261. "Congressman Apologizes For Affair in TV Ad," *NBC News* [database online] available from http://www.nbcnews.com/id/15132240/ns/politics/t/congressman-apologizes-affair-tv-ad/ ; Internet; accessed July 20, 2013, 1.

262. Ibid.

263. Dana Milbank, "During National Character Counts Week, Bush Stumps for Philanderer," *The Washington Post* [database online] available from http://www.washingtonpost.com/wp-dyn/content/article/2006/10/19/AR2006101901621.html ; Internet; accessed July 20, 2013, 1.

264. John Byrne, "Anti-gay Congressman David Dreier, Said to be Gay, 'Lived With Male Chief of Staff,'" *The Raw Story* [database online] available from http://www.rawstory.com/exclusives/ byrne/david_dreier_outed_brad_smith_gay_920.htm ; Internet; accessed July 2013, 1 and "Representative David Dreier To Retire After 32 Years In Congress," *San Bernardino County Sentinel* [database online] available from http://sbsentinel.com/2012/03/representative-david-dreier-to-retire-after-32-years-in-congress/ ; Internet; accessed July 20, 2013, 1.

265. John Byrne, "Anti-gay Congressman David Dreier, Said to be Gay, 'Lived With Male Chief of Staff,'" *The Raw Story* [database online] available from http://www.rawstory.com/exclusives/byrne/david_dreier_outed_brad_smith_gay_920.htm ; Internet; accessed July 2013, 1.

266. John Byrne, "Anti-gay Congressman David Dreier, Said to be Gay, 'Lived With Male Chief of Staff,'" *The Raw Story* [database online] available from http://www.rawstory.com/

exclusives/byrne/david_dreier_outed_brad_smith_gay_920.htm ; Internet; accessed July 2013, 1 and "Representative David Dreier To Retire After 32 Years In Congress," *San Bernardino County Sentinel* [database online] available from http://sbsentinel.com/2012/03/representative-david-dreier-to-retire-after-32-years-in-congress/ ; Internet; accessed July 20, 2013, 1.

267. "Representative David Dreier To Retire After 32 Years In Congress," *San Bernardino County Sentinel* [database online] available from http://sbsentinel.com/2012/03/representative-david-dreier-to-retire-after-32-years-in-congress/ ; Internet; accessed July 20, 2013, 1.

268. "Representative David Dreier To Retire After 32 Years In Congress," *San Bernardino County Sentinel* [database online] available from http://sbsentinel.com/2012/03/representative-david-dreier-to-retire-after-32-years-in-congress/ ; Internet; accessed July 20, 2013, 1 and "Rep. Dreier Won't Seek Reelection," *LA Observer* [database online] available from http://www.laobserved.com/archive/2012/02/rep_david_dreier_wont_see.php ; Internet; accessed July 20, 2013, 1.

269. "Ex-Rep. David Dreier Finds a New Role with Annenberg Group," *Los Angeles Times* [database online] available from http://articles.latimes.com/2013/feb/20/local/la-me-pc-rep-david-dreier-20130220 ; Internet; accessed July 20, 2013, 1.

270. Ken Rudin, "Sanford The Latest In A Series Of Political Sex Scandals," *NPR* [database online] available from http://www.npr.org/blogs/politicaljunkie/2009/06/sanford_just_the_latest_sex_sc.html ; Internet; accessed July 20, 2013, 1 and "Virginia G.O.P. Congressman Pulls Out of Race," The New York Times [database online] available from http://www.nytimes.com/2004/08/31/ politics/31virginia.html ; Internet; accessed July 20, 2013, 1.

271. Michael D. Shear and Chris L. Jenkins, "Va. Legislator Ends Bid for 3rd Term," *The Washington Post* [database online] available from http://www.washingtonpost.com/wp-dyn/articles/A47194-2004Aug30.html ; Internet; accessed July 20, 2013, A02.

272. "Virginia G.O.P. Congressman Pulls Out of Race," *The New York Times* [database online] available from http://www.nytimes.com/2004/08/31/politics/31virginia.html ; Internet; accessed July 20, 2013, 1.

273. Michael D. Shear and Chris L. Jenkins, "Va. Legislator Ends Bid for 3rd Term," The Washington Post [database online] available from http://www.washingtonpost.com/wp-dyn/articles/A47194-2004Aug30.html ; Internet; accessed July 20, 2013, A02 and "This Week Injustice - Edward Schrock," The Daily Show [database online] available from http://www.thedailyshow.com/watch/thu-september-16-2004/this-week-injustice---edward-schrock ; Internet; accessed July 20, 2013.

274. Michael D. Shear and Chris L. Jenkins, "Va. Legislator Ends Bid for 3rd Term," *The Washington Post* [database online] available from http://www.washingtonpost.com/wp-dyn/articles/A47194-2004Aug30.html ; Internet; accessed July 20, 2013, A02.

275. Ibid.

276. Michael D. Shear and Chris L. Jenkins, "Va. Legislator Ends Bid for 3rd Term," *The Washington Post* [database online] available from http://www.washingtonpost.com/wp-dyn/articles/A47194-2004Aug30.html ; Internet; accessed July 20, 2013, A02 and "Virginia G.O.P. Congressman Pulls Out of Race," *The New York Times* [database online] available from http://www.nytimes.com/2004/08/31/politics/31virginia.html ; Internet; accessed July 20, 2013, 1.

277. Michael D. Shear and Chris L. Jenkins, "Va. Legislator Ends Bid for 3rd Term" *The Washington Post* [database online] available from http://www.washingtonpost.com/wp-dyn/articles/A47194-2004Aug30.html ; Internet; accessed July 20, 2013, A02.

278. . Katy Kay, "Profile: Gary Condit," *BBC News* [database online] available from http://news.bbc.co.uk/2/hi/americas/1447661.stm ; Internet; accessed July 22, 2013, 1.

279. Ibid.

280. "Chandra Levy Murder Case Gets Fresh Look In Closed Door Meetings," *Huffington Post* [database online] available from http://www.huffingtonpost.com/2013/01/24/chandra-levy-murder-case-meetings_n_2542007.html ; Internet; accessed July 22, 2013, 1.

281. "Guilty Verdict in handra Levy Murder Case," *NBC News* [database online] available from http://www.nbcnews.com/id/40317461/ns/us_news-crime_and_courts/t/guilty-verdict-chandra-levy-murder-case/#.Ue1eDhafemE; Internet; accessed July 22, 2013, 1.

282. Katy Kay, "Profile: Gary Condit," *BBC News* [database online] available from http://news.bbc.co.uk/2/hi/americas/1447661.stm ; Internet; accessed July 22, 2013, 1.

283. Ibid.
284. Geraldine Sealey, "Condit Affair: The Latest D.C. Sex Scandal," *ABC News* [database online] available from http://abcnews.go.com/Politics/story?id=121497&page=2 ; Internet; accessed July 22, 2013, 1.
285. Katie McCarthy, "Gary Condit's Son: Dad Got a 'Bad Deal,' Didn't Deserve What Happened," *ABC News* [database online] available from http://abcnews.go.com/blogs/politics/2010/11/gary-condits-son-dad-got-a-bad-deal-didnt-deserve-what-happened/ ; internet; accessed July 22, 2013, 1.
286. "Chandra Levy's Remains Found in D.C. Park," *CNN* [database online] available from http://archives.cnn.com/2002/US/05/22/levy.body/ ; Internet; accessed July 2013, 1.
287. Ibid.
288. Geraldine Sealey, "Condit Affair: The Latest D.C. Sex Scandal," *ABC News* [database online] available from http://abcnews.go.com/Politics/story?id=121497&page=2 ; Internet accessed July 22, 2013, 1.
289. Sari Horwitz, Scott Higham, and Sylvia Moreno, "Who Killed Chandra Levy," *The Washington Post* [database online] available from http://www.washingtonpost.com/wp-srv/metro/specials/chandra/ch10_1.html ; accessed July 22, 2013, 1.
290. "Guilty Verdict in Chandra Levy Murder Case," *NBC News* [database online] available from   http://www.nbcnews.com/id/40317461/ns/us_news-crime_and_courts/t/guilty-verdict-chandra-levy-murder-case/ ; Internet; accessed July 22, 2013, 1.
291. Ibid.
292. "Chandra Levy's Parents Have Doubts That Convicted Killer Ingmar Guandique Murdered Their Daughter," *Huffington Post* [database online] available from http://www.huffingtonpost.com/2013/04/20/chandra-levy-killer-ingmar-guandique-murder_n_3104657.html ; Internet; accessed July 22, 2013.
293. "Guilty Verdict in Chandra Levy Murder Case," *NBC News* [database online] available from   http://www.nbcnews.com/id/40317461/ns/us_news-crime_and_courts/t/guilty-verdict-chandra-levy-murder-case/ ; Internet; accessed July 22, 2013, 1.
294. Ibid.
295. Katie McCarthy, "Gary Condit's Son: Dad Got a 'Bad Deal,' Didn't Deserve What Happened," *ABC News* [database online] available from http://abcnews.go.com/blogs/politics/2010/11/gary-condits-son-dad-got-a-bad-deal-didnt-deserve-what-happened/ ; Internet; accessed July 22, 2013, 1.
296. Ibid.
297. Champ Clark, "INSIDE STORY: Gary Condit After Chandra Levy Case," *People* [database online] available from http://www.people.com/people/article/0,,20264057,00.html ; Internet; accessed July 22, 2013, 1.
298. "The Petraeus Scandal: What We Know," *CNN* [database online] available from http://www.cnn.com/2012/11/14/us/petraeus-what-we-know ; Internet; accessed July 22, 2013, 1.
299. Nancy Dillon, "Ex-CIA Director David Petraeus Apologizes for Affair in First Public Speech Since Resignation," *Daily News* [database online] available from http://www.nydailynews.com/news/politics/petraeus-apologize-affair-speech-resigning-article-1.1299224#ixzz2ZocoYUue ; Internet; accessed July 22, 2013, 1.
300. "The Petraeus Scandal: What We Know," *CNN* [database online] available from http://www.cnn.com/2012/11/14/us/petraeus-what-we-know ; Internet; accessed July 22, 2013, 1.
301. "The Petraeus Scandal: What We Know," *CNN* [database online] available from http://www.cnn.com/2012/11/14/us/petraeus-what-we-know ; Internet; accessed July 22, 2013, 1.
302. Ibid.
303. Nancy Dillon, "Ex-CIA Director David Petraeus Apologizes for Affair in First Public Speech Since Resignation," *Daily News* [database online] available from http://www.nydailynews.com/news/politics/petraeus-apologize-affair-speech-resigning-article-1.1299224#ixzz2ZocoYUue ; Internet; accessed July 22, 2013, 1 and "David Petraeus Apologizes for Career-Ending Affair With Biographer Paula Broadwell," *CBS News* [database online] available from http://www.cbsnews.com/8301-201_162-57576484/david-petraeus-apologizes-for-career-ending-affair-with-biographer-paula-broadwell/ ; Internet; accessed July 22, 2013. 1.

304. Ibid, 1.

305. Ibid.

306. "David Petraeus Affair Began After He Left Army: Former Spokesman," *Huffington Post* [database online] available from http://www.huffingtonpost.com/2012/11/12/david-petraeus-affair_n_2116790.html ; Internet; accessed July 22, 2013, 1.

307. Michael Daly, "Scott Broadwell Proves to Be a Class Act in the Wake of His Wife's Affair," *The Daily Beast* [database online] available from http://www.thedailybeast.com/articles/ 2012/11/21/scott-broadwell-proves-to-be-a-class-act-in-the-wake-of-his-wife-s-affair .html; Internet; accessed July 22, 2013, 1.

308. Howard Kurtz, "Gen. John Allen, Caught Up in David Petraeus Scandal, Is Bypassing NATO Post and Retiring," *The Daily Beast* [database online] available from http:// www.thedailybeast.com/articles/2013/02/19/gen-john-allen-caught-up-in-david-petraeus-scandal-is-bypassing-nato-post-and-retiring.html ; Internet; accessed July 22, 2013, 1.

Chapter Three

Non-Sex Based Political Scandals of the 21st Century

This chapter centers on non-sex based scandals between 2000 and 2011. This chapter includes non-sex based scandals that involved Lewis Libby, Bernard Kerik, Samuel "Sandy" Berger, Claude Alexander Allen, II, Kyle Foggo, Jack Abramoff, Lurita Alexis Doan, Alphonso Jackson, General Alberto Gonzales, Kwame Kilpatrick and Jesse Jackson, Jr. and other notable non-sex government scandals. This section of the research provides a written account of thirty-four public servants or government officials who participated in unethical professional behavior in the workplace (i.e. United States Congress, Department of Health and Human Services, Department of Justice, and The Environmental Protection Agency). Lastly, this chapter also details allegations made against government officials who allegedly conspired against the United States government.

The goal of this chapter is threefold. The author will provide a discussion of non-sex based scandals from 2000-1011. Furthermore, this chapter will identify the consequences associated with the decisions elected and public officials made to engage in professionally unethical behavior. Moreover, this research will identify the impact the scandal had on the official and others associated with the persons at the center of the sex scandal (i.e., spouse, children, employees, etc.).

JESSE JACKSON, JR. (D)

Jesse Jackson, son of former Rainbow Push Coalition founder[1] Jesse Jackson, Sr., had a promising political career prior to becoming tangled in the

Blagojevich corruption scandal, accusations of an extramarital affair and allegations of using campaign funds for personal use.

Jesse Jr. was elected to the United States House of Representatives in 1995.[2] He represented the 2nd Congressional District of Illinois from 1995-2012 before his political career and reputation began to unravel. Many, including his wife Sandy, believed Jackson would one day serve in the United States Senate. Those hopes and dreams were dashed in 2008 when accusations were made that Jesse Jr attempted to bribe his way into the Senate seat Obama once held. Although, he admitted he was interested in representing Illinois in the Senate, Mr. Jackson vehemently denied trying to buy his way into the United States Senate by paying Robert "Rod" Blagojevich.[3] Although he was not charged with wrongdoing in the Blagojevich scandal, Jackson became known as "Candidate #5."[4] Despite surviving the Blagojevich scandal, Jackson's career was seemingly under a cloud of suspicion.

As if that were not bad enough, in 2010 Jesse Jackson, Jr. admitted to having an affair with Giovanna Huidobro. Giovanna Huidobro was employed as a hostess in a Washington, D.C. restaurant.[5] Jackson found himself in the midst of two federal investigations one by the United States House Ethics Committee and the Federal Bureau of Investigation (FBI). The House Ethics Committee was still trying to determine whether Jackson engaged in wrongdoing while trying to secure the Senate seat vacated by Barack Obama. In September 2010, Federal Bureau of Investigation (FBI) began its investigating into allegations Jackson asked businessmen to purchase airlines tickets for his mistress to travel from DC to Chicago. They also began to scrutinize the politician's finances in connection with allegations that emerged after Jackson admitted to having an affair.[6] It was rumored that Jackson used campaign funds to pay for lavish gifts for Ms. Huidobro and helped to furnish her Washington, D.C. apartment. When asked about whether he requested businessmen purchase airline tickets for Ms. Huidobro, Jesse Jr. remarked, "The reference to a social acquaintance is a personal and private matter between me and my wife that was handled some time ago."[7] He then asked the media to respect he and his wife's need for "privacy."[8]

As his private lifestyle became more transparent and questions about his financial stability arose, the congressman from Chicago began to crack under the pressure. Jackson took a leave of absence for medical reasons in June 2010 around the time his affair and his personal finances were being scrutinized. In October 2010, he remained on medical leave and began treatment at the world renowned Mayo Clinic for "bipolar II disorder."[9] Despite impending investigations of misconduct and revelations about his extramarital affair, the junior Jackson was reelected to Congress on November 7, 2012.[10] Less than one month after winning his reelection bid for Congress, Jesse Jackson Jr resigned from the House of Representatives saying he was leaving for medical reasons. However, he did acknowledge he was the subject of a "federal criminal investigation into the possible misuse of campaign funds" in his letter of resignation. [11]

The forty-seven year old Jackson's letter to John Boehner, Speaker of the House of Representatives, also highlighted his many years of "public service." [12] Additionally, the ill and disgraced politician wrote, "However, over the past several months, as my health has deteriorated, my ability to serve the constituents of my district has continued to diminish. Against the recommendations of my doctors, I had hoped and tried to return to Washington and continue working on the issues that matter most to the people of the Second District. I know now that will not be possible." [13]

Subsequently, in January 2013, Sandi Jackson, wife of Jesse Jackson Jr., announced her resignation from Chicago's City Council citing her need to help her husband in his recovery. [14] The former Alderwoman of Chicago told the media, "As a representative of the people of the 7th Ward, I value the public trust which has been bestowed upon me and take my responsibility to safeguard the interests of my constituents seriously." [15] Moreover, Sandi Jackson said she was "unapologetically a wife and a mother and I cannot deny my commitment to those most important personal responsibilities." [16] Finally, she concluded, "after much consideration and while dealing with very painful family health matters I have met with my family and determined that the constituents of the 7th Ward, as well as you Mr. Mayor, and my colleagues in the City Council deserve a partner who can commit all of their energies to the business of the people." [17]

On February 20, 2013, the former congressman plead guilty in a federal court related to charges he misused his campaign funds. Jackson told the judge, "I used monies that should have been used for campaign purposes." [18] Furthermore, the forty-seven year old admitted he transferred "$750,000" [19] of his campaign funds to his person account over a seven year period. [20]

Undoubtedly, February 20, 2013 was an extremely dark day in the lives of the Jackson family. While the junior Jackson was in court owning up to his illegal behavior, his wife Sandi Jackson was in another courtroom pleading guilty "falsifying a tax return and reporting less income than she made." [21] Mrs. Jackson also failed to disclose income she received while on her husband's payroll. For much of her husband's congressional career, Sandi Jackson received a "$5,000 a month check from her husband as his political consultant." [22]

In August, 2013, Mr. Jackson received "two and a half years in prison" [23] for using congressional campaign funds for personal expenses including household bills, household items, high-end trips and lux items. The judge admonished the forty-eight year old saying, "As a public official, you are supposed to live up to a higher standard of ethics and integrity." [24]

Sandi Jackson was sentenced to 12 months in jail for her part in the financial scheme. [25] After receiving his sentence, Jesse Jackson said, "I take responsibility for my actions."[26] He also admitted to misleading the public. A tearful Sandi Jackson addressed the court saying, "My heart breaks every day with the pain it has caused my babies."[27] The judge was not moved by her tears and reminded Sandi Jackson "It's not the government that put your children in this position."[28] Both Jesse Jackson, Jr. and Sandi Jackson pleaded with the court to think of the impact their sentences would have on their two children who are "13 and 9"[29] years of age. Mr. Jackson will serve his prison term first. Once he returns home, his wife Sandi will go to prison to serve her one year prison sentence.[30] Unfortunately, the Jackson children and family members will have to pick up the broken pieces of the family's legacy which now includes adultery, corruption and fraud.

CHARLES B. RANGEL (D-NY)

Former Ways and Means Committee Chairman, Charles B. Rangel (D-NY) became the focus of a congressional ethics probe in March 2010 after allegations surfaced he had engaged in misconduct. After serving 40 years in the United States House of Representatives, Rangel was charged with misconduct by the very committee he had chaired or served as ranking member.[31]

Representative Rangel was charged with 13 counts of wrongdoing including misuse of Congressional letterhead, using staff to solicit contributions for an academic institution that bears his name. Many of the people his staff asked for money had worked with him when he chaired the House Ways and Means Committee.[32] The senior member of Congress with forty years of service was also charged with violating the House gift rule and violating of United States postal and franking laws. The Ethics Committee also maintained Rangel broke regulations set by Congress' House Office Building Commission when he allowed his staffers to solicit money for the school named in his honor. Additionally, Rangel was charged with violating the "purpose law" and the "Congressional Handbook" when he solicited contributions for the school on government grounds.[33]

Moreover, the 80 year old member was charged with breaking regulations in House Rule 16 and the Ethics in Government Act when he failed to provide "complete Financial Disclosure statements on income, rent on property, gifts, and other financial assets"[34] he possessed. The House Ethics Committee found Rangel guilty on 11 of the 13 ethics violations with which he was charged. The Committee ruled the senior member failed to pay taxes on income he secured from renting property he owned in the Dominican Republic. The Ethics Committee also decided Rangel broke the law when he failed to disclose more than $600,000 in financial assets when he filed his Financial Disclosure statements.[35]

At the beginning of the Ethics probe, Rangel maintained he was innocent of wrongdoing and welcomed the opportunity to address the allegations made against him. Immediately following the verdict in his Ethics Subcommittee trial, Rangel released an unapologetic statement disagreeing with the committee's ruling. The professional politician wrote, "How can anyone have confidence in the decision of the Ethics Subcommittee when I was deprived of due process rights, right to counsel and was not even in the room?"[36] The Member of Congress remained hopeful the full Committee would treat him "more fairly, and take into account my entire 40 years of service to the Congress."[37] The likelihood the full committee would reach a different verdict was slim considering eight members of the trial subcommittee are members of the Full Ethics Committee.

Shortly after the committee ruled on Rangel's case, the 80 year old former Ways and Means chair told his peers and the media, "At long last, sunshine has pierced through this cloud that has been over my head for more than two years."[38] Rangel also admitted engaging in abusing the tax laws saying, "I mean, this is wrong to abuse the tax system."[39] Despite previous assertions of innocence, the 20 term member had to admit defeat. On December 2, 2010, the full House of Representatives voted 333-79 to censure Rangel as a consequence of being found guilty on 11 counts of ethics misconduct. House Speaker Nancy Pelosi (D) announced the decision to censure Representative Charles B. Rangel (D-NY). Congress also ordered him to pay taxes on the money earned from his rental property in the Dominican Republic. Pelosi also said Rangel was required to provide proof of payment to the appropriate taxing bodies.[40]

On December 2, 2010, Rangel addressed his colleagues in the House after being officially censured. He told member of the House of Representatives, "I stand to say that I have made serious mistakes."[41] However, in a voice of defiance Rangel told the body, "None of the presidents of the history of this great country, has anyone ever suffered the humiliation of a censure when the record is abundantly clear and never challenged that, in those two years of investigations which I called for, counsel and the committee found no evidence at all of corruption, found no evidence of self-enrichment, found no evidence that there was an intention on my part to evade my responsibility, whether in taxes or whether in financial disclosures."[42] Representative Charles Rangel acknowledged his failures to abide by the rules of the United States Congress. He argued they were represented unintentional errors on his part. Despite his defiance, Rangel did eventually say I brought it on myself."[43]

Despite apologizing for his wrongdoing, Rangel filed a lawsuit against the U.S. House Ethics Committee that found him guilty of 11 ethics violations in an attempt to get the committee's ruling overturned on April 25, 2013. Apparently, the legislator still believes censure is excessive despite the fact he could have been expelled from Congress for his abuse of the tax laws he helped to pass. The lawsuit claims Representative Rangel was denied substantive due process and suffered a series of injuries that were "a result of constitutional violations."[44]

Moreover, Representative Rangel claims he continues "to suffer irreparable harm by reason of the sanction of censure...."[45] The fall of career politician Charles B. Rangel paints a portrait of a man who became accustomed to making laws that he did not believe applied to him. Instead of accepting the consequences of his actions willingly, he continues to compound the situation by refusing to subject himself to the authority of his peers and refusing to truly acknowledge his wrongdoing. Although the member's political career and legacy have been tainted by his behavior and censure, Representative Rangel plans to run for reelection in 2014.[46]

JOE WILSON (R-SC)

The member of Congress from South Carolina interrupted a major televised speech about health care reform by President Barack Obama to a joint session of Congress. After Obama said that no illegal aliens would be accepted under his health plan, Rep. Wilson shouted, "You lie!" The incident resulted in a formal rebuke by the House of Representatives. He later admitted that the outburst was "inappropriate." Congressman Wilson is serving his sixth term in the House of Representatives. He is a member of several committees including:

The Committee on Education and Workforce, the House of Representatives Armed Services Committee, the Armed Services Committee's Subcommittee on Military Personnel, and the Committee on Foreign Affairs.[47]

G. THOMAS PORTEOUS

G. Thomas Porteous was a federal judge in eastern Louisiana when he found himself in the middle of a corruption scandal in September 2010. Members of the United States House of Representatives declared Porteous "unfit to serve on the bench."[48] The House in its Articles of Impeachment[49] maintained the judge had engaged in behavior unbecoming of a jurist for decades. Members of the House of Representatives alleged the judge engaged in "taking cash, expensive meals and other gifts from lawyers and a bail bondsman."[50] They also maintained Porteous lied to members of the House. Finally, members of the House of Representatives said the judge filed "for bankruptcy under false name."[51]

Porteous admitted accepting meals from attorneys and a bail bondsman. However, he and his attorney, Jonathan Turley maintained accepting meals did not constitute an illegal act. Turley acknowledged Porteous' behavior "reflected poor judgment."[52] Nevertheless, both Porteous and Turley argued the allegations leveled against the judge did not amount to "high crimes and misdemeanors" which is the Constitutional requirement for impeachment.[53]

Despite Porteous' belief that he had not committed high crimes and misdemeanors, the House passed the Articles of Impeachment. A Senate panel heard the arguments made by Representatives Adam Schiff (D-CA) and Bob Goodlatte (R-VA) for impeachment. Representative Schiff told the U.S. Senate panel, "It is the unanimous view of the House of Representatives that his conduct is not only wrong but so violative of the public trust that he cannot be allowed to remain on the bench without making a mockery of the court system."[54]

The Senate investigated the allegations made against the judge and discovered he had problems with drinking and gambling. He racked up more than $100,000 debt from "cash advances spent in casinos."[55] The Senate also identified two attorneys (Robert Creely and Jacob Amato) with whom Porteous maintained an especially close relationship. Moreover, Creely and Amato acknowledged giving Porteous "thousands of dollars."[56] The attorneys also acknowledged taking the judge on excursions to "Las Vegas for Porteous' son's bachelor party."[57] Both Creely and Amato paid for expensive meals, hotel accommodations and a visit to a strip club.

At the conclusion of its investigation, a Senate panel unanimously agreed to impeach G. Thomas Porteous for misconduct.[58] Consequently, Porteous was removed from the bench. Turley, Porteous' legal counsel disagreed with the Senate's decision and declared "Judge Porteous has never been indicted, let alone convicted, of any crime."[59] Mr. Turley declared the judge was impeached based on "an appearance of impropriety."[60] After years of inappropriate behavior on the bench, G. Thomas Porteous was deemed unfit to sit as a jurist.

KWAME KILPATRICK

Kwame Kilpatrick's political career appeared to be on the fast track when he was elected to the Detroit City Council in January 1996. Kilpatrick's mother previously held the city council seat but vacated her position as a councilwoman when she was elected to the United States House of Representatives.[61] According to Michigan prosecuting attorneys, Mr. Kilpatrick's questionable actions began early in his political career. Prosecutors allege Kilpatrick ensured "$500,000" in state grants were awarded to a nonprofit organization developed by one of his friends. His wife, Carlita Kilpatrick, allegedly received some money from the grant award as well.[62]

On November 6, 2001, the former city council member's career was catapulted when he was elected Mayor of Detroit. Kilpatrick was thirty-one years old at the time he assumed the leadership position.[63] Two years later, the public began asking questions about $160,000 on a city-issued credit card."[64] He allegedly utilized the card to pay for parties at nightclubs, limousine rental and more than 50 personal trips. Furthermore, Kilpatrick allegedly used the card to lease a luxury vehicle for his wife Carlita.[65]

Despite his questionable use of city funds for personal use, Mr. Kilpatrick successfully defended his position when he defeated Mr. Hendrix on November 8, 2005. Hendrix was in the lead in the beginning of the election. Kilpatrick modified his appearance by removing his signature accessory, a diamond stud earring. The mayor also appealed to voters saying he would be a better leader.[66]

In May 2003, the Deputy Chief of Police Gary Brown was fired from his post. Brown accused the mayor of terminating his employment because he conducted a probe into Kilpatrick's alleged misconduct. Gary Brown and another policeman Harold Neltrope filed a lawsuit against the mayor claiming they were wrongfully fired. In 2007, a jury decided in favor of the officers and awarded them "$6.5 million."[67] During the trial allegations were made accusing the mayor of having an extramarital affair with Ms. Christine Beatty, who served as the mayor's Chief of Staff. Despite denying the affair, Kwame Kilpatrick offered to settle the case with Brown and Neltrope for "$8.4 million."[68]

Four months after the settlement was reached, text messages sent between Mr. Kilpatrick and his chief of staff, Ms. Beatty, were published in a Detroit newspaper for everyone to read. The messages proved the two had engaged in an affair. Additionally, the texts also proved Kilpatrick and Beatty tried to cover up the affair. Moreover, the text messages proved that both Kilpatrick and Ms. Beatty "lied under oath."[69] At the end of January 2008, Kilpatrick admitted he was unfaithful to his wife and violated his marriage vows on local television. His wife Carlita was present and sat beside him holding his hand.[70]

In March 2008, Prosecutor Kym Worthy charged Mr. Kilpatrick with eight felony counts including "perjury, obstruction of justice and misconduct in office."[71] His former chief of staff, Ms. Beatty, was charged with seven felony counts. Initially, Kilpatrick refused to resign from his post. However, he announced his resignation on September 24, 2008.[72]

After a 5 month trial, the former mayor was convicted on a slew of charges including fraud, racketeering, and extortion. Kilpatrick's father, Bernard Kilpatrick, a co-defendant in the case, was also convicted on charges he used his son's position to enhance his financial position. Bernard Kilpatrick was convicted of "filing a false tax return."[73] The second co-defendant, Mr.

Ferguson, Kilpatrick's friend, was convicted on "9 of 11 counts filed against him, including racketeering."[74]

The former mayor of Detroit seemed surprised and dismayed when the guilty verdict was read in court. A number of the jurors spoke with the media following the court proceeding. One juror told the press, "There was no one piece of evidence that sealed the deal."[75] said one juror, who like the other members declined to be quoted by name. "We weighed all the evidence as a whole."[76] One juror who admitted to voting for Kilpatrick on two occasions said, "I was disappointed having done that."[77] She continued, "Sitting on this trial for the last six months, I really, really saw a lot that turned my stomach."[78]

In July 2013, a Detroit news station reported on the financial challenges Mrs. Carlita Kilpatrick faced while her husband was serving his jail term. After losing her job and her husband's income, the Kilpatrick's lease on the home expired and was not renewed. Kwame Kilpatrick and Carlita Kilpatrick rented the "5,000-square-foot home"[79] she and her husband leased for $2,600 a month,"[80] in Dallas, Texas. Neighbors told the media that many of the Kilpatrick's personal belongings were placed on the curb a few days before the former first lady of Detroit moved from the neighborhood.[81] Obviously, Mr. Kilpatrick's corruption has detrimentally harmed his family, specifically his wife, and father. His mother, former Congresswoman Cheeks-Kilpatrick, has been silent regarding her son's sorted political career and conviction.

On October 11, 2013, news broadcasters reported Mr. Kilpatrick had been sentenced to 28 years in federal prison for his blatantly unethical conduct while serving as mayor of Detroit. The former Mayor of Detroit was "convicted of 24 counts of racketeering, bribery, extortion, mail fraud,"[82] and other corruption charges. Perhaps one of the most disturbing aspects of this case of misuse and abuse of power lies in Kwame Kilpatrick's refusal to accept responsibility for his actions. His address to the court was described as a "non-apology apology"[83] because he never acknowledged any wrongdoing. His lack of remorse leads one to ask whether Kilpatrick is a morally and ethically bankrupt individual incapable of accepting responsibility for his corrupt behavior.

LEWIS LIBBY:
CHIEF OF STAFF TO VICE PRESIDENT DICK CHENEY (R)

Lewis "Scooter" Libby, former Cheney Chief of Staff, was charged and convicted for perjuring himself and "lying to a grand jury" and federal agents in 2003. Libby allegedly lied about leaked information about Valerie Wilson, a CIA agent.[84] The scandal was referred to as the "Plame Affair." The scandal led to a four-year investigation into how Ms. Wilson's real name (Valerie

Plame) was leaked to the public. Scooter Libby said he became aware of Mrs. Plame's identity from Tim Russert during an interview for NBC news conducted in mid-July 2003. However, Libby actually learned the CIA operative's identity from other officials who worked for Vice-President Dick Cheney. [85] The scandal was intriguing because it involved a member of the Vice-President's staff, other administration officials, and a host of questions about the Iraq war. [86]

In March 2007, the jury in Libby's case did not believe his "claims of memory lapses." [87] Consequently, Scooter Libby was convicted of "obstruction of justice, giving false statements to the Federal Bureau of Investigation," and two counts of perjury. He was acquitted of one count of "making false statements" [88] to members of the Federal Bureau of Investigation. [89] On March 6, 2007, the former Cheney Chief of Staff was sentenced to 22 months in prison. [90] He was also ordered to pay $250,000 in fines. [91]

Shortly after leaving the federal courthouse, Mr. Libby's attorney, Theodore Wells, told reporters he planned to appeal the decision. He said Libby was "totally innocent and that he did not do anything wrong." [92] President George W. Bush reportedly "was saddened for Scooter Libby and his family." [93] Bush's disagreement with the verdict was reflected by his decision on July 1, 2007, to commute Lewis "Scooter" Libby's sentence. President Bush did not go as far as to pardon the former Cheney chief of staff. Thus, Libby's felony conviction remains on his criminal record [94] and his high profile political career and legacy were detrimentally damaged.

The leak of the CIA operative's true identity and Mr. Libby's involvement implicated 23 other high ranking public officials [95] including Karl Rove, Condoleezza Rice, Stephen Hadley, Andrew Card, Alberto Gonzales, Mary Matalin, Ari Fleischer, Colin Powell, Karen Hughes, Adam Levine, Bob Joseph, Vice-President Dick Cheney, President George W. Bush, Susan Ralston, Israel Hernandez, John Hannah, Scott McClellan, Dan Bartlett, Claire Buchan, Catherine Martin, Jennifer Millerwise and David Wurmser. [96]

ALPHONSO JACKSON (R)

George W. Bush neighbor and political appointee, [97] Alphonso Jackson (R) was appointed to head the U.S. Department of Housing and Urban Development. In 2008, the FBI began investigating the housing secretary for allegedly wrongdoing and corruption. [98] Allegations leveled against Secretary Jackson primarily focused on his use of his political clout to ensure contracts were given to his friends. [99] It was alleged Jackson retaliated against the Philadelphia Housing Authority when it refused to sell real estate property to a developer with whom he was friendly. Mr. Jackson contacted Philadelphia's mayor in 2006. Jackson's sole purpose for contacting the mayor of

Philadelphia was to "demand the transfer to the developer Kenny Gamble."[100] Jackson wanted the housing authority to sell the $2 million property to his friend dirt-cheap. The housing authority director explained Jackson also had HUD staff members contact his office about his request for almost a year. Carl Greene, director Philadelphia Housing Authority, maintained Jackson's staff made threatening calls and wrote threatening letters about housing programs.[101] Moreover, Greene maintained the Philadelphia Housing Authority was punished for not complying with Jackson's demand. The housing authority was told it was going to be stripped of "its ability to spend some federal funds, a move that the authority said could raise rents for most of its 84,000 low-income tenants and force the layoffs of 250 people."[102]

Amid rumors of corruption and ineptitude, and an FBI investigation into possible misconduct, Alphonso Jackson "involuntarily"[103] resigned from the United States Department of Housing and Urban Development in April 2008 because the Bush Administration determined there were "too many controversies swirling around him."[104] Jackson's effectiveness was called into question and President Bush doubted Jackson's ability "to be an effective Cabinet member."[105]

ATTORNEY GENERAL ALBERTO GONZALES AND "LAWYERGATE"

On December 7, 2006, nine U.S. attorneys were abruptly fired from the Department of Justice under the leadership of former Attorney General Alberto Gonzales.[106] Gonzales was appointed by President George W. Bush in November 2004.[107] The attorneys maintained they were terminated without cause and no explanation was given.[108] Among those fired without explanation were: Former U.S. District Attorneys H.E. "Bud" Cummins, Cindy Lam, John McKay, David Iglesias, and Daniel Bogden.[109] All of the fired attorneys were political appointees who were hired at the pleasure of President George W. Bush. Likewise, they could be fired at will by the Chief Executive.[110]

According to Alberto Gonzales, the DOJ attorneys were fired for a number of reasons although he never supplied a rationale for the terminations. The terminated attorneys were replaced by others Gonzales deemed more suitable. Many speculated that the real reason the attorneys were terminated was political. On a number of occasions, the lawyers failed to "bring charges that might have helped Republican candidates."[111] In one instance, former U.S. Attorney Paul Charlton did not believe a murder case warranted the death penalty. His superiors disagreed and moved forward with a request for the death penalty in the case.[112]

The allegations of inappropriate use of power against then Attorney General Alberto Gonzales were investigated by the Inspector General of the

Department of Justice. At the conclusion of the 18 month investigation, a grand jury failed to indict Mr. Gonzales of wrongdoing.[113]

Congress conducted a probe into Gonzales actions, but the investigation was met with resistance. A number of high ranking Department of Justice appointees refused to testify invoking "executive privilege."[114] Among those who refused to answer questions raised by Congress were: Mr. Alberto Gonzales (R), Attorney General of the United States, Karl Rove (R) Advisor to President Bush, and Harriet Miers (R) Legal Counsel to President Bush, Mr. Michael A. Battle (R), Director of Executive Office of US Attorneys in the Justice Department, Attorney Bradley Schlozman (R), Director of Executive Office of US Attorneys who replaced Battle, Mr. Michael Elston (R), Chief of Staff to Deputy Attorney General Paul McNulty, Mr. Paul McNulty (R), Deputy Attorney General to William Mercer, Mr. William W. Mercer (R), Associate Attorney General to Alberto Gonzales, Mr. Kyle Sampson (R), Chief of Staff to Attorney General Alberto Gonzales, Ms. Monica Goodling (R), Liaison between President Bush and the Justice Department, Mr. Joshua Bolten (R), Deputy Chief of Staff to President Bush was found in contempt of Congress, and Ms. Sara M. Taylor (R) Aid to Presidential Advisor Karl Rove. A number of those who refused to testify were held in contempt by Congress. Among those held in contempt for not complying with the legislative body's request for information included Harriet Miers (R) and Mr. Joshua Bolten (R) were charged with contempt.[115]

BUSH WHITE HOUSE E-MAIL CONTROVERSY

During the Lawyergate investigation, it was discovered that the Bush administration used Republican National Committee (RNC) web servers for millions of emails, which were then destroyed, lost or deleted in possible violation of the Presidential Records Act and the Hatch Act. George W. Bush, Dick Cheney, Karl Rove, Andrew Card, Sara Taylor and Scott Jennings all used RNC web servers for the majority of their emails. Of 88 officials, no emails at all were discovered for 51 of them. As many as 5 million e-mails requested by Congressional investigators of other Bush administration scandals were therefore unavailable, lost, or deleted. Although no one was charged with a crime, those named in news reports as having been involved in the scandal were left to live with the cloud of suspicion that was levied against them.

LURITA ALEXIS DOAN (R)

Lurita Alexis Doan was appointed by President George W. Bush to head the General Services Administration (GSA) in 2006. The chief administrator is responsible for heading an agency "with 12,000 employees and a $20 million annual budget."[116] Doan was also responsible for oversight of GSA infrastructure, which included "thousands of buildings and properties."[117]

Following an 11-month investigation by the Inspector General of the General Services Administration (GSA), President Bush's support for Doan appeared to wane. The investigation findings suggested Lurita Doan failed to abide by the Hatch Act in 2007 when she asked employees to "help our candidates."[118] The investigation also turned up evidence that Doan may have violated the Hatch Act in January 2007 by allegedly asking political appointees how they could "help our candidates" at an agency briefing conducted by a White House official, according to several of the appointees present for the briefing.[119]

Moreover, the U.S. Office of Special Counsel conducted an independent investigation into Doan's actions. Scott J. Bloch, Special Counsel, appealed to the president encouraging him to "discipline Doan."[120] Among the corrective actions Bloch suggested, included firing Doan for engaging in illegal political activity in the workplace.[121]

Despite telling a congressional oversight committee she "did not recall asking the political appointees to help Republican candidates," Ms. Doan resigned from her post. In response to Doan's resignation, Representative Waxman said, "I know this decision was difficult for the White House and Lurita Doan, but it was the right thing to do."[122] Ultimately, Lurita Alexis Doan's political career was ruined because she broke the law when she engaged in political activities by fundraising on behalf of Republican candidates.[123]

JACK ABRAMOFF

Jack Abramoff was an influential lobbyist before acknowledging he broke campaign finance laws.[124] The former lobbyist pled guilty to a number of "crimes related to the Indian gaming lobby."[125] Prior to receiving his punishment for his illegal activities, Abramoff told court onlookers he "happily and arrogantly engaged"[126] in corruption as a lobbyist.[127] Abramoff received a plea agreement in exchange for pleading guilty to one count of fraud, one count of tax evasion and one count of conspiracy to bribe public officials.[128] The plea deal also required Abramoff to name members of Congress with whom he engaged in illegal campaign finance activities. In September 2008, United States District Court Judge Ellen Huvelle sentenced the "once-powerful"[129] Abramoff to serve four years in a federal prison for his part in "corruption scandal."[130]

Alice Fisher, head of the Department of Justice Criminal Division, told the media, "The corruption scheme with Mr. Abramoff is very extensive."[131]

Fisher declared the Department of Justice (DOJ) would continue to "follow this wherever it goes."[132]

The list Abramoff provided the Department of Justice with consisted of a number of key political leaders, with whom he admitted engaging in corrupt activities. Among those implicated in the scandal were:

1. Tom DeLay (R-TX) was investigated in October 2005 in connection with the Abramoff scandal. The congressman was not indicted because the investigation did not reveal any wrongdoing on his part. However, on June 9, 2006, Representative DeLay resigned from the United States House of Representatives. It was later discovered that he had illegally moved funds from a PAC named "Americans for a Republican Majority" to Republican Party candidates running for state legislative positions. The former member of Congress was convicted on two counts of money laundering and conspiracy in 2010. DeLay was sentenced to 3 years in prison.[133]

2. James W. Ellis (R) was the executive director of the PAC "Americans for a Republican Majority" when he was indicted on money laundering charges.[134]

3. John D. Calyandro (R) was another employee of "Americans for a Republican Majority" who admitted guilt in the Abramoff lobbying scandal.[135]

4. Representative Bob Ney (R-OH) pleaded guilty to conspiracy and making false statements about trips and gifts he received from Jack Abramoff in exchange for legislative favors. For his part in the scandal, the Ohio legislator was sentenced to 30 months in prison.[136]

5. Robert E. Coughlin (R) was Deputy Chief of Staff with the Department of Justice Criminal Division when he pled guilty to accepted bribes from the lobbyist.[137]

6. David Safavian was employed as Chief of Staff by the General Services Administration (GSA) when he was found guilty of obstructing justice and perjury. The former chief of staff received an 18-month sentence for his illegal behavior.[138]

7. Roger Stillwell (R) worked for the Department of Interior when he pleaded guilty to participating in the lobbying scandal. The former Bush Administration employee was sentenced to a two year suspended sentence.[139]

8. Susan B. Ralston (R) served as Special Assistant to President Bush and Senior Advisor to Karl Rove. She resigned from her post on October 6, 2006, for accepting gifts and supplying pertinent information to her previous employer Jack Abramoff.[140]

9. J. Steven Griles (R) had previously been employed as an assistant to the head of the Department of Interior when he pleaded guilty to

obstruction of justice charges. The former Assistant Deputy received a 10-month sentence for his part in the Abramoff scandal. [141]

10. Italia Federici (R) worked for the United States Secretary of Interior. She also served as the president of the Council of Republicans for Environmental Advocacy. She acknowledged her part in the scandal and pleaded guilty to tax evasion and obstruction of justice charges. Ms. Federici received four years' probation for her illegal activity. [142]

11. Robert Jared Carpenter (R) was Vice-President of the Council of Republicans for Environmental Advocacy when his name surfaced in the lobbying scandal. Carpenter pleaded guilty to income tax evasion. For his illegal behavior, Mr. Carpenter was sentenced to 45 days in jail. He also received 4 years probation for engaging in illegal activity. [143]

12. Michael Scanlon (R) was a legislative aide for Congressman Tom DeLay when he began to engage in illegal activity with Abramoff. He took a job working for the lobbyist and became Jack Abramoff's business partner. Mr. Scanlon pleaded guilty to bribery. [144] As a part of his plea agreement, he was sentenced to 2 years in prison [145] and was required to pay $20 million in restitution. Additionally, the plea agreement required $17.7 million had to be given to his former employer, Greenberg Taurig, LLP. The remaining $2.5 million had to be given to a number of Native American tribes in the U.S. that suffered tremendously because of Scanlon's unscrupulous actions. [146]

13. Tony Rudy (R), former legislative assistant to Representative Tom DeLay, pleaded guilty to conspiracy. [147]

14. Neil Volz (R) former legislative assistant to Representative Robert Ney, pleaded guilty to one count of conspiracy in 2006. One year later, Volz received two years probation for his part in the scandal. Furthermore, the former legislative assistant was required to complete 100 hours community service and pay fines in the amount of $2,000. [148]

15. Mark Zachares (R) was employed by the United States Department of Labor when he accepted a bribe from Jack Abramoff. He pleaded guilty to conspiracy charges. [149]

16. William Heaton (R) was the Chief of Staff for Bob Ney (R) when he began to engaging in illegal activities with Abramoff. Heaton pleaded guilty to one count of conspiracy for taking a trip to Scotland paid for by the unscrupulous lobbyist Jack Abramoff. Heaton admitted he accepted expensive gifts over a two-year period in exchange for assisting Abramoff's clients. [150]

17. Kevin A. Ring (R) was employed by Congressman John Doolittle (R-CA) when he Began to participate in illegal acts with Abramoff. Mr. Ring was indicted on eight counts of corruption. However, a mistrial was declared in his case. [151]

18. John Albaugh (R) former chief of staff to Ernest Istook (R-OK) pled guilty to accepting bribes connected to the Federal Highway Bill. Istook was not charged with wrongdoing. [152]

19. James Hirni (R) had been employed by Rep. Tim Hutchinson (R-AR) when he became acquainted with Abramoff. The former legislative staffer was charged with wire fraud because he admitted bribing one of Don Young's (R-Alaska) staffers in exchange for getting amendments added to the Federal Highway Bill. [153]

KYLE DUSTY FOGGO

Kyle Dusty Foggo was third in command of the CIA when the FBI began investigating whether he had engaged in professional misconduct by using his influence to ensure his high school friend, Brent R. Wilkes, was awarded government contracts. [154] Wilkes was "named as a co-conspirator" [155] in a corruption case against United States Representative Randy Cunningham. [156] Foggo admitted he attended poker parties hosted by Wilkes. Federal investigators conducted an investigation into whether Foggo's friend supplied prostitutes for men who attended the poker parties. Foggo denied engaging in sex acts with prostitutes. [157] The high-ranking official resigned from his position in mid May 2006, shortly after CIA Director Porter Goss resigned. Foggo notified CIA employees of his intention to leave the agency by way of email. [158]

Foggo was indicted on 11 charges including wire fraud, depriving taxpayers of honest services, conflict of interest, money laundering and conspiracy. [159] Foggo was one of a number of people indicted and convicted of conspiring against the government. A federal judge accepted Foggo's guilty plea despite his failure to accept full responsibility for misusing his power and clout to help a longtime friend secure government contracts. Mr. Foggo was sentenced to 37 months in prison and two years supervised probation. [160] The former CIA executive director is the highest ranking public official convicted of felony charges of bribery. [161]

JULIE MACDONALD (R)

Deputy Assistant Secretary of Fish and Wildlife Services, Julie MacDonald, resigned on April 30, 2007, after being investigated by the Inspector General for allegedly using her position and influence to limit endangered species protection. The Inspector General's investigation revealed a number of unethical issues with the manner in which MacDonald carried out her duties. The former Deputy Assistant Secretary was accused of rewriting "scientific reports," and harassing employees. Moreover, she was accused of scheming with an attorney to generate "lawsuits against" the very agency she was hired to be an advocate.[162] Oddly enough, MacDonald allegedly spent a lot of time "blocking agency efforts to place imperiled species on the endangered list"[163] and removing endangered species on the government's endangered species list. She was also diligent at minimizing the amount of land recognized as "critical habitat."[164]

The senior Bush appointee resigned on May 1, 2007, after the Inspector General of the U.S. Fish and Wildlife Services found her guilty of providing "non-public information" to lobbyists, which is tantamount to ethical misconduct.[165] She was also found guilty of leaking "internal Fish and Wildlife documents to business groups" that were opposed to environmental priorities and the agency as a whole.[166]

Following the announcement that she was leaving the U.S. Fish and Wildlife Service, Kieran Suckling told reporters, "Julie MacDonald's reign of terror over the U.S. Fish and Wildlife Service is finally over."[167]

Despite being deemed unethical by the Inspector General, the former Deputy Assistant Secretary maintained she vacated her position "for personal reasons, including illness in her family."[168] She told reporters she respected the employees who worked at the U.S. Fish and Wildlife Services.[169] MacDonald did comment on whether her resignation was prompted by potential disciplinary actions for sharing private documents and information with the public.[170]

CLAUDE ALEXANDER ALLEN, II (R)

Claude Alexander Allen was an attorney and Domestic Policy advisor to President George W. Bush when news broke that he was a suspect in a "refund fraud" case. Allen allegedly swindled an upscale Target and a department store at least 25 times before he was charged. The high-ranking official would buy an item and take the item home. Sometime later, Allen would return to the store, remove an identical item from the shelves and use the receipt for the item he bought to get a refund credited to his credit card. This scandal seemed weird considering the 45 year-old husband, father of four, and White House advisor yielded a salary of $161,000 annually[171] and lived in an upscale home valued at $1,000,000.[172] Reporters were left speculating about the rationale behind Allen's "refund fraud" scheme. We may never really know why the Bush advisor committed such a seemingly senseless crime, but his behavior led to his quick demise.

In January 2006, Claude Allen told the Chief of Staff and Harriet Meyers, White House Chief Counsel, "there had been a mix-up."[173] Allen resigned from his White House position on February 9, 2006,[174] citing "long work hours and a desire to spend more time with his family."[175] Allen was charged with "felony theft"[176] for shoplifting $5,000 worth of merchandise from Target in 2005.[177] Claude A. Allen II quietly exited from public life and all hopes of political prominence were lost.

As if Claude A. Allen's scandal was not humiliating enough, Allen's son, Claude A. Allen, III, has made headline news as a suspect in a Gaithersburg, Maryland murder case. On May 28, 2013, news reports suggested Allen's son allegedly killed an unarmed 25-year-old man, Michael P. Harvey, with a hatchet after an argument over marijuana and PCP. It was presumed the killing was drug related.[178] According to law enforcement authorities, the twenty-year-old Allen "confessed to killing Harvey."[179] Harvey's body was found in a wooded area behind Allen's Gaithersburg, Maryland home. The twenty year old was charged with homicide and held without bond. Allen's father did not attend his son's arraignment.[180]

LESTER CRAWFORD (R)

Dr. Lester M. Crawford was appointed Commissioner of the Food and Drug Administration (FDA) by President George W. Bush in February 2005.[181] As the head of the FDA, he provided leadership for a number of offices including Office of Chief Scientist, Office of Chief Counsel, Office of Executive Secretariat, Office of External Affairs, the Office of Legislation, and Office of Minority Health and Office of Women's Health.[182] In 2004, Dr. Crawford and his wife, Catherine W. Crawford, were accused of selling stock in companies (e.g., Telefax, Inc., Sysco Corporation, Wendy's, Embrex, WalMart Stores, Inc. and PepsiCo Inc.) regulated by the Federal and Drug Administration. Each company was involved in pharmaceutical and agricultural biotechnology. Their behavior constituted a conflict of interest. Shares sold by the couple ranged from "$1,001 to $100,000."[183] According to an interview with a Forbes journalist, Crawford said he sold his stock in FDA regulated companies in 2004 prior to assuming the helm as Commissioner of the Food and Drug Administration.[184]

Dr. Crawford was previously employed as a Deputy Commissioner with the Food and Drug Administration. He served in that capacity for more than three years before being appointed FDA Commissioner. His rise to power was short-lived. After serving two months as Commissioner.[185] Dr. Crawford announced his resignation on September 23, 2005.[186] Despite being adamant, his resignation was not related to accusations of financial misconduct,[187] the former FDA Commissioner pleaded guilty to conflict of interest charges in October 2006 following a criminal investigation. As a consequence of his actions, Crawford received 3 years suspended sentence and fined $90,000.[188]

YELLOWCAKE SCANDAL

In September 2002, members of Congress were deliberating on whether to pass legislation that would allow President George W. Bush to deploy U.S. troops to Iraq. The U.S. Senate Committee on Foreign Relations received information from high-ranking intelligence officials about "Iraq's weapons capability."[189] Although members of the Republican Party were disproportionately supportive of the legislative measure, Democratic members of Congress had reservations and needed to be convinced going to war with Iraq was the right decision. Many Democrats had doubts about whether Iraq was a legitimate danger to the United States. Moreover, members of the Democratic Party had questions about whether Iraq "possessed weapons of mass destruction."[190] Democrats were not convinced Saddam Hussein had weapons of mass destruction at his disposal. Thus, they did not agree with the Bush administration's desire to engage in a "preemptive war."[191] A handful of Democrats even contemplated proposing an alternative to the Republican drafted resolution.

However, information was presented to the national lawmakers that suggested Iraq had tried to purchase uranium at least five times over a three-year period (1999-2001). Central Intelligence Agency officials told Congress that Iraq tried to purchase "five hundred tons of uranium oxide from Niger."[192] The chemical Iraq allegedly tried to purchase is referred to as "yellowcake"[193] and is used to create fuel for nuclear reactors. Yellowcake can also be used to develop nuclear weapons. According to news reports, the amount of the chemical Saddam Hussein was attempting to purchase could create a bomb.

Around the same time U.S. governmental leaders were faced with deciding whether to engage in war with Iraq, the British government shared information suggesting Iraq had attempted to buy "significant quantities of uranium."[194] The allegation attracted immediate attention; a headline in the London *Guardian* declared, "african gangs offer route to uranium."[195]

Several days after Tony Blair, Prime Minister of Britain, disclosed documents that led many Brits to believe Saddam Hussein was trying to build a nuclear bomb, Colin Powell met with members of the U.S. Senate Foreign Relations Committee in a closed-door session. The former Secretary of State told committee members Iraq repeatedly tried to acquire uranium. He suggested Iraq's actions demonstrated the country's intent to build nuclear weapons. Democrats who were previously opposed to the Bush resolution were swayed by Powell's testimony. By continuously telling the story Saddam Hussein was attempting to buy uranium combined with telling members of Congress Iraq had weapons of mass destruction changed the direction of the debate on the legislative matter. Despite the fact Iraq and Niger persistently denied being in negotiations over uranium, U.S. officials were persuaded to believe Iraq was trying to build nuclear weapons. In less than fourteen days, the U.S. House of Representatives and U.S. Senate voted in favor of the resolution and U.S. troops were deployed to Iraq.[196]

The United States was engaged in military battle with Iraq for almost a year before it was revealed Bush administration officials fabricated the story in order to convince Congress to authorize the war with Iraq. In July 2003, White House officials admitted the president's statement that suggested Iraq tried to buy uranium in his 2001 State of the Union Address was not true. The White House team maintained President George W. Bush was unaware the information was false. Bush officials argued high-ranking officials in the Central Intelligence Agency (CIA) had repeatedly verified the information.[197] The deception began when President Busch's Press Secretary, Ari Fleischer admitted the allegation that Iraq tried to buy yellowcake uranium was based on falsified documents. Nevertheless, Fleischer tried to justify President Bush's statement declaring, "I see nothing that goes broader that would indicate that there was no basis to the President's broader statement."[198]

Although, the Bush administration's argument the president did not know the information that helped convince Congress to approve the resolution to go to war with Iraq was false, an official at the Central Intelligence Agency (CIA), told reporters the president was aware the information was wrong long before President Bush made his State of the Union address and lied to Congress and the American public.[199]

Ultimately, the "yellowcake" scandal deceived national lawmakers, the American electorate and the public. Not only did they deceive citizens into believing Iraq was a threat to the United States, the financial cost associated with the war was astronomical. Ten years after engaging in war with Iraq, the United States has spent approximately "$1.7 trillion."[200] The actual cost is much higher than the "$50 billion to $60 million"[201] initially projected by the Bush administration in 2002. Perhaps, the yellowcake scandal was one of the most expensive lies ever told and once again diminished the degree to which the American public trusts the United States government and its leaders.

COALITION PROVISIONAL AUTHORITY
CASH PAYMENT SCANDAL

The Coalition Provisional Authority Cash Payment Scandal began in April 2003. The illegal activity continued until June 2004. Shortly thereafter, it was discovered that approximately $12 million U.S. dollars had been shipped from the United States Federal Reserve to Baghdad, Afghanistan. The majority of the funds belonged to the people of Iraq. The money never reached the people but the Coalition Provisional Authority used the money to fund their projects. According to news reports, "$9 million" could not be located.[202]

Representative Henry Waxman's staffers on the Committee on Government Reform to write a report on June 20, 2005. The committee report maintained $12 billion in cash had been delivered to Iraq by C-130 planes on shrink-wrapped pallets of US $100 bills."[203]

Although the money was sent to aid in rebuilding Iraq, a few people wasted the funds and pocketed the money for themselves. In response to the revelation of corruption, United States Congressman Henry Waxman commented, "Who in their right mind would send 363 tons of cash into a war zone?"[204] According to the representative, the largest payment consisted of "$1.5 billion in cash."[205]

All involved made out like bandits by accepting money and luxury items. The Washington Post reported one U.S. government official received "$546,000" of the illegal money for acquiring "$13 million" in additional deals for a U.S. entrepreneur. In 2005, Mr. Robert Stein, the former comptroller of Coalition Provisional Authority, was arrested along with a Philip Bloom a Romanian businessman in connection to the corruption scandal. A series of emails between Stein and Bloom demonstrates their bribery scheme. In one email dated January 3, 2004, Stein writes, "I love to give you money."[206] Stein and Bloom were arrested and charged with "fraud, money-laundering and conspiracy."[207] Moreover, Bloom allegedly maintained a house in Baghdad where women would report to perform "sexual favors"[208] in exchange for participating in the corruption scheme.

Stein pleaded guilty to charges of "bribery, conspiracy, money laundering" and a number of other charges for his part in the Iraq corruption scandal. Overall, four American citizens, including Stein, were arrested for their participation in illegal activities associated with stealing government funds that were intended to aid in the restructuring of Iraq.[209] Additionally, two senior level Army reservists, Lt. Col. Debra Harrison and Lt. Col. Michael Wheeler, were arrested in the conspiracy and bribery plot.

For his part in the scheme, Stein could have received as much as 30 years in prison for his unscrupulous behavior. However, Stein cooperated with federal investigators and in exchange received a lighter sentence. Robert Stein was 52 at the time of sentencing. He received "nine years in jail"[210] for misusing his position and influence to enhance his personal finances by "accepting bribes for contracts during the rebuilding of Iraq."[211] Assistant Attorney General Alice S. Fisher from the Department of Justice's Criminal Division told the media, "The Department of Justice will protect the integrity of the federal contracting process by aggressively prosecuting fraud, bribery and other crimes that taint missions as critical as the reconstruction of Iraq."[212] As a part of his punishment, Robert Stein was mandated to turn over "$3.6 million."[213] This scandal demonstrates how temporary monetary gain made illegally can lead to the demise of lives. Stein, Bloom and a few U.S. Army reservists risked everything for a few million dollars and expensive gifts, and sexual favors. Their temporary gain, lead to major losses and felony criminal records.

BUSH ADMINISTRATION'S PAYMENT OF COLUMNISTS

In January 2005, the Bush Administration found itself at the center of a media scandal. According to news reports, the Bush Administration contracted Maggie Gallagher (R), Michael McManus (R) and Armstrong Williams (R) to promote policy initiatives formulated by President George W. Bush.

Michael McManus, a "syndicated newspaper columnist,"[214] was paid approximately $4,000 from the United States Department of Health and Human Services for advocating Bush's marriage initiative by coaching "marriage mentors."[215] He was paid "$10,000"[216] to train "Marriage Savers" mentors. Additionally, one of McManus' non-profit businesses was awarded "$49,000 from a group"[217] that received money from the Department of Health and Human Services"[218] to encourage unmarried couples with children to marry. After receiving payment, the columnist increased his discussion of the marriage initiative in his syndicated column. McManus repeatedly quoted Mr. Wade Horn, an HHS official and former board member of "Marriage Savers,"[219] contracted Mr. McManus' services.

In 2005, the U.S. Department of Health and Human Services acknowledged hiring Mr. McManus to advocate for the Bush Administration's marriage initiative.[220] Department of Health and Human Services officials maintained they contracted the columnist for his expertise. Mr. Horn, an HHS official, told the press, 'Thirty years ago, if you were a columnist, you were employed full time by a newspaper most likely, and it was very clear."[221]

He went on to say, "With the explosion of media outfits today, there are a lot of people who wear a lot of hats. Where's the line? What if you have your own blog? Are you a journalist?"[222]

In 2002, syndicated columnist Maggie Gallagher was contracted to work with the Department of Health and Human Services. He worked with the department from January through October 2002. She frequently pushed the marriage initiative in her column. In defense of the initiative, she wrote, "The Bush marriage initiative would emphasize the importance of marriage to poor couples" and "educate teens on the value of delaying childbearing until marriage," she wrote in National Review Online, for example, adding that this could "carry big payoffs down the road for taxpayers and children."[223] Maggie Gallagher received in excess of $21,000 from HHS to promote President Bush's "$300 million initiative" advocating marriage to draft articles for the HHS officials handling the marriage initiative. She also wrote brochures and conducted briefings for HHS officials.[224]

On January 25, 2005, the columnist was asked about the contract. She boldly responded, "Did I violate journalistic ethics by not disclosing it? I don't know. You tell me."[225] Furthermore, she told reporters it never occurred to her that she disclose the information.[226] Shortly thereafter, Maggie Gallagher changed her tune and wrote, "I should have disclosed a government contract when I later wrote about the Bush marriage initiative. I would have, if I had remembered it. My apologies to my readers,"[227] in her column.

Finally, Armstrong Williams, a conservative African-American syndicated columnist was also named in the scandal. Williams accepted "$240,000"[228] from the United States Department of Education to promote "No Child Left Behind."[229] In response to critics who argued his behavior was unscrupulous, Mr. Williams said, "I wanted to do it because it's something I believe in."[230]

One must raise the question, did the Bush administration contract with the columnists for the purpose of propaganda. The three columnists Maggie Gallagher, Michael McManus and Armstrong Williams have effectively discredited themselves within the journalism community. Their behavior has caused some to wonder if journalists and columnists can be trusted when they assume an advocacy tone in favor of a president's political initiatives. Despite the scandal, each of the columnists involved has moved beyond the incident and continue to write columns on a regular basis.

SAMUEL "SANDY" BERGER (D)

In July 2004, Samuel "Sandy" Berger was accused of stealing "classified" national security documents and notes from the National Archives in Washington, DC.[231] The former Clinton national security advisor allegedly stole the documents in preparation for a hearing on the September 11 attack on the United States.[232] After months of being investigated, Sandy Berger pleaded guilty of taking the "classified material" saying, "It was a mistake and it was wrong."[233] Despite admitting taking the documents, the former Clinton aide still "denied criminal wrongdoing."[234] Berger's lawyer admitted the former top Clinton advisor, "knowingly removed the handwritten notes by placing them in his jacket and pants and inadvertently took copies of actual classified documents in a leather portfolio."[235] Although, many of the documents were returned to the National Archives. A number of classified government documents have yet to be returned.[236]

In September 2008, a District Court judge sentenced the former Clinton advisor, to perform "100 hours of community service."[237] Berger was also ordered to "$50,000 in fines"[238] and "$6,905 for the administrative costs of his two-year probation."[239] Following sentencing, Samuel "Sandy" Berger told the media, "I deeply regret the actions that I took at the National Archives two years ago, and I accept the judgment of the court."[240] He also told reporters, "I'm glad that the 9/11 Commission has made clear that it received all the documents that it sought, all the documents that it needed, and I'm pleased to finally have this matter resolved." Mr. Berger received a plea agreement in exchange for admitting he removed the documents.[241]

Although, Samuel Berger's public political career ended in disgrace, he seems to have retained some of his influence. He currently serves as chairman of a firm that develops global strategy. The Albright Stoneridge Group has ties to the investment firm "Albright Capital Management." He handles Albright's strategic engagements in Central Asia, the Middle East, Asia and Russia.[242]

BERNARD KERIK (R)

In 2004, President George W. Bush nominated Bernard Kerik (R) to head the Department of Homeland Security position which oversees "twenty-two federal agencies."[243] Shortly after receiving the presidential nomination, Kerik found himself in the midst of a scandal surrounding his employing an illegal immigrant as his children's nanny and housekeeper. The former New York Police Commissioner relinquished his nomination citing, "he feared an embarrassing nanny scandal."[244] Kerik told reporters he found information that made him question the immigration status of his nanny. Furthermore, he maintained, "It has also been brought to my attention that for a period of time during such employment required tax payments and related filings had not been made."[245] President Bush was caught off guard because the FBI background check should have revealed the issue.

Kerik said he withdrew his name from consideration for the Department of Homeland Security post due to media scrutiny would only draw attention away from "the vital efforts of the Department of Homeland Security."[246] After telephoning President George W. Bush to inform him of his intention to withdraw, he sent a letter explaining, "I am convinced that, for personal reasons, moving forward would not be in the best interests of your administration, the Department of Homeland Security or the American people."[247]

Kerik was married to his third wife when he found himself in the "hotseat" when it was revealed that he had simultaneously engaged in two extramarital affairs at a Battery Park City apartment he rented for his "passionate liaisons."[248] He was engaged in an extramarital affair with Jeanette Pinero, a local corrections officer, and Judith Regan, a well-known publisher. Kerik and Regan's affair lasted less than 12 months. Pinero found out about his relationship with Regan when she discovered a love letter in the apartment Kerik had penned to Judith Regan.[249]

The forty-nine year old father of two attempted to minimize the damage his nanny scandal and double affair would have on his career. Nevertheless, a District Court judge sentenced the former New York Police Commissioner to "four years in federal prison."[250]

On November 4, 2009, Bernard Kerik "pleaded guilty to two counts of tax fraud, one count of making a false statement on a loan application and five counts of making false statements to the federal government while being vetted for senior posts."[251] In exchange for pleading guilty, the government dropped all the corruption charges filed against Kerik. District Judge Stephen Robinson went well beyond federal sentencing guidelines, which suggested 27 to 33 months. He said the guidelines do not take into account "the almost operatic proportions of this case."[252] On March 28, 2013, after serving a little more than three years in prison, Mr. Kerik was released from a Maryland prison.[253] In response to his early release, Kerik said, "I'm not wasting one minute. I can't wait to get back and hold my kids.[254] Mr. Kerik was on "house arrest" and required to "wear an ankle bracelet until his official October release"[255] date.

WATERBOARDING TORTURE SCANDAL

In 2004, many Americans were horrified when the media revealed U.S. military officials were using a "waterboarding" torture technique as a means to gather information from prisoners detained in Iraq. Waterboarding is "an interrogation technique simulating the experience of drowning, in which a person is strapped, face up, to a board that slopes downward at the head, while large quantities of water are poured over the face into the breathing passages."[256]

In 2004, *TIME* magazine published a story on the use of the torture technique by American soldiers in Iraq. The story discussed torture strategies U.S. military used to acquire intelligence or critical information from detainees in Guantanamo Bay, Cuba. The news account also included images of U.S. military officials cheering and rejoicing while waterboarding detainees.

There were approximately "550 people detained"[257] at the U.S. Naval base in Guantanamo Bay prison in 2004. A number of the prisoners had not been charged but had been detained for years without access to legal representation.[258] According to FBI reports, waterboarding was only one severe interrogation technique U.S. military engaged in when torturing detainees at Guantanamo Bay in Cuba. Many detainees were chained to the floor for "more than 24 hours at a time."[259] Detainees were also denied water and food. Moreover, the prisoners were also "allowed to defecate on themselves."[260] The Federal Bureau of Investigation (FBI) adamantly denied engaging in cruel and dehumanizing intelligence gathering techniques. Officials from the FBI and the Pentagon maintained the order to use torture techniques like waterboarding and withholding food came from the United States Secretary of Defense, Donald H. Rumsfeld. The order was given in December 2002. Following concerns expressed by military lawyers that the orders violated domestic and international law, Rumsfeld modified the order.[261] Despite allegations the order came from Rumsfeld, the United States Department of Defense maintained Secretary Rumsfeld never recommended the utilization of torture tactics as a means to extract information from detainees.[262]

Despite use of the aggressive intelligence techniques, at least one FBI agent voiced his disagreement with the use of torture techniques in writing on December 5, 2003 claiming, "These tactics have produced no intelligence of a threat neutralization nature to date and . . . have destroyed any chance of prosecuting" prisoners.[263]

Former Vice-President Dick Cheney told reporters he had "no regrets"[264] about the use of waterboarding and other aggressive interrogation practices used by the Bush administration following the September 11, 2001 attack on the United States that demolished the Twin Towers in New York City and caused the deaths of hundreds of American people. The former Vice-President said he "would strongly support using it again if circumstances arose where we had a high-value detainee and that was the only way we could get him to talk."[265]

Similarly, when questioned by Central Intelligence Agency officials, President George W. Bush admitted he authorized the "waterboarding" of Khalid Sheik Mohammed.[266] The 44th president of the United States took responsibility for U.S. military interrogation tactics used at Guantanamo Bay, Cuba. Bush wrote about giving the authorization to use waterboarding in his memoir titled, *Decision Points*. Mr. Bush wrote about the day he was approached by CIA officials about using waterboarding to attempt to get information from Khalid Sheik Mohammed. The former president expressed no concern about compliance with domestic or international law. In his memoir, Bush makes it clear that if he had to do it all again, he would make the same decision when he writes, 'Damn right."[267] He explained, "I'd do it again to save lives."[268] Despite acknowledging giving permission to engage in horrific interrogation techniques, former President George W. Bush rejected the notion the procedures were tantamount to torture.[269] Despite the Bush administration's assertion aggressive interrogation procedures were needed, the excessive use of waterboarding, subjecting detainees to excessive cold and excessive heat, withholding food and not allowing bathroom breaks is diametrically opposed to the notion of American civil liberties so heavily espoused by the United States.

Shortly after assuming leadership of the White House, President Barack Obama said his administration would monitor the use of aggressive interrogation tactics in Guantanamo Bay. In November 2011, the Commander-in-Chief told the press, "Waterboarding is torture. It's contrary to America's traditions, it's contrary to our ideals, it's not who we are, it's not how we operate."[270] President Obama continued saying, "We did the right thing by ending that practice."[271] Although some may agree with the use of aggressive interrogation strategies on our enemies, the question becomes, are extreme interrogation measures like waterboarding and starvation tactics appropriate. Moreover, does the U.S. government have a responsibility to abide by domestic and international law as it relates to the civil rights and civil liberties of prisoners alleged to have engaged in terrorist activity against the people of the United States?

NSA WARRANTLESS SURVEILLANCE SCANDAL

Under a presidential order signed in 2002, the intelligence agency has monitored the international telephone calls and international e-mail messages of hundreds, perhaps thousands, of people inside the United States without warrants over the past three years in an effort to track identify people linked to Al Qaeda. The agency maintained they still pursue warrants to monitor entirely domestic communications.

In 2002, information was leaked to the media suggesting President George W. Bush authorized National Security officials to spy on American citizens in response to September 11th attack on the United States. Bush admitted giving the National Security Agency (NSA) permission "to eavesdrop on Americans communicating with people overseas"[272] and to monitor email communications.[273] President Bush justified his behavior saying it was acceptable. However, he argued the leaking of the security matter constituted an illegal act.[274] The Chief Executive addressed the nation in a rare live weekly address telling the American people he was well within his "constitutional responsibilities and authorities."[275] According to the president, the program was classified due to the sensitive nature of national security. He maintained the goal of the program was not to monitor citizens' calls for the sake of spying but rather "to detect and prevent terrorist attacks."[276] Moreover, Bush repeatedly used his "spy powers."[277] Despite his attempt to justify his decision to eavesdrop on thousands of citizens calls, Senator Charles Schumer told the press, "Today's revelation that the government listened in on thousands of phone conversations without getting a warrant is shocking and has greatly influenced my vote."[278] In March 31, 2010, federal judge Vaughn Walker ruled that the government had violated a 1978 federal statute requiring court approval for domestic surveillance when it intercepted phone calls of Al Haramain, a now-defunct Islamic charity in Oregon, and of two lawyers representing it in 2004.[279] Judge Walker determined the surveillance or spying on Al Haramain was "unlawful."[280] Consequently, governmental authorities were ordered to pay the victims for damages.[281]

No one knows to what degree the National Security Agency has continued with warrantless surveillance. One thing is true, the creative license of David Marconi's in the film *Enemy of the State* has truly come upon us.

KENNETH LAY (R) AND THE ENRON SCANDAL

Kenneth Lay (R) cofounder of Enron Corp found himself in the middle of one of the largest corporation scandals in United States history. Lay was at the helm of Enron for the bulk of the company's existence serving as its chair and chief executive from January 1987 to February 2001 and again from August 2001 to January 2002.[282]

In an effort to defend himself, Mr. Lay told the media the task force investigating the company's illegal activity was guilty of plunging him in a "wave of terror."[283] In another response about his knowledge and involvement in the Enron scheme Lay said, "I have said before I accept full responsibility for everything that happened at Enron. Having said that I can't take full responsibility for illegal activity . . . for all 30,000 employees at Enron, particularly those engaged in illegal activities."[284]

The cofounder and chief executive was indicted on seven (7) criminal charges in connection with "lying about Enron's financial health before the company crumbled into bankruptcy in December 2001," inflating Enron profits and withholding information about company debt. Lay was charged with conspiring "to commit securities and wire fraud"[285] for his involvement from 1999 to 2001.[286] Lay was also charged with committing "bank fraud and three counts of making false statements to banks"[287] about his personal banking accounts. The son of a minister allegedly received "$75 million in loans from three banks." According to the lenders, Mr. Lay failed to adhere to the terms of the loan agreements. [288]

Despite denying his involvement in Enron's illegal activities, Mr. Lay was found guilty conspiracy and fraud. Consequently, the former Enron CEO could have been sentenced to 165 years for his illegal actions. Kenneth Lay's sentencing hearing was scheduled for October 23, 2006. However, Mr. Lay died of a heart disease while vacationing with his family at a ski resort in July 2006.[289] Shortly after his death, Lay's conviction was vacated by United States District Court Judge Sim Lake. His conviction was "erased" based on a "2004 ruling that a defendant's death pending appeal extinguished his entire case, based on "a 2004 ruling that found that a defendant's death pending appeal extinguished his entire case, as he hadn't had a full opportunity to challenge the conviction."[290]

The Enron scandal led to the demise and disgrace of more than one company executive. A number of company officials were implicated and indicted for their participation in the scheme. A number of executives were implicated in the scandal.

Richard Causey, former Enron chief of accounting, pleaded guilty to "securities fraud"[291] in December 2005. A former Enron trading executive admitted to "participating in an asset sale scheme to recognize earnings prematurely and improperly."[292] Additionally, an executive in the "trading"[293] division named Christopher Calger acknowledged he was guilty of helping carry out "an asset sale scheme to recognize earnings prematurely and improperly."[294]

Moreover, the company's former assistant to the treasurer, Timothy DeSpain, "pleaded guilty to conspiracy."[295] DeSpain also acknowledged he lied to and withheld crucial information from "credit rating agencies at the request of multiple superiors so the energy giant's financial picture appeared healthier."[296]

Kevin Hannon, head of Enron's broadband unit, also "pleaded guilty to conspiracy charges."[297] Mark Koenig, former leader of investor relations, "pleaded guilty to aiding and abetting securities fraud."[298] The company's former energy traders, John Forney and Timothy Belden, "pleaded guilty to wire fraud."[299] They both admitted to "manipulating energy markets during California's power crisis of 2000-2001."[300] Additionally, Kenneth Rice, former Chief Executive Officer of the broadband unit, "pleaded guilty to securities fraud."[301] Ms. Paula Rieker, former top executive for investor relations, came clean about her guilt and involvement in "insider trading."[302]

The husband and wife team of Andrew Fastow and Lea Fastow were charged in the Enron case. Andrew Fastow, former Chief of Finance, was charged with "98 counts of fraud, conspiracy, insider trading, money laundering and others."[303] Mr. Fastow, admitted guilt in two of the conspiracy counts lodged against him. Moreover, he acknowledged "orchestrating myriad schemes to hide Enron debt and inflate profits while enriching himself with millions."[304] Despite cooperating with government officials, Fastow was sentenced to 10 years in prison and required to hand over "$30 million in cash and property."[305] Lea Fastow, wife of Andrew Fastow and Enron's former assistant treasurer initially admitted they were guilty of "a felony tax crime."[306] She also admitted to assisting her husband in his corrupt behavior by hiding money her husband earned from illegal activity.[307]

Additionally, David Delainey admitted to participating in "insider trading."[308] Former Enron Treasurer, Ben Gilsan Jr., "pleaded guilty to conspiracy."[309] Gilsan received five-years in prison for his participation in the scheme. Former trader, Jeffrey Richter admitted guilt related "to wire fraud"[310] charges filed against him. Larry Lawyer admitted he filed "false tax returns" neglecting to report approximately $80,000 in income and accepting gifts for his participation in the Enron scheme. Finally, Michael Kopper, former assistant to Andrew Fastow "pleaded guilty to two counts of conspiracy." Kopper told officials he helped "Fastow carry out schemes to help Enron manipulate its books while skimming millions for himself, Fastow and selected friends and colleagues."[311]

The scope and level of involvement in the Enron scandal surpassed other schemes devised by corporations to defraud investors, the government, and employees. Enron Employees lost their jobs and financial security. The financial losses were insurmountable. Employee retirement plans were obliterated by poor leadership, poor management and reckless abandon on the part of company executives. Enron employees lost approximately "$2.1 billion in assets."[312] According to a New York Times article some employees were "married couples who both worked who lost as much as $800,000 or $900,000."[313]

JANET REHNQUIST (R)

In August 2001, President George W. Bush appointed Janet Rehnquist (R) Inspector General of the Department of Health and Human Services (HHS).[314] Her appointment was controversial because she comes from a prominent family with strong governmental ties. She is the daughter of Supreme Court Justice William Rehnquist.[315] As Inspector General of HHS she was responsible for supervising approximately 1,600 employees. The role is nonpartisan and functions as the Department of Health and Human Services (HHS) "internal watchdog."[316]

Janet Rehnquist's time with the Department of Health and Human Services (HHS) was short lived and riddled with questionable actions on her part. She demonstrated poor decision-making and poor leadership when she adhered to a request made by Governor Jeb Bush's Chief of Staff Kathleen Shanahan. Ms. Shanahan asked Inspector General Janet Rehnquist to delay the probe into Florida "federal overpayment" accounting practices. At the time, Florida had allegedly received federal overpayments in excess of $500 million.[317] Despite the fact the role of the Inspector General is nonpartisan in nature, Ms. Rehnquist complied with Kathleen Shanahan's request to delay the investigation which ensured the findings would not be made public until after Florida Governor Jeb Bush's reelection bid. Ms. Rehnquist used her clout to halt the audit by instructing her staff to begin the audit after Florida's gubernatorial election.[318] There were also allegations made by congressional staffers that Rehnquist bought and kept a handgun in her office.[319] According to government officials, "kept a gun in her office without authorization and whether she violated personnel rules."[320] Finally, Rehnquist was accused of removing longstanding HHS employees. Both the United States Senate Finance Committee and the U.S. Government Accounting Office (GAO) conducted investigations of Rehnquist based on allegations of professional misconduct.[321]

Janet Rehnquist abruptly resigned following the commencement of congressional and GAO probes into her conduct as Inspector General.[322] On March 4, 2003, Ms. Rehnquist penned a letter to the president announcing she was resigning effective June 1st citing a desire "to spend more time with her teenage daughters and pursue other professional opportunities."[323] She continued, "I am proud of the record of accomplishment during my tenure."[324]

According to a draft report issued on June 6, 2003 by the Government Accounting Office in Washington, D.C., Ms. Rehnquist's behavior essentially "undermined the independence of the office, showed poor judgment and created an atmosphere of anxiety and distrust."[325] The former Inspector General of HHS denounced GAO's depiction of her leadership claiming it "consists largely of opinions, speculation, hearsay and predetermined conclusions not supported by the weight of the evidence."[326] Furthermore, the GAO report found she created a hostile work environment. Moreover, the findings suggest Janet Rehnquist was prejudiced by Medicare and Medicaid officials. Additionally, Rehnquist bypassed Civil Service procedures in hiring an individual to fill a key position, inappropriately obtained credentials identifying her as a law enforcement official and 'exhibited serious lapses in judgment."[327] Despite the numerous findings of professional misconduct, Ms. Janet Rehnquist maintains she was not guilty of misconduct or conflict of interest in her role as Inspector General of the Department of Health and Human Services.

JOHN YOO (R)

John Yoo was employed as the Deputy Assistant Attorney General by the Department of Justice[328] (DOJ) Office of Legal Counsel when he wrote a series of memorandums that led to his being referred to as the "torture lawyer."[329] The former DOJ lawyer provided a legal strategy for President Bush on how to torture war prisoners without "avoid breaking Geneva Convention Restrictions"[330] in his January 9, 2002 memorandum. Yoo suggested rationales about how to "keep United States officials from being charged with war crimes for the way prisoners were detained and interrogated."[331] Furthermore, the memo offered arguments maintaining President Bush did not have to conform to the Geneva Convention regulations when dealing with war prisoners or military detainees in Afghanistan.[332] Finally, former Deputy

Assistant Attorney General also suggested ways in which interrogators could avoid legal culpability from "The Convention Against Torture and the Anti-Torture Act."[333]

Mr. Yoo maintained President Bush had a right as commander-in-chief to suspend sections of the ABM Treaty without informing Congress and to bypass the Foreign Intelligence Surveillance Act allowing warrantless wire-tapping of US Citizens within the United States by the National Security Agency. Based on his interpretation of the USA Patriot Act, Mr. Yoo also argued the First Amendment, Fourth Amendment and the Takings Clause did not apply to the Chief Executive in wartime. Finally, he instructed Bush administration officials they could engage in "Enhanced Interrogation Techniques" otherwise known as torture techniques because provisions of the "War Crimes Act," the Third Geneva Convention, and the "Anti-Torture Convention" did not apply to interrogation strategies.[334]

The University of California Berkley law professor was sued by a Jose Padilla a "convicted terrorist" who argued Yoo's memos encouraged the U.S. military officials to torture him to obtain intelligence information. Padilla "was arrested in 2002."[335] He was accused of "conspiring to detonate a radioactive dirty bomb."[336] Padilla remained in the custody of military officials for almost four years. Padilla's lawsuit against John Yoo was dismissed by an appellate court in May 2012.

Yoo is on the faculty at the University of California Berkley Law School.[337] He is also the author of "The Powers of War and Peace: The Constitution and Foreign Affairs after 9/11" published in 2005 by University of Chicago Press, "War by Other Means: An Insider's Account of the War on Terror" published in 2006 by Grove/Atlantic Publishers. In 2012, Yoo wrote "Taming Globalization: International Law, the U.S. Constitution, and the New World Order" published by Oxford University served as a co-editor of "Confronting Terror: 9/11 and the Future of American National Security."[338]

RICK RENZI (R)

United States Representative Rick Renzi (R) was elected to Congress in 2002. He represented the 1st congressional district in Arizona from 2003 through 2009.[339] Renzi served on the Intelligence Committee and Resources and Financial Services.[340] In 2008, the legislator became the subject of Department of Justice (DOJ) investigation for alleged misconduct and misuse of his position for personal gain.[341] The three-term member of Congress pleaded not guilty to charges he abused his position as a legislator for personal economic gain.[342]

In 2008, Renzi was indicted on 32 felony counts of conspiracy, extortion, racketeering, money laundering, lying to insurance regulators and wire fraud.[343] Initially, the then 49 year old member of Congress denied wrongdoing and told reporters, "I will not resign and take on the cloak of guilt because I am innocent."[344] However, the three term[345] Arizona representative did announce his decision not to seek another term.[346]

Congressman Renzi was accused of assisting a business pay back an $800,000 loan. Renzi received more than $700,000 from James W. Sandlin in 2005. He was also accused of moving money between a number of personal accounts. The Arizona legislator allegedly used more than $300,000 of the $700,000 he received from Sandlin to pay off his taxes. Moreover, the indictment maintains the member of Congress failed to claim the money he received from his business associate as income in his financial disclosure forms in 2006.[347]

On February 22, 2008, the former Congressman pleaded not guilty to all of the charges filed against him. On June 11, 2013, the former legislator was "convicted on 17 of the 32"[348] charges filed against him. He is scheduled to receive his sentence on August 19, 2013.

Former congressman Rick Renzi was sentenced to serve three years in prison for his corrupt actions. Judge David Bury told the court he could not explain why Mr. Renzi and Mr. Sandlin engaged in criminal activity. Judge Bury told the people in the courtroom, "I'm not wise enough to know why good people do bad things — I think character and avarice have something to do with it,"[349] The judge went on to say, "That's what happened here. Two good men committed bad acts."[350] Renzi's co-conspirator James Sandlin was sentenced to 18 months in prison for his participation is the scheme. Both Renzi and Sandlin are expected to begin their prison sentences in January 2014.[351]

JOHN DOOLITTLE (R-CA)

Congressman John Doolittle was elected to Congress in 1990. He represented the 14th congressional district of California from 1991-1992 and the 4th congressional district from 1993 to 2009.[352] He served on the House Appropriations Committee.

Representative Doolittle was implicated in the Abramoff lobbying scandal. On January 10, 2008, the member of the House of Representatives announced his retirement. He told reporters and supportive constituents, he planned to retire at the end of his term. The nine-term member said, "My wife, Julie, and I have made this decision after much prayer and deliberation. It was not my initial intent to retire, and I fully expected and planned to run again right up until very recently."[353] After recounting his years of public service, Doolittle told the press he and his wife "are at peace with this choice and look forward to starting a new chapter in our lives."[354]

The former member of Congress became the subject of a Department of Justice investigation. The probe focused on his relationship with the infamous Jack Abramoff. Doolittle allegedly received monthly payments of $5,000 from Abramoff. The payments were delivered to Mrs. Doolittle on behalf of the representative. Federal investigators also investigated allegations that the former member of Congress helped a defense contractor obtain "$37 million in federal funds."[355]

In April 2007, Federal Bureau of Investigation officers searched Congressman John Doolittle's home in Virginia. The search allowed investigators to gather evidence that suggested he took money from the lobbyist Jack Abramoff and failed to report other extravagant gifts Abramoff gave him and his wife, Julie Doolittle. Information from the raid also suggested Julie Doolittle accepted "$67,000 from Abramoff's lobbying firm for event-planning work, including a March 2003 fundraiser at the Spy Museum in Washington, D.C. The event never happened because of the launch of the war in Iraq."[356] Representative Doolittle issued a statement declaring his support for his wife. He also said, he and his wife were "optimistic that truth will win out in the end."[357]

In June 2010, following a lengthy investigation, Department of Justice (DOJ) ended its investigation concluding the former representative and his wife had not engaged in illegal activity. Today, John Doolittle is employed as a lobbyist.[358]

RANDY CUNNINGHAM (R-CA)

In 2003, Representative Randy "Duke" Cunningham became the focus of a federal investigation when he sold his home in California to a defense contractor. The sale drew attention because the price of the home was well above the market value.[359] "Duke" Cunningham, a former member of the United States Navy, served the 50th district in California for fourteen years before he resigned in disgrace."[360]

Mr. Cunningham was charged with "conspiracy to commit bribery, mail and wire fraud and tax evasion."[361] Cunningham's plea agreement with federal prosecutors stemmed from an investigation of the 2003 sale of his California home to a defense contractor for an inflated price. He was sentenced to eight years in federal prison and ordered to pay "$1.8 million in restitution for back taxes."[362]

On November 28, 2005, U.S. Representative Randy "Duke" Cunningham announced his resignation shortly after pleading guilty to accepting approximately "$2 million in bribes"[363] from defense contractors. When the judge asked if Cunningham received gifts including cash in exchange for using his political clout to "influence the Defense Department"[364] on the behalf of his sponsors the former member of Congress replied, 'Yes, your honor."[365] Moreover, the disgraced politician told the judge prior to receiving his sentence, "Your honor I have ripped my life to shreds due to my actions, my actions that I did to myself."[366] The sixty-four year old had one request. He asking the judge if he could be allowed to spend some time with his "91 year-old mother"[367] before beginning his prison term.

Cunningham also addressed the media saying, 'The truth is I broke the law, concealed my conduct and disgraced my office,"[368] he told reporters, his voice strained with emotion. "I know I will forfeit my reputation, my worldly possessions, most importantly the trust of my friends and family."[369] After serving the bulk of his sentence, the former legislator was released to a halfway house in December 2012[370] as he prepares to return to some semblance of normalcy.

CYNTHIA MCKINNEY (D-GA)

U.S. Representatives Cynthia McKinney (D-GA) was involved in a physical altercation with a member of the U.S. Capitol Police Department on March 29, 2006. She represented the 11th district that covers suburban Atlanta, Georgia.[371] She served on the House Committee on International Relations. McKinney also worked with the Women's Caucus Task Force on Children, Youth and Families.[372]

The officer did not recognize Congresswoman McKinney because she was not wearing her member's pin when she approached the security check point.[373] McKinney allegedly hit the officer when she was told she could not go around the security station. The Capitol Police maintained she failed to present identification and struck him with her cellphone.[374] Although there was disparity between McKinney and the officer's accounts of events, one thing is clear, the member lost her composure and struck the officer.

The Georgia representative apologized saying, "I know that Capitol Hill Police are securing our safety, and I appreciate the work that they do. I have demonstrated my support for them in the past and I continue to support them now."[375] She also maintained that she was inappropriately touched by the officer.[376]

A spokesperson for the Capitol Hill police told the media the matter was under investigation. Everyone is required to walk through security check points; no one is permitted to walk around a checkpoint like McKinney attempted.[377] Ultimately, the U.S. Capitol Police decided not to file charges against the national legislator.

She lost her primary election to Dekalb County Commissioner Hank Johnson. She only received 49% of the votes while her opponent Hank Williams received 59% of the votes. McKinney spoke against electronic machines claiming they "are a threat to our democracy."[378] She also declared, "we will not accept any more stolen elections.'[379] In 2008, the former member of Congress resurfaced as a presidential candidate for the Green Party.[380] Cynthia McKinney still resides in Dekalb County in Atlanta, Georgia.

WILLIAM J. JEFFERSON (D-LA)

William Jefferson was elected to represent Louisiana's 2nd district in 1981. The senior member of Congress became the focus of an FBI probe in 2005 when allegations were made that he utilized his position as a U.S. Representative "to solicit bribes from American companies"[381] that wanted to conduct business in West Africa.

According to the FBI investigation, over a five-year period Representative Jefferson soliciting "hundreds of millions of dollars"[382] from companies that needed government approval in order to gain approval to do business in Africa. He shared the money with others who were in cahoots with him in his bribery scheme. The legislator received more than "$478,000"[383] in exchange for agreeing to use his power and influence to ensure companies could do business in the continent of Africa. Moreover, Mr. Jefferson allegedly wasted government resources when he engaged in criminal activities.

Not only did Representative William J. Jefferson accept bribes, he also bribed others to go along with his scheme. On one occasion he was videotaped accepting "$100,000 in cash"[384] from an FBI informant to bribe a West African government official. Authorities obtained a search warrant and retrieved "$90,000"[385] in the congressman's home freezer.

The former member of Congress was charged with a total of "16 federal counts of bribery, racketeering, fraud and money laundering."[386] United States Attorney told reporters, "Mr. Jefferson traded on his good office to enrich himself and his family through a pervasive pattern of fraud, bribery and corruption that span many years and two continents."[387]

Despite the evidence against him and the appearance of impropriety and corruption, Representative William J. Jefferson refused to resign from Congress. Moreover, he ran for reelection despite the cloud of suspicion that surrounded his leadership and integrity. Apparently, his constituents had no problem with his unethical behavior because he successfully defeated his opponent in the 2006 congressional election.[388] However, Congressman Jefferson's attempt to revitalize his political career was short-lived. The Louisiana voters rejected the member of Congress when he ran in 2008.[389]

The former member of Congress and Harvard Law School graduate was depicted in his trial as being void of integrity and driven by greed. Mr. Jefferson was 62 years old when he was convicted on 11 counts "of bribery, racketeering and money laundering involving business ventures in Africa."[390] On November 13, 2009, the former legislator was sentenced to serve "13 years"[391] in a federal prison for inappropriately using his position on the House Ways and Means Trade Subcommittee to line his pockets and family member's pockets.[392]

Additionally, Mr. Brett Pfeffer, Jefferson's former chief of staff, was found to have been complicit in the bribery scheme. In 2006, Mr. Pfeffer pleaded guilty to charges of "aiding and abetting the bribery of a public official and conspiracy to commit bribery."[393] Judge T.S. Ellis, III sentenced Pfeffer to eight-years in prison. The judge believed "there is no doubt that his cooperation was substantial."[394] According to his attorney Paul Knight, Brett Pfeffer's downfall was caused by his inability to "stand up to Congressman Jefferson."[395] Both the former member of Congress and Pfeffer became the butt of many jokes. Ultimately, this scandal teaches us how the actions of one man implicated and negatively impacted the lives of others. It also teaches us it is imperative individuals develop a sense of ethical boundaries they are unwilling to compromise.

BILL JANKLOW (R-SD)

On August 16, 2003, U.S. Representative Bill Janklow was involved in a driving accident in South Dakota that led to the death of motorcyclist, Randolph Scott. The victim was fifty-three years old. Mr. Scott was a resident of Minnesota. The fatal accident occurred on a rural dirt road near the member's hometown at 4:30 p.m. on Saturday, August 16, 2003. He was charges with felony "manslaughter in the second degree."[396] He was also charged with "failing to stop at a stop sign,"[397] and speeding and "reckless driving."[398]

The member of Congress was found guilty of "manslaughter in the second degree"[399] on January 22, 2004. The Circuit Court judge could have sentenced the senior legislator to a maximum of ten years in jail. The sixty-four year old legislator was sentenced to less than 4 months in jail. Additionally, Janklow three year probation. The judge who presided over the case gave Janklow a reduced sentence largely due to the testimony of character witnesses. His many years of public service also factored into the judge's decision.

The fatal traffic accident caused him to live inside a prison for three months. The conviction ruined the likelihood of a prolonged tenure in Congress.[400] Prior to the speeding accident that led to Mr. Scott's death, Bill Janklow had a stellar career as South Dakota's "attorney general, governor"[401] and representative.

In November 2012, Mr. Janklow announced he was dying from cancer. He told the media he had one regret in life and that was running a stop sign and killing Randolph Scott. The former South Dakota governor said, 'If I had it to do over, I'd do everything I did, but I'd stop at a stop sign."[402] On January 12, 2012, the former Congressman died at seventy-two years of age from inoperable brain cancer.[403]

ROBERT TORRICELLI, SENATOR (D-NJ)

Robert Torricelli was serving his first term in the U.S. House of Representatives when the ethics questions emerged about his fundraising tactics. Before being elected to the U.S. Senate, Robert Torricelli served seven terms in the United States House of Representatives.[404]

On July 30, 2002, the U.S. House Ethics Committee ruled Senator Robert Torricelli engaged in inappropriate behavior. The former legislator was found guilty of misconduct because he accepted gifts from Mr. David Chang who was found guilty of breaking campaign finance laws regulated by the Federal Election Commission. Chang sold the representative a "television, CD player and bronze statutes."[405] Chang lent the member of Congress the statutes and they were displayed in Toricelli's congressional office. The television and CD player were sold to the legislator "below market value."[406]

The panel also concluded that the senator's sister and one of her friends violated Senate rules governing gifts when they accepted "earrings" from the infamous donor. According to Senate Rule 35.1 (a). "No Member, officer, or employee shall knowingly accept a gift except as provided by the Gifts Rule."[407] Senators and their staff are prohibited from accepting gifts (presents or cash) from "registered lobbyist, foreign agent, or private entity that retains or employs such individuals."[408] The total value of gifts from the general public "must not exceed $100"[409] in any calendar year. Traditionally, gifts valued at "$10 or less"[410] are not calculated in the annual limit.

The Senate Ethics Committee issued a multiple page verdict highlighting inappropriate activities which represented "poor judgment"[411] on Senator Torriccelli's part. The seasoned politician also used his office and political clout to contact and write "government officials"[412] on Mr. Chang's behalf. The senator also went as far as to allow Mr. Chang to participate in official meetings with representatives of foreign governments.[413]

The six member panel maintained in its report, "After evaluating the extensive body of evidence before it and your testimony, the committee is troubled by incongruities, inconsistencies and conflicts, particularly concerning actions taken by you which were, or could have been, of potential benefit to Mr. Chang."[414] The Senate Ethics Committee reprimanded the senator telling him "Your actions and failure to act led to violations of Senate rules (and related statutes) and created at least the appearance of impropriety."[415]

Consequently, the senator was required to compensate Chang for the items he accepted as gifts. He was made to "pay fair market value" for the TV and CD player. The veteran legislator was mandated to pay interest on the value of the gifts he wrongfully accepted. Torricelli was also required to give the statues back to his campaign donor and political ally.[416]

The U.S. attorney, Ms. Mary Jo White, ended the probe into Torricelli and Chang's relationship. Despite his admittance to official misconduct, charges were not filed against Mr. Torricelli because she did not believe the government could convict Torricelli.[417]

The scandal detrimentally affected his political career in the United States Senate. After serving one term, Torricelli announced he would not run for another term. Shortly after hearing the committee's ruling, Torricelli spoke on the Senate floor saying, "The day that I was elected to the United States Senate remains among the most cherished of my life."[418] He added, "During recent weeks, I have spent long nights tormented by the question of how I could have allowed such lapses of judgment to compromise all that I have fought to build."[419] Moreover, the disgraced senator realized "It might take a lifetime to answer that question to my own satisfaction."[420]

In October 2002, the Democratic Party tapped former U.S. Senator Frank Lautenberg, then 79 years of age, to replace disgraced Robert Torricelli. New Jersey Governor Jim McGreevey announced the Democratic Party's intention to file a petition on behalf of the party requesting Torricelli's name be replaced with Lautenberg's name on the ballot.[421] McGreevey told the media, "I am confident, based upon a thorough and vigorous debate, the citizens of the state of New Jersey will elect Senator Lautenberg to the United States Senate, preserving quality representation on behalf of our state, and ensuring a Democratic majority in the United States Senate.'[422]

Lautenberg went on to win the congressional election and served constituents in New Jersey for a decade following the Torricelli scandal. His political career came to a halt when the eighty-nine year old senator became ill and died from pneumonia on June 3, 2013,[423] leaving Democrats to scramble to find a replacement candidate.[424]

JIM TRAFICANT (D-OH)

In 2002, nine term U.S. Representative James "Jim" Traficant was accused of tax evasion, conspiracy, and bribery.[425] The House Ethics Committee launched an investigation to determine whether Congressman James Traficant engaged in official misconduct on April 17, 2002.[426] The inquiry was conducted by the full Ethics Committee and an "investigative" subcommittee charged to gather information regarding the allegations made against Traficant.[427]

On July 30, 2002, a federal grand jury indicted the outspoken and flamboyant representative on 10 felony counts of "conspiracy to violate bribery statutes, filing false income tax returns, and others for obstruction of justice, conspiracy to defraud the United States and racketeering."[428] A number of the bribery charges suggest the congressman accepted gifts in the form of free labor "in exchange for intervening with federal and state authorities on behalf of contractors."[429] Additional charges alleged he made members of his congressional staff complete chores and work on his boat during regular business days.[430]

Shortly after receiving the news that he'd been indicted, the representative from Youngstown told the press, "investigators were pressing potential witnesses to tell them what they wanted to hear."[431] He declared the full committee and the investigative subcommittee were not interested in "the truth."[432] Despite not being an attorney, Traficant represented himself during his corruption trial. The verdict in the case was announced on April 12, 2002. After hearing all of the evidence presented in the trial, the jury found the national law maker guilty on all ten counts. He was declared guilty of accepting bribes, racketeering, making his congressional and district staff do personal chores unrelated to their job description and "filing false tax returns."[433] Upon hearing the verdict, Traficant addressed the court saying, "I accept your verdict."[434]

Shortly after the trial, the United States House of Representatives began the process to expel Traficant from the legislative body. Despite the then 61 year olds' arguments against expulsion, four hundred twenty House members voted in favor of expulsion. Only one member, Gary Condit, voted against removing the Youngstown native from Congress. As a consequence of his official misconduct, James "Jim" Traficant became "the fifth"[435] member of Congress to be removed from office by his peers in more than two hundred years. He was expelled from the House of Representatives on July 24, 2002.[436]

During the sentencing phase of his trial, the former legislator received the news that he would have to pay for his illegal activity by serving "eight years" in jail on July 30, 2002. He was also ordered to pay "$150,000" in fines related to his illegal activity. The U.S. District Court judge that presided over the case told the disgraced politician, "You've done a lot of good in your years in Congress ... the good you have done does not excuse you of the crime you were convicted of."[437] The disgraced former member of the House of Representatives served seven years of his eight year sentence for engaging in corrupt activities including racketeering, tax evasion and taking bribes.[438] The sixty-eight year old exited the prison carrying his personal belongings in a bag and was transported home by taxi.[439]

Although, it appeared the former member of Congress' political future was over. Nevertheless, in May 2010, a defiant James Traficant announced his plan to run for the 17th congressional district seat he once held prior to his conviction.[440] He was successful at getting his name on the ballot for the November 2010 congressional election.[441] In the end, James Traficant was unsuccessful in his attempt to come back from his fall from his political disgrace. Incumbent Tim Ryan (D-OH) retained his seat in the House of Representatives.[442] Voters in Ohio seemingly had enough of Traficant's antics and his display of poor character. The seventy-two year old disgraced politician has disappeared from the political scene and resides in Youngstown, Ohio with his wife Patricia Choppa Traficant.[443]

CONCLUSION

The section of the study treated thirty-four (34) non-sex scandals involving a diverse group of government officials. It is safe to say that many of the officials faced public embarrassment due to media coverage of their scandalous and illegal activity. Some officials involved in sex scandals lost their political career. Consequently, a number of government officials resigned from political office. Among those who resigned from their political posts were: Julie McDonald, Claude Alexander Allen, II, Lester Crawford, Bernard Kerik, and Jesse Jackson, Jr. A large number of government officials involved in non-sex scandals were indicted for illegal activity. Among those indicted for breaking the law were: Lewis Libby, Lurita Alexis Doan, Jack Abramoff, Kyle Foggo, Samuel Berger, Bernard Kerik, Kenneth Lay (Enron Scandal), Rick Renzi, Randy Cunningham, William J. Jefferson, Jim Traficant, Jesse Jackson, Jr, G. Thomas Porteous and Kwame Kilpatrick. A significant number of officials were convicted and sentenced to prison for their illegal behavior. Among those convicted and sentenced to prison included: Lewis Libby, Jack Abramoff, Kyle Foggo, Lester Crawford, Bernard Kerik, Rick Renzi, Randy Cunningham, William J. Jefferson, Bill Janklow, Robert Torricelli, Jesse Jackson, Jr., and Kwame Kilpatrick. Congressman Charles Rangel was censured by Congress as a consequence of his unethical and illegal behavior (withholding income on his tax return). Judge G. Thomas Porteous was impeached by the United States Congress due to his unethical and illegal activity. Ultimately, every government official or public servant involved or implicated in a non-sex scandal addressed in this chapter damaged his/her professional credibility which led to the demise of his/her professional or political career. Each individual involved in a non-sex scandal was publicly exposed for participating in unethical and illegal behavior. Ultimately, the consequences associated with their inappropriate, unprofessional, illegal actions are all their own making because they refused to harness or control their desire for more power and money. In conclusion, these scandals serve as examples of what happens to an individual who is unwilling or unsuccessful at overcoming greed and the need for increased power.

NOTES

1. Monica Davey, "For a Soaring Political Career, Uncertain Turns," *The New York Times* [database online] available from http://www.nytimes.com/2012/07/12/us/for-a-soaring-political-career-uncertain-turns.html?pagewanted=all&_r=0 ; Internet; accessed August 22, 2013, 1.

2. Ed O'Keefe, "The Rise and Fall of Jesse Jackson Jr.," *The Washington Post* [database online] available from http://www.washingtonpost.com/blogs/the-fix/wp/2013/02/20/the-rise-and-fall-of-jesse-jackson-jr/ ; Internet; accessed August 22, 2013, 1.

3. Monica Davey, "For a Soaring Political Career, Uncertain Turns," *The New York Times* [database online] available from http://www.nytimes.com/2012/07/12/us/for-a-soaring-political-career-uncertain-turns.html?pagewanted=all&_r=0 ; Internet; accessed August 22, 2013, 1.

4. Steven Gray, "Jesse Jackson Jr.: The Trouble with Being Candidate 5," *TIME* [database online] available from http://www.time.com/time/politics/article/0,8599,1866058,00.html ; Internet; accessed August 22, 2013, 1.

5. Andrew Greiner, "Jesse's Girl?," *NBC Chicago* [database online] available from http://www.nbcchicago.com/blogs/ward-room/Jesse-Jackson-Responds-to-New-Allegations-103457694.html ; Internet; accessed August 22, 2013, 1.

6. "Jesse Jackson Jr. Investigation: Feds Target Congressman's Finances In New Probe," *Huffington Post* [database online] available from http://www.huffingtonpost.com/2012/10/13/jesse-jackson-jr-investig_n_1963714.html; Internet; accessed August 21, 2013, 1.

7. Andrew Greiner, "Jesse's Girl?," *NBC Chicago* [database online] available from http://www.nbcchicago.com/blogs/ward-room/Jesse-Jackson-Responds-to-New-Allegations-103457694.html ; Internet; accessed August 22, 2013, 1.

8. Ibid.

9. Rachel Weiner, "Jesse Jackson Jr. Undergoing Treatment for Bipolar Disorder," *The Washington Post* [database online] available from http://www.washingtonpost.com/blogs/the-fix/post/jesse-jackson-jr-undergoing-treatment-for-bipolar-disorder/2012/08/13/e2dabca6-e575-11e1-8741-940e3f6dbf48_blog.html ; Internet; accessed August 21, 2013, 1.

10. Andrew Greiner, "Jesse Jackson Jr. Wins Reelection From Mayo Clinic," *NBC Chicago* [database online] available from http://www.nbcchicago.com/blogs/ward-room/Jesse-Jackson-Jr-Wins-Reelection--175717941.html ; Internet; accessed August 21, 2013, 1.

11. Monica Davey, "Jesse Jackson Jr. Resigns, Facing Illness and Inquiry," *The New York Times* [database online] available from http://www.nytimes.com/2012/11/22/us/jackson-jr-to-resign-house-seat.html ; Internet; accessed August 21, 2013, 1.

12. Ibid.

13. Monica Davey, "Jesse Jackson Jr. Resigns, Facing Illness and Inquiry," *The New York Times* [database online] available from http://www.nytimes.com/2012/11/22/us/jackson-jr-to-resign-house-seat.html , November 21, 2012, accessed August 21, 2013, 1.

14. B.J. Lutz, "Alderman Sandi Jackson Resigns," *NBC Chicago* [database online] available from   http://www.nbcchicago.com/blogs/ward-room/chicago-alderman-sandi-jackson-resign-186527151.html ; Internet; accessed August 21, 2013, 1.

15. Ibid.

16. Ibid.

17. B.J. Lutz, "Alderman Sandi Jackson Resigns," *NBC Chicago* [database online] available from   http://www.nbcchicago.com/blogs/ward-room/chicago-alderman-sandi-jackson-resign-186527151.html ; Internet; accessed August 21, 2013, 1.

18. Carol Cratty and Tom Cohen, "Jesse Jackson Jr., Wife Plead Guilty to Charges Involving Campaign Funds," *CNN* [database online] available from http://www.cnn.com/2013/02/20/politics/jackson-plea-deal ; Internet; accessed August 21, 2013, 1.

19. Ibid.

20. Ibid.

21. Phil Rogers, "Sandi Jackson Pleads Guilty To Tax Fraud," *NBC Chicago* [database online] available from http://www.nbcchicago.com/blogs/ward-room/Sandi-Jackson-Jesse-Jackson-Jr-Plea-192091691.html ; Internet; February 20, 2013, 1.

22. Phil Rogers, "Sandi Jackson Pleads Guilty To Tax Fraud," *NBC Chicago* [database online] available from http://www.nbcchicago.com/blogs/ward-room/Sandi-Jackson-Jesse-Jackson-Jr-Plea-192091691.html ; Internet; accessed August 22, 2013, 1.

23. Fredreka Schouten, "Ex-Rep. Jesse Jackson Jr. Gets 30 Months in Prison," *USA Today* [database online] available from http://www.usatoday.com/story/news/politics/2013/08/14/jesse-jackson-sentenced-sandi-jackson-misusing-campaign-funds/2650453/ ; Internet; accessed August 22, 2013, 1.

24. Ibid.

25. Ibid.

26. Ibid.

27. Ibid.

28. Ibid.

29. Fredreka Schouten, "Ex-Rep. Jesse Jackson Jr. Gets 30 Months in Prison," *USA Today* [database online] available from http://www.usatoday.com/story/news/politics/2013/08/14/jesse-jackson-sentenced-sandi-jackson-misusing-campaign-funds/2650453/ ; Internet; accessed August 22, 2013, 1.

30. Katherine Skiba, "Both Jacksons Get Prison Terms; He'll Serve First," *Chicago Tribune* [database online] available from http://articles.chicagotribune.com/2013-08-14/news/chi-jesse-jackson-jr-sentence-20130814_1_both-jacksons-sandi-jackson-jackson-jr ; Internet; accessed August 22, 2013, 1.

31. S.A. Miller, "Scandal-stained Rangel Quits Post," *New York Post* [database online] available from http://www.nypost.com/p/news/national/just_don_o4LUuhrmDip5pcpADAecPK ; Internet; accessed August 6, 2013, 1.

32. Jordan Fabian, "Charles Rangel at IRS Hearing: "Wrong to Abuse the Tax System," *ABC News* [database online] available from http://abcnews.go.com/ABC_Univision/Politics/congressman-charlie-rangel-wrong-abuse-tax-system/story?id=19201621 ; Internet; accessed August 6, 2013, 1.

33. Jill Jackson, "Charlie Rangel: List of Charges," *CBS News* [database online] available from http://www.cbsnews.com /8301-503544_162-20012179-503544.html; Internet; accessed August 6, 2013, 1.

34. Ibid.

35. Jill Jackson, "Charlie Rangel: List of Charges," *CBS News* [database online] available from http://www.cbsnews.com /8301-503544_162-20012179-503544.html; Internet; accessed August 6, 2013, 1.

36. Paul Kane, "Rep. Charlie Rangel Found Guilty of 11 Ethics Violations," *The Washington Post* [database online] available from http://www.washingtonpost.com/wp-dyn/content/article/2010/11/16/AR2010111604000.html ; Internet; accessed August 6, 2013, 1.

37. Ibid.

38. Carol D. Leonnig and Paul Kane, "Rep. Charles Rangel Broke Ethics Rules, House Panel Finds," *The Washington Post* [database online] available from http://www.washingtonpost.com/ wp-dyn/content/article/2010/07/22/AR2010072204704.html , July 23, 2010, accessed August 6, 2013, 1.

39. Jordan Fabian, "Charles Rangel at IRS Hearing: "Wrong to Abuse the Tax System," *ABC News* [database online] available from http://abcnews.go.com/ABC_Univision/Politics/congressman -charlie-rangel-wrong-abuse-tax-system/story?id=19201621 ; Internet; accessed August 6, 2013, 1.

40. "Congress Censures Charlie Rangel," *ABC News* [database online] available from http://abcnews.go.com/Politics/video/congress-censures-charlie-rangel-12299325 ; Internet; accessed August 6, 2013.

41. "Rare House Censure Ends 2-Year Ordeal for Rangel House Censure Ends 2-Year Ordeal for Rangel House," *Public Broadcast System* [database online] available from http://www.pbs.org/newshour/bb/politics/july-dec10/rangel_12-02.html ; Internet; accessed August 6, 2013.

42. "Rare House Censure Ends 2-Year Ordeal for Rangel House Censure Ends 2-Year Ordeal for Rangel House," *Public Broadcast System* [database online] available from http://www.pbs.org/newshour/bb/politics/july-dec10/rangel_12-02.html ; Internet; accessed August 6, 2013.

43. Ibid.

44. Johnathan Capehart, "Censured Charles Rangel Can't Help Himself," *The Washington Post* [database online] available from http://www.washingtonpost.com/blogs/post-partisan/wp/2013/04/25/censured-charles-rangel-cant-help-himself/ ; Internet; accessed August 6, 2013, 1.

45. Ibid.

46. Dan Friedman, "Rep. Charles Rangel Will Run For Reelection In 2014 — For Now," *New York Daily News* [database online] available from http://www.nydailynews.com/news/politics/rep-charles-rangel-run-reelection-2014-article-1.1407246; Internet; accessed August 15, 2013.

47. "U.S. Congressman Joe Wilson Biography," Congressman Joe Wilson [database online] available from http://joewilson.house.gov/biography/default.aspx; Internet; accessed November 20, 2013.

48. Bob Evans, "Judge G. Thomas Porteous Faces Impeachment Trial In Congress," *Huffington Post* [database online] available from accessed August 6, 2013, 1.

49. Bob Evans, "Judge G. Thomas Porteous Faces Impeachment Trial In Congress," *Huffington Post* [database online] available from http://www.huffingtonpost.com/2010/09/13/judge-g-thomas-porteous-impeachment-trial_n_715336.html; Internet; accessed August 6, 2013, 1 and "H.Res. 1031," *OpenCongress* [database online] available from http://www.opencongress.org/ bill/111-hr1031/text; Internet; accessed August 6, 2013, 1-2.

50. Ibid., 1.

51. Ibid.

52. Ibid.

53. Ibid.

54. Ibid., 1.

55. Ibid.

56. Ibid.

57. Ibid.

58. Patricia Murphy, "Senate Removes Judge G. Thomas Porteous, Jr. Following Impeachment Trial," *Politics Daily* [database online] available from http://www.politicsdaily.com/2010/12/08/senate-impeaches-judge-thomas-porteous-removes-him-from-office/ ; Internet; accessed August 6, 2013, 1.

59. Bob Evans, "Judge G. Thomas Porteous Faces Impeachment Trial In Congress," *Huffington Post*, http://www.huffingtonpost.com/2010/09/13/judge-g-thomas-porteous-impeachment-trial_n_715336.html; Internet; accessed August 6, 2013, 1.

60. Ibid.

61. "Interactive Timeline: Kwame Kilpatrick Corruption Case," Detroit News [database online] available from http://www.detroitnews.com/article/99999999/SPECIAL01/130226003 ; Internet; accessed August 24, 2013, 1.

62. Ibid., 2.

63. Ibid., 3.

64. Ibid., 5.

65. Ibid.

66. Ibid., 6.

67. Ibid., 7.

68. Ibid.

69. "Interactive Timeline: Kwame Kilpatrick Corruption Case," *Detroit News* [database online] available from http://www.detroitnews.com/article/99999999/SPECIAL01/130226003 ; Internet; accessed August 24, 2013, 9 and Madison Gray, S. James Snyder and M.J. Stephen, "Sinful Stateman: Kwame Kilpatrick," *TIME* [database online] available from http://www.time.com/time/specials/2007/article/0,28804,1721111_1721210_1721124,00.html ; Internet; accessed August 24, 2013, 1.

70. "Interactive Timeline: Kwame Kilpatrick Corruption Case," *Detroit News* [database online] available from http://www.detroitnews.com/article/99999999/SPECIAL01/130226003 ; Internet; accessed August 24, 2013, 9.

71. Ibid.

72. Ibid.

73. Mary Chapman, "Former Mayor of Detroit Guilty in Corruption Case," *The New York Times* [database online] available from http://www.nytimes.com/2013/03/12/us/kwame-kilpatrick-ex-mayor-of-detroit-convicted-in-corruption-case.html?_r=0 ; Internet; accessed August 24, 2013, 1.

74. Ibid.

75. Mary Chapman, "Former Mayor of Detroit Guilty in Corruption Case," *The New York Times* [database online] available from http://www.nytimes.com/2013/03/12/us/kwame-kilpatrick-ex-mayor-of-detroit-convicted-in-corruption-case.html?_r=0 ; Internet; accessed August 24, 2013, 1.

76. Ibid.

77. Ibid.

78. Ibid.

79. Tresa Baldas, "Kwame Kilpatrick's Wife Evicted From Texas Home," *NewsTalk WCHB News* [database online] available from http://wchbnewsdetroit.com/2808214/kwame-kilpatricks-wife-evicted-from-texas-home/ ; Internet; accessed August 24, 2013, 1.

80. Ibid.

81. Ibid.

82. Ashley Woods, "Kwame Kilpatrick 28-Year Prison Sentence For Corruption Is Long, But Not 'Extreme': Experts," *Huffington Post* [database online] available from http://www.huffingtonpost.com/2013/10/11/kwame-kilpatrick-sentence-jail-corruption_n_4080171.html ; Internet; accessed October 13, 2013, 1.

83. Ibid.

84. Neil A. Lewis, "Libby Guilty of Lying in C.I.A. Leak Case," *New York Times* [database online] available from http://www.nytimes.com/2007/03/07/washington/ 07libby.html?pagewanted=all&_r=0 ; Internet; accessed August 5, 2013, 1.

85. Ibid.

86. Ibid.

87. Ibid.

88. Carol D. Leonning and Amy Goldstein, "Libby Found Guilty in CIA Leak Case," *The Washington Post* [database online] available from http://www.washingtonpost.com/wp-dyn/content/article/2007/03/06/AR2007030600648.html ; Internet; accessed August 5, 2013, 1 and Neil A. Lewis, "Libby Guilty of Lying in C.I.A. Leak Case," New York Times [database online] available from http://www.nytimes.com/2007/03/07/washington/ 07libby.html?pagewanted=all&_r=0 ; Internet; accessed August 5, 2013,1.

89. Neil A. Lewis, "Libby Guilty of Lying in C.I.A. Leak Case," *New York Times* [database online] available from http://www.nytimes.com/2007/03/07/washington/ 07libby.html?pagewanted=all&_r=0 ; Internet; accessed August 5, 2013, 1.

90. "Key Players in the CIA Leak Investigation," *The Washington Post* [database online] available from http://www.washingtonpost.com/wp-srv/politics/special/plame/Plame_Key Players.html ; Internet; accessed August 5, 2013, 1.

91. Jim Rutenberg and Scott Shane, "Libby Pays Fine; Judge Poses Probation Query," *The New York Times* [database online] available from http://www.nytimes.com/2007/07/06/washington/06libby.html?_r=1&oref=slogin ; Internet; accessed August 5, 2013, 1.

92. Carol D. Leonning and Amy Goldstein, "Libby Found Guilty in CIA Leak Case," *The Washington Post* [database online] available from http://www.washingtonpost.com/wp-dyn/content/article/2007/03/06/AR2007030600648.html ; Internet; accessed August 5, 2013, 1.

93. Neil A. Lewis, "Libby Guilty of Lying in C.I.A. Leak Case," *New York Times* [database online] available from http://www.nytimes.com/2007/03/07/washington/ 07libby.html?pagewanted=all&_r=0 ; Internet; accessed August 5, 2013, 1.

94. Neil A. Lewis, "Libby Guilty of Lying in C.I.A. Leak Case," *New York Times* [database online] available from http://www.nytimes.com/2007/03/07/washington/ 07libby.html?pagewanted=all&_r=0 ; Internet; accessed August 5, 2013, 1.

95. Faiz Shakir, "23 Administration Officials Involved in Plame Affair," ThinkProgress [database online] available from http://thinkprogress.org/report/leak-scandal/ ; Internet; accessed August 5, 2013, 1.

96. Ibid.

97. Dan Eggen and Carol D. Leonnig, "Jackson Resigns as HUD Secretary," *The Washington Post* [database online] available from http://articles.washingtonpost.com/2008-04-01/politics/ 36878302_1_jackson-dan-bartlett-hud-contractors; Internet; accessed August 7, 2013, 1.

98. "HUD Chief Resigns Amid Ethics Investigations," *CNN* [database online] available from http://www.cnn.com/2008/POLITICS/03/31/hud.resignation/ ; Internet; accessed August 7, 2013, 1.

99. Charlie Savage, "No Charges for Ex-Head of Housing Under Bush," *New York Times* [database online] available from http://www.nytimes.com/2010/05/04/us/politics/ 04jackson.html?_r=0 ; Internet; accessed August 7, 2013, 1.

100. Carol Leonnig, "HUD Chief Accused of Retaliation," *The Washington Post* [database online] available from http://articles.washingtonpost.com/2008-02-04/news/36892229_1_carlgreene-jackson-authority ; Internet; accessed August 7, 2013, 1.

101. Ibid.

102. Carol Leonnig, "HUD Chief Accused of Retaliation," *The Washington Post* [database online] available from http://articles.washingtonpost.com/2008-02-04/news/36892229_1_carlgreene-jackson-authority ; Internet; accessed August 7, 2013, 1.

103. Peter Dreier, "HUD Secretary Alphonso Jackson's Resignation," *Huffington Post* [database online] available from http://www.huffingtonpost.com/peter-dreier/hud-secretary-alphonso-ja_b_94787.html ; Internet; accessed August 7, 2013, 1.

104. Dan Eggen and Carol D. Leonnig, "Jackson Resigns as HUD Secretary," *The Washington Post* [database online] available from http://articles.washingtonpost.com/2008-04-01/politics/ ; Internet; accessed August 7, 2013, 1.

105. Ibid.

106. "Top Ten Political Scandals: U.S. Attorney Firings - 'Lawyergate,'" *Rolling Stone* [database online] available from http://www.rollingstone.com/politics/pictures/top-ten-political-scandals-20110926/lawyergate-0371211 ; Internet; accessed August 20, 2013, 1.

107. "Bush Attorney General Pick is Alberto Gonzales," *CNN* [database online] available from http://www.cnn.com/2004/ALLPOLITICS/11/10/bush.cabinet/ ; Internet; accessed August 20, 2013, 1.

108. "Top Ten Political Scandals: U.S. Attorney Firings - 'Lawyergate,'" *Rolling Stone* [database online] available from http://www.rollingstone.com/politics/pictures/top-ten-political-scandals-20110926/lawyergate-0371211 ; Internet; accessed August 20, 2013, 1.

109. Adam Zagorin, "Why Were These U.S. Attorneys Fired?," *TIME* [database online] available from http://www.time.com/time/nation/article/0,8599,1597085,00.html ; Internet; accessed August 20, 2013, 1.

110. Ibid.

111. Richard A. Serrano , Ralph Vartabedian and Sam Howe Verhovek , "Outrage, Questions Persist on Firing of U.S. Attorneys," *The Seattle Times* [database online] available from http:// seattletimes.com/html/nationworld/2003613762_attorneys12.html ; Internet; accessed August 20, 2013, 1.

112. Richard A. Serrano , Ralph Vartabedian and Sam Howe Verhovek , "Outrage, Questions Persist on Firing of U.S. Attorneys, *The Seattle Times* [database online] available from http:// seattletimes.com/html/nationworld/2003613762_attorneys12.html ; Internet; accessed August 20, 2013, 1.

113. Carrie Johnson, "No Grand Jury for Gonzales," *The Washington Post* [database online] available from http://www.washingtonpost.com/wp-dyn/content/article/2008/09/28/ AR2008092801057.html ; Internet; accessed August 20, 2013, 1.

114. "Bush attorney general pick is Alberto Gonzales," *CNN* [database online] available from http://www.cnn.com/2004/ALLPOLITICS/11/10/bush.cabinet/ ; Internet; accessed August 20, 2013, 1.

115. "House Approves Contempt Citations for Miers, Bolten," *Fox News* [database online] available from http://www.foxnews.com/story/2008/02/14/house-approves-contempt-citations-for-miers-bolten/ ; Internet; accessed August 20, 2013, 1.

116. "Lurita Doan Finally Forced Out at GSA," *Politico* [database online] available from http://www.politico.com/blogs/thecrypt/0408/Lurita_Doan_forced_out_at_GSA.html ; Internet; accessed August 6, 2013, 1.

117. Ibid.

118. Robert O'Harrow Jr. and Scott Higham, "Doan Ends Her Stormy Tenure as GSA Chief," *The Washington Post* [database online] available from http://www.washingtonpost.com/wp-dyn/content/article/2008/04/30/AR2008043001271.html ; Internet; accessed August 6, 2013, 1.

119. Ibid.

120. Robert O'Harrow Jr. and Scott Higham, "Doan Ends Her Stormy Tenure as GSA Chief," *The Washington Post* [database online] available from http://www.washingtonpost.com/wp-dyn/content/article/2008/04/30/AR2008043001271.html ; Internet; accessed August 6, 2013, 1.

121. Ibid.

122. Ibid.

123. Ibid.

124. "Jack Abramoff Urges Ethics Reform In NCSL Speech," *Huffington Post* [database online] available from http://www.huffingtonpost.com/2012/08/09/jack-abramoff-ethics-reform ncsl_n_1762154.html ; Internet; accessed August 6, 2013, 1.

125. Ibid.

126. Richard B. Schmitt, "Ex-GOP Lobbyist Abramoff Sentenced to 4 Years in Prison," *Los Angeles Times* [database online] available from http://articles.latimes.com/2008/sep/05/nation/na-abramoff5 ; Internet; accessed August 6, 2013, 1.

127. Ibid.

128. Susan Schmidt and James V. Grimaldi, "Abramoff Pleads Guilty to 3 Counts," *The Washington Post* [database online] available from http://www.washingtonpost.com/wp-dyn/content/article/2006/01/03/AR2006010300474.html ; Internet; accessed August 6, 2013, 1.

129. Ibid.

130. Richard B. Schmitt, "Ex-GOP Lobbyist Abramoff Sentenced to 4 Years in Prison," *Los Angeles Times* [database online] available from http://articles.latimes.com/2008/sep/05/nation/na-abramoff5 ; Internet; accessed August 6, 2013, 1.

131. Ibid.

132. Jeffrey Smith, "Tom DeLay, Former U.S. House Leader, Sentenced to 3 Years in Prison," *The Washington Post* [database online] available from http://www.washingtonpost.com/wp-dyn/content/article/2011/01/10/AR2011011000557.html ; Internet; January 10, 2011, 1.

133. U.S. Congress, House of Representatives Government Reform Committee, "Staff Report" [database online] available from http://oversight-archive.waxman.house.gov/abramoff/docs/abramoff.pdf ; Internet; accessed August 6, 2013, 10-11 and "A Guide To The Abramoff and DeLay Investigations," *The New York Times* [database online] available from http://graphics8.nytimes.com/packages/pdf/politics/04cnd-marsh3.pdf ; Internet; accessed August 6, 2013, 1.

134. Jeffrey Smith and Christopher Lee, "DeLay Booked in Houston on Money-Laundering, Conspiracy Charges," *The Washington Post* [database online] available from http://www.washingtonpost.com/wp-dyn/content/article/2005/10/20/AR2005102000248.html ; Internet; accessed August 6, 2013, 1.

135. Ibid.

136. Philip Shenon, "Ney Is Sentenced to 30 Months in Prison," *The New York Times* [database online] available from http://www.nytimes.com/2007/01/19/washington/19cnd-ney.html ; Internet; accessed August 6, 2013, 1.

137. James V. Grimaldi, "Ex-Official Linked to Abramoff Pleads Guilty," *The Washington Post* [database online] available from http://www.washingtonpost.com/wp-dyn/content/article/2008/04/22/AR2008042202430.html ; Internet; accessed August 6, 2013, 1.

138. Susan Schmidt, "Official in Abramoff Case Sentenced to 18 Months," *The Washington Post* [database online] available from http://www.washingtonpost.com/wp-dyn/content/article/2006/10/27/AR2006102700486.html ; Internet; accessed August 6, 2013, 1.

139. Susan Schmidt and James V. Grimaldi, "Official Charged in Abramoff Scandal," *The Washington Post* [database online] available fromhttp://www.washingtonpost.com/wp-dyn/content/article/2006/06/28/AR2006062802069.html ; Internet; accessed August 6, 2013, 1.

140. Peter Baker and James V. Grimaldi, "Rove Aide Linked To Abramoff Resigns," *The Washington Post* [database online] available from http://www.washingtonpost.com/wp-dyn/content/article/2006/10/06/AR2006100600965.html ; Internet; accessed August 6, 2013, 1.

141. Edmund L. Andrews, "Ex-Deputy of Interior Dept. Pleads Guilty," *The New York Times* [database online] available from http://www.nytimes.com/2007/03/23/washington/23cnd-giles.html ; Internet; accessed August 6, 2013, 1.

142. "Environmental Activist Federici Pleads Guilty to Tax Evasion in Abramoff Probe," *Fox News* [database online] available from http://www.foxnews.com/story/2007/06/08/environmental-activist-federici-pleads-guilty-to-tax-evasion-in-abramoff-probe/ ; Internet; accessed August 6, 2013, 1.

143. Susan Schmidt, "Republican With Links to Abramoff Is Sentenced," *The Washington Post* [database online] available from http://www.washingtonpost.com/wp-dyn/content/article/2007/12/14/AR2007121402008.html ; Internet; accessed August 6, 2013, 1.

144. U.S. Congress, House of Representatives Government Reform Committee, "Staff Report," *U.S. Congress* [database online] available from http://oversight-archive .waxman.house.gov/ ; Internet; accessed August 6, 2013, 10.

145. Ibid.

146. Megan Stride, "Abramoff Lobbyist Sentenced To 20 Months," *Law 360* [database online] available from http://www.law360.com/articles/225511/abramoff-lobbyist-sentenced-to-20-months ; Internet; accessed August 7, 2013, 1.

147. U.S. Congress, House of Representatives Government Reform Committee,"Staff Report," U.S. Congress [database online] available from http://oversight-archive .waxman.house.gov/ ; Internet; accessed August 6, 2013, 11.

148. Ibid.

149. Spencer S. Hsu, "Aide Sentenced in Abramoff Scandal," *The Washington Post* [database online] available from http://www.washingtonpost.com/wp-dyn/content/article/2010/11/22/AR2010112207038.html ; Internet; accessed 6, 2013, 1.

150. James V. Grimaldi and Carol D. Leonnig, "Former Aide to Ex-Congressman Ney Pleads Guilty in Abramoff Case," *The Washington Post* [database online] available from http:/www.washingtonpost.com/wp-dyn/content/article/2007/02/26/AR2007022601631.html ; Internet; accessed August 6, 2013, 1.

151. "Former Abramoff Colleague Kevin Ring Sentenced to 20 Months in Prison for Conspiracy, Honest Services Fraud and Payment of Gratuities Related to Illegal Lobbying Scheme," The United States Department of Justice, [database online] available from http://www.justice.gov/ ; Internet; accessed August 6, 2013, 1.

152. "Ex-Aide Gets Probation in Lobbying Scandal," *The New York Times* [database online] available from http://www.nytimes.com/2011/04/08/us/politics/08brfs-Washington.html_r=0&gwh=C78F3C581F32158ECE9642589858F0E7; Internet; accessed August 6, 2013, 1.

153. Derek Kravitz, "Another Ex-Abramoff Aide Charged," *The Washington Post* [database online] available from http://voices.washingtonpost.com/washingtonpostinvestigations/2009/01/ex-abramoff_aide_charged.html ; Internet; accessed August 6, 2013, 1.

154. Dan Eggen and Charles R. Babcock, "Official Quits; FBI Probes Role in Defense Contracts," *The Washington Post* [database online] available from http://www.expose-the-warprofiteers.org/archive/media/2006/20060509.htm ; Internet; accessed August 7, 2013, 1.

155. Ibid.

156. Ibid.

157. Brian Ross and Richard Esposito, "Foggo Out at CIA," *ABC News* [database online] available fromhttp://abcnews.go.com/US/Investigation/story?id=1938864&page=1 ; Internet; accessed August 7, 2013, 1.

158. Ibid.

159. Kelli Arena and Terry Frieden, "Former CIA No. 3 Indicted For Steering Contracts to Friend," *CNN.com* [database online] available from http://www.cnn.com/2007/LAW/02/13/cia.foggo/ ; Internet; accessed August 7, 2013, 1.

160. Matthew Barakat, "Kyle 'Dusty' Foggo, Former CIA #3, Gets More Than 3 Years In Prison," *Huffington Post* [database online] available from http://www.huffingtonpost.com/2009/02/26/kyle-dusty-foggo-former-c_n_170240.html ; Internet; accessed August 7, 2013, 1 and Marcus Stern, "Disgraced Senior CIA Official Heads to Prison Still Claiming He's a Patriot," *ProPublica* [database online] available from http://www.propublica.org/article/disgraced-senior-cia-official-heads-to-prison-still-claiming-hes-a-patriot ; Internet; accessed August 7, 2013, 1.

161. David Johnston, "Ex-C.I.A. Official Admits Corruption," *The New York Times* [database online] available from http://www.nytimes.com/2008/09/30/washington/30inquire.html?_r=0 ; Internet; accessed August 7, 2013, 1.

162. "Embattled Interior Official Julie MacDonald Resigns In Wake of Inspector General Report," *Environmental News Network* [database online] available from http://www.enn.com/press_releases/1945 ; Internet; accessed August 7, 2013, 1.

163. "Embattled Interior Official Julie MacDonald Resigns In Wake of Inspector General Report," *Environmental News Network* [database online] available from http://www.enn.com/press_releases/1945 ; Internet; accessed August 7, 2013, 1.

164. Ibid.

165. "Reign of Bush Fish and Wildlife Official Ends in Disgrace," *Environmental News Service* [database online] available from http://www.ens-newswire.com/ens/may2007/2007-05-01-03.asp ; Internet; accessed August 7, 2013, 1.

166. Ibid.

167. "Embattled Interior Official Julie MacDonald Resigns In Wake of Inspector General Report," *Environmental News Network* [database online] available from http://www.enn.com/press_releases/1945 ; Internet; accessed August 7, 2013, 1.

168. Elizabeth Williamson, "Interior Dept. Official Facing Scrutiny Resigns," *The Washington Post* [database online] available from http://www.washingtonpost.com/wp-dyn/content/article/2007/05/01/AR2007050101920.html ; Internet; accessed August 7, 2013, 1.

169. Ibid.

170. Elizabeth Williamson, "Interior Dept. Official Facing Scrutiny Resigns," *The Washington Post* [database online] available from http://www.washingtonpost.com/wp-dyn/content/article/2007/05/01/AR2007050101920.html ; Internet; accessed August 7, 2013, 1.

171. "20 Forgotten Bush Scandals," *The Daily Beast* [database online] available from http://www.thedailybeast.com/articles/2009/01/06/forgotten-bush-scandals.html ; Internet; accessed August 8, 2013, 1.

172. "Ex-White House Aide Arrested in Alleged Refund Scam," *CNN.com* [database online] available from http://www.cnn.com/2006/US/03/11/claude.allen.arrest/ ; Internet; accessed August 8, 2013, 1.

173. "Bush Advisor Claude Allen Arresting for Shoplifting Scam," YouTube [database online] available from http://www.youtube.com/watch?v=CamqKMLa-pk ; Internet; accessed August 8, 2013.

174. Rachel Schteir, "Former Bush Aide Charged in Felony Theft," *Slate Magazine* [database online] available from http://www.slate.com/articles/news_and_politics/this_just_in/ 2006/03/former_bush_aide_charged_in_felony_theft.html ; Internet; accessed August 8, 2013, 1 and "20 Forgotten Bush Scandals," *The Daily Beast* [database online] available from http://www.thedailybeast.com/articles/2009/01/06/forgotten-bush-scandals.html ; Internet; accessed August 8, 2013, 1.

175. "Bush Advisor Claude Allen Arrested for Shoplifting Scam," YouTube [database online] available from http://www.youtube.com/watch?v=CamqKMLa-pk ; Internet; accessed August 8, 2013.

176. Rachel Schteir, "Former Bush Aide Charged in Felony Theft," *Slate Magazine* [database online] available from http://www.slate.com/articles/news_and_politics/this_just_in/2006/03/former_bush_aide_charged_in_felony_theft.html ; Internet; accessed August 8, 2013, 1.

177. Ibid.

178. "Claude Alexander Allen, III In Court," YouTube [database online] available from http://www.youtube.com/watch?v=7yWZVk6jC94 ; Internet; accessed August 8, 2013.

179. "Gaithersburg Murder Suspect Appears in Court," *NBC 4 Washington* [database online] available from http://www.nbcwashington.com/news/local/Gaithersburg-Murder-Suspect-Appears-in-Court-209168621.html , May 28, 2013, accessed August 8, 2013, 1.

180. Ibid.

181. Gardiner Harris, "Ex-Head of F.D.A. or Wife Sold Stock in Regulated Area," *The New York Times* [database online] available from http://www.nytimes.com/2005/10/27/politics/27fda.html?_r=0 ; Internet; accessed August 8, 2013, 1.

182. "About the Office of the Commissioner," United States Health and Human Services, *The Food and Drug Administration* [database online] available from http://www.fda.gov/ AboutFDA/CentersOffices/oc/default.htm ; Internet; accessed August 8, 2013, 1.

183. Gardiner Harris, "Ex-Head of F.D.A. or Wife Sold Stock in Regulated Area," *The New York Times* [database online] available from http://www.nytimes.com/2005/10/27/politics/27fda.html?_r=0 ; Internet; accessed August 8, 2013, 1.

184. Ibid.

185. Ibid.

186. "Embattled FDA Chief Lester Crawford Resigns," *NBC News* [database online] available from http://www.nbcnews.com/id/9455426/ns/health-health_care/t/ embattled-fda-chief-lester-crawford-resigns/#.UgVXKBafemE, September 23, 2005, accessed August 8, 2013, 1.

187. "Embattled FDA Chief Lester Crawford Resigns," *NBC News* [database online] available fromhttp://www.nbcnews.com/id/9455426/ns/health-health_care/t/embattled-fda-chief-lester-crawford-resigns/#.UgVXKBafemE ; Internet; accessed August 8, 2013, 1.

188. "Ex-FDA Chief Pleads Guilty to Conflict of Interest," *NBC News* [database online] available from http://www.nbcnews.com/id/15291650/ns/health-health_care/t/ex-fda-chief-pleads-guilty-conflict-interest/ ; Internet; accessed August 8, 1023, 1 and "Former FDA Chief Crawford Gets Supervised Probation, Fine for Stock Scandal," *Fox News* [database online] available from http://www.foxnews.com/story/2007/02/27/former-fda-chief-crawford-gets-supervised-probation-fine-for-stock-scandal/ ; Internet; accessed August 2013, 1.

189. Seymour Hersh "Annals of National Security: Who Lied To Whom?," *The New Yorker Magazine* [database online] available from http://www.newyorker.com/archive 2003/03/31/030331fa_fact1 ; Internet; accessed August 27, 2013, 1.

190. Ibid.

191. Ibid.

192. Ibid.

193. Ibid.

194. Seymour Hersh "Annals of National Security: Who Lied To Whom?," *The New Yorker Magazine* [database online] available from http://www.newyorker.com/archive 2003/03/31/030331fa_fact1 ; Internet; accessed August 27, 2013, 1.

195. Ibid.

196. Ibid.

197. "Bush and Iraq: Follow the Yellow Cake Road," *TIME* [database online] available from http://www.time.com/time/world/article/0,8599,463779,00.html ; Internet; accessed August 27, 2013, 1.

198. "White House 'Warned Over Iraq Claim,'" *BBC News* [database online] available from http://news.bbc.co.uk/2/hi/americas/3056626.stm ; Internet; accessed August 27, 2013, 1.

199. "White House 'Warned Over Iraq Claim,'" *BBC News* [database online] available from http://news.bbc.co.uk/2/hi/americas/3056626.stm ; Internet; accessed August 27, 2013, 1.

200. Kim Peterson, "Real Cost of US War With Iraq: $1.7 Trillion," *MSN Money* [database online] available from http://money.msn.com/now/post.aspx?post=c6dd9699-4865-4242-852e-0773529464fc%20 ; Internet; accessed August 27, 2013, 1.

201. Ibid.

202. "The Spoils of War: Billions over Baghdad," *Vanity Fair* [database online] available from http://www.vanityfair.com/politics/features/2007/10/iraq_billions200710 ; Internet; accessed August 26, 2013, 1.

203. Ibid.

204. Ibid.
205. Ibid.
206. James Glanz, "Former U.S. Official in Iraq to Plead Guilty to Corruption," *The New York Times* [database online] available from http://www.nytimes.com/2006/02/01/international/ middleeast/01cnd-reconstruct.html?_r=0 ; Internet; accessed August 26, 2013, 1.
207. Charles R. Babcock and Renae Merle, "U.S. Accuses Pair of Rigging Iraq Contracts," *The Washington Post* [database online] available from http://www.washingtonpost.com/wp-dyn/content/article/2005/11/17/AR2005111701879.html ; Internet; accessed August 26, 2013, 1.
208. James Glanz, "Former U.S. Official in Iraq to Plead Guilty to Corruption," *The New York Times* [database online] available from http://www.nytimes.com/2006/02/01/international/ middleeast/01cnd-reconstruct.html?_r=0 ; Internet; accessed August 26, 2013, 1.
209. Ibid.
210. "Prison Term for Fraud in Iraq," *The Los Angeles Times* [database online] available from http://articles.latimes.com/2007/jan/30/nation/na-contractor30 ; Internet; accessed August 26, 2013, 1.
211. Ibid.
212. Ibid.
213. Ibid.
214. Dan Collins,"3rd Columnist On Bush Payroll," *CBS News* [database online] available from http://www.cbsnews.com/2100-250_162-669432.html ; Internet; accessed August 24, 2013, 1.
215. Ibid.
216. Anne Kornblut, "Third Journalist Was Paid to Promote Bush Policies," *The New York Times* [database online] available from http://www.nytimes.com/2005/01/29/politics/ 29column.html ; Internet; accessed August 24, 2013, 1.
217. Dan Collins,"3rd Columnist On Bush Payroll," CBS News, [database online] available http://www.cbsnews.com/2100-250_162-669432.html ; Internet; accessed August 24, 2013, 1.
218. Ibid.
219. Ibid.
220. Anne Kornblut, "Third Journalist Was Paid to Promote Bush Policies," *The New York Times* [database online] available from http://www.nytimes.com/2005/01/29/politics/ 29column.html ; Internet; accessed August 24, 2013, 1.
221. Ibid.
222. Ibid.
223. Howard Kurtz, "Writer Backing Bush Plan Had Gotten Federal Contract," *The Washington Post* [database online] available from http://www.washingtonpost.com/wp-dyn/articles/ A36545-2005Jan25.html ; Internet; accessed August 24, 2013, 1.
224. Ibid.
225. Ibid.
226. Ibid.
227. Ibid.
228. "3rd Columnist On Bush Payroll," *CBS News* [database online] available from http:// www.cbsnews.com/2100-250_162-669432.html ; Internet; accessed August 24, 2013, 1 and Greg Toppo, "Education Dept. Paid Commentator to Promote Law," *USA Today* [database online] available from http://usatoday30.usatoday.com/news/washington/2005-01-06-williams-whitehouse_x.htm ; Internet; accessed August 24, 2013, 1.
229. "3rd Columnist On Bush Payroll," *CBS News* [database online] available from http:// www.cbsnews.com/2100-250_162-669432.html ; Internet; accessed August 24, 2013, 1.
230. Greg Toppo, "Education Dept. Paid Commentator to Promote Law," *USA Today* [database online] available from http://usatoday30.usatoday.com/news/washington/2005-01-06-williams-whitehouse_x.htm ; Internet; accessed August 24, 2013, 1.
231. "Former Clinton Aide Pleads Guilty to Taking Classified Docs," *Fox News* [database online] available from http://www.foxnews.com/story/2005/04/03/former-clinton-aide-pleads-guilty-to-taking-classified-docs/ ; Internet; accessed August 8, 2013, 1.

232. Kevin Johnson and Susan Page, "Clinton Adviser Probed About Removing Classified Terror Memos," *USA Today* [database online] available from http://usatoday30.usatoday.com/news/washington/2004-07-19-berger-probe_x.htm?POE=NEWISVA ; Internet; accessed August 8, 2013, 1.

233. "Former Clinton Aide Pleads Guilty to Taking Classified Docs," *Fox News* [database online] available from http://www.foxnews.com/story/2005/04/03/former-clinton-aide-pleads-guilty-to-taking-classified-docs/ ; Internet; accessed August 8, 2013, 1.

234. "Clinton Adviser Berger Cops Plea," *CBS News* [database online] available from http://www.cbsnews.com/2100-250_162-684458.html ; Internet; accessed August 8, 2013, 1.

235. Ibid.

236. Ibid.

237. "Sandy Berger Fined $50,000 For Taking Documents," *CNN* [database online] available from http://www.cnn.com/2005/POLITICS/09/08/berger.sentenced/ ; Internet; accessed August 8, 2013, 1.

238. "Berger to Pay $50,000 Fine for Taking Papers," *The New York Times* [database online] available from http://www.nytimes.com/2005/09/08/politics/08wire-berger.html?_r=0 ; Internet; accessed August 2013, 1.

239. Ibid.

240. Ibid.

241. "Former Clinton Aide Pleads Guilty to Taking Classified Docs," Fox News [database online] available from http://www.foxnews.com/story/2005/04/03/former-clinton-aide-pleads-guilty-to-taking-classified-docs/ ; Internet; accessed August 8, 2013, 1.

242. "Samuel R. "Sandy" Berger," Biography, *The Aspen Institute* [database online] available from   http://www.aspeninstitute.org/policy-work/homeland-security/ahsg/members/berger   ; Internet; accessed August 8, 2013, 1.

243. Leo Standora , David Saltonstall and Kenneth R. Bazinet , "Kerik Bows Out: Nanny Flap Ruins Ex-N.Y.C. Top Cop's Bid To Head Homeland Security," *Daily News* [database online] available from http://www.nydailynews.com/news/kerik-bows-nanny-flap-ruins-ex-n-y-top-bid-head-homeland-security-article-1.340785 ; Internet; accessed August 14, 2013, 1.

244. Ibid.

245. Ibid.

246. Ibid.

247. Russ Buettner, "Bernard Kerik's Double Affair Laid Bare," *Daily News* [database online] available from http://www.nydailynews.com/news/bernard-kerik-double-affair-laid-bare-article-1.340899 ; Internet; accessed August 14, 2013, 1.

248. Ibid.

249. Ibid.

250. Jim Fitzgerald, "Bernie Kerik Sentenced To Four Years In Prison," *Huffington Post* [database online] available from http://www.huffingtonpost.com/2010/02/18/bernie-keriks-jail-senten_0_n_467097.html ; accessed August 14, 2013, 1.

251. Cindy Adams, "Kerik Now Out, Gave Tips In Jail," *The New York Times* [database online] available from http://www.nytimes.com/2009/11/06/nyregion/06kerik.html?_r=0 ; Internet; accessed August 14, 2013, 1.

252. Ibid.

253. Daniel Beekman, "Former NYPD Commissioner Bernard Kerik To Be Released From Federal Prison Tuesday: Report," *Daily News* [database online] available from http://www.nydailynews.com/new-york/ex-top-bernard-kerik-released-prison-report-article-1.1356153 ; Internet; accessed August 14, 2013, 1.

254. Ibid.

255. Cindy Adams, "Kerik Now Out, Gave Tips In Jail," *The New York Times* [database online] available from http://www.nytimes.com/2009/11/06/nyregion/06kerik.html?_r=0 ; Internet; accessed August 14, 2013, 1.

256. "The Definition of waterboarding," Oxford Dictionaries [database online] available from   http://oxforddictionaries.com/us/definition/american_english/waterboarding,   accessed August 28, 2013, 1.

257. Dan Eggen and R. Jeffrey Smith, "FBI Agents Allege Abuse of Detainees at Guantanamo Bay," *The Washington Post* [database online] available from http://www.washingtonpost.com/ wp-dyn/articles/A14936-2004Dec20.html ; Internet; accessed August 28, 2013, 1.

258. Ibid.

259. Dan Eggen and R. Jeffrey Smith, "FBI Agents Allege Abuse of Detainees at Guantanamo Bay," *The Washington Post* [database online] available from http://www.washingtonpost.com/ wp-dyn/articles/A14936-2004Dec20.html ; Internet; accessed August 28, 2013, 1.

260. Ibid.

261. Ibid.

262. Ibid.

263. Dan Eggen and R. Jeffrey Smith, "FBI Agents Allege Abuse of Detainees at Guantanamo Bay," *The Washington Post* [database online] available from http://www.washingtonpost.com/ wp-dyn/articles/A14936-2004Dec20.html ; Internet; accessed August 28, 2013, 1.

264. R. Jeffrey Smith, "In New Memoir, Bush Makes Clear He Approved Use of Waterboarding," *The Washington Post* [database online] available from http://www.washingtonpost.com/wp-dyn/content/article/2010/11/03/AR2010110308082.html?hpid=topnews ; Internet; accessed August 28, 2013, 1.

265. Ibid.

266. Ibid.

267. R. Jeffrey Smith, "In New Memoir, Bush Makes Clear He Approved Use of Waterboarding," *The Washington Post* [database online] available from http://www.washingtonpost.com/wp-dyn/content/article/2010/11/03/AR2010110308082.html?hpid=topnews ; Internet; accessed August 28, 2013, 1.

268. Ibid.

269. Ibid.

270. Mary Bruce, "Obama Says GOP Candidates Are Wrong, Waterboarding is 'Torture,'" *ABC News* [database online] available from http://abcnews.go.com/blogs/politics/2011/11/obama-says-gop-candidates-are-wrong-waterboarding-is-torture/ ; Internet; accessed August 28, 2013, 1.

271. Ibid.

272. "Bush Says He Signed NSA Wiretap Order," *CNN* [database online] available from http://www.cnn.com/2005/POLITICS/12/17/bush.nsa/ ; Internet; accessed August 28, 2013, 1.

273. James Risen and Eric Lichtbau, "Bush Lets U.S. Spy on Callers Without Courts," The New York Times [database online] available from http://www.nytimes.com/2005/12/16/politics/ 16program.html?pagewanted=all&_r=0; Internet; accessed August 28, 2013, 1.

274. "Bush Says He Signed NSA Wiretap Order," *CNN* [database online] available from http://www.cnn.com/2005/POLITICS/12/17/bush.nsa/ , December 17, 2005, accessed August 28, 2013, 1.

275. Ibid.

276. Ibid.

277. Ibid.

278. Ibid.

279. Charlie Savage and James Risen, "Federal Judge Finds N.S.A. Wiretaps Were Illegal," *The New York Times* [database online] available from http://www.nytimes.com/2010/04/01/us/01nsa.html ; Internet; accessed August 28, 2013, 1.

280. Ibid.

281. Ibid.

282. Richard Partington, "The Enron Cast: Where Are They Now?," *Financial News* [database online] available from http://www.efinancialnews.com/story/2011-12-01/enron-ten-years-on-where-they-are-now?ea9c8a2de0ee111045601ab04d673622 ; Internet; accessed August 14, 2013, 1.

283. Marius Meland, "Lay Points Finger At Fastow For Enron Collapse," *Law 360* [database online] available from http://www.law360.com/articles/6261/lay-points-finger-at-fastow-for-enron-collapse ; Internet; accessed August 14, 2013, 1.

284. Ibid.

285. "The Enron Trials," *USA Today* [database online] available from http://usatoday30.usatoday.com/money/industries/energy/2006-01-27-charges_x.htm; Internet; accessed August 14, 2013, 1.

286. Ibid.

287. Ibid.

288. Ibid.

289. "Enron Founder Ken Lay Dies of Heart Disease," *NBC News* [database online] available from http://www.nbcnews.com/id/13715925/ns/business-corporate_scandals/t/enron-founder-ken-lay-dies-heart-disease/#.UgvWShafemE; Internet; accessed August 14, 2013, 1.

290. Richard Partington, "The Enron Cast: Where Are They Now?," *Financial News* [database online] available from http://www.efinancialnews.com/story/2011-12-01/enron-ten-years-on-where-they-are-now?ea9c8a2de0ee111045601ab04d673622 ; Internet; accessed August 14, 2013, 1.

291. "A Look At Those Involved In The Enron Scandal," *USA Today* [database online] available from http://usatoday30.usatoday.com/money/industries/energy/2005-12-28-enron-participants_x.htm ; Internet; accessed August 14, 2013, 1.

292. Ibid.

293. Ibid.

294. Ibid.

295. Ibid.

296. Ibid.

297. Ibid.

298. Ibid.

299. Ibid.

300. Ibid.

301. Ibid.

302. Ibid.

303. Ibid.

304. Ibid.

305. Ibid.

306. "A Look At Those Involved In The Enron Scandal," *USA Today* [database online] available from http://usatoday30.usatoday.com/money/industries/energy/2005-12-28-enron-participants_x.htm ; Internet; accessed August 14, 2013, 1.

307. Ibid.

308. Ibid.

309. Ibid.

310. Ibid.

311. Ibid.

312. Richard Oppel, Jr., "Employees' Retirement Plan Is a Victim as Enron Tumbles," *The New York Times* [database online] available from http://www.nytimes.com/2001/11/22/business/ employees-retirement-plan-is-a-victim-as-enron-tumbles.html ; accessed August 14, 2013, 1.

313. Ibid.

314. "Janet Rehnquist Resigns," *CBS News* [database online] available from http://www.cbsnews.com/2100-250_162-542782.html ; Internet; accessed August 15, 2013, 1.

315. Ibid.

316. Jonathan Karl and George Cooper, "Chief Justice's Daughter To Resign Government Post," *CNN* [database online] available from http://www.cnn.com/2003/ALLPOLITICS/03/04/janet.rehnquist/ ; Internet; accessed August 15, 2013, 1.

317. "Janet Rehnquist Resigns," *CBS News* [database online] available from http://www.cbsnews.com/2100-250_162-542782.html ; Internet; accessed August 15, 2013, 1.

318. Ibid.

319. Robert Pear, "Inquiries on Gun and Ousters Focus on Health Dept. Official," *New York Times* [database online] available from http://www.nytimes.com/2002/11/13/politics/ 13REHN.html ; Internet; accessed August 15, 2013, 1.
320. Ibid.
321. Jonathan Karl and George Cooper, "Chief Justice's Daughter To Resign Government Post, *CNN* [database online] available from http://www.cnn.com/2003/ALLPOLITICS/03/04/ janet.rehnquist/ ; Internet; accessed August 15, 2013, 1.
322. Ibid.
323. Ibid.
324. Ibid.
325. "Draft GAO Report Criticizes Former HHS Inspector General Rehnquist," *Kaiser Health News* [database online] available from http://www.kaiserhealthnews.org/daily-reports/ 2003/june/06/dr00018130.aspx ; Internet; accessed August 15, 2013, 1.
326. "Draft GAO Report Criticizes Former HHS Inspector General Rehnquist," *Kaiser Health News* [database online] available from http://www.kaiserhealthnews.org/daily-reports/ 2003/june/06/dr00018130.aspx ; Internet; accessed August 15, 2013, 1.
327. Ibid.
328. "California: Court Throws Out Suit Against Bush Lawyer," *The New York Times* [database online] available from http://www.nytimes.com/2012/05/03/us/politics/lawsuit-against-john-yoo-is-thrown-out.html ; Internet; accessed August 14, 2013, 1 and "John Yoo, Former Justice Department Lawyer, Protected From Torture Lawsuit, Rules Appeals Court," *Huffington Post* [database online] available from http://www.huffingtonpost.com/2012/05/02/john-yoo-torture-bush-administration-jose-padilla_n_1471587.html ; Internet; accessed August 14, 2013, 1.
329. "Torture Lawyer John Yoo Drafted Legal Rationale For NSA Spying, Protesters Targeting His Talk in SF Tonight," *San Francisco Bay Guardian Online* [database online] available from http://www.sfbg.com/politics/2013/07/10/torture-lawyer-john-yoo-drafted-legal-rationale-nsa-spying-protesters-targeting- ; Internet; accessed August 14, 2013, 1.
330. "Memorandum for William J. Haynes II, General Counsel of the Department of Defense," The United States Department of Justice, http://www.aclu.org/pdfs/safefree/ yoo_army_torture _memo.pdf ; Internet; accessed August 14, 2013.
331. "A Guide to the Memos on Torture," *The New York Times* [database online] available from http://www.nytimes.com/ref/international/24MEMO-GUIDE.html ; Internet; accessed August 14, 2013, 1.
332. Office of the Deputy Assistant Attorney General, "Memorandum for William J. Haynes II, General Counsel of the Department of Defense," *The United States Department of Justice* [database online] available from http://www.aclu.org/pdfs/safefree/yoo_army_torture _memo.pdf; Internet; accessed August 14, 2013.
333. Ibid.
334. Office of the Deputy Assistant Attorney General, "Memorandum for William J. Haynes II, General Counsel of the Department of Defense," *The United States Department of Justice* [database online] available from http://www.aclu.org/pdfs/safefree/yoo_army_torture _memo.pdf; Internet; accessed August 14, 2013.
335. "California: Court Throws Out Suit Against Bush Lawyer," *The New York Times* [database online] available from http://www.nytimes.com/2012/05/03/us/politics/lawsuit-against-john-yoo-is-thrown-out.html ; Internet; accessed August 14, 2013, 1 and "John Yoo, Former Justice Department Lawyer, Protected From Torture Lawsuit, Rules Appeals Court," *Huffington Post* [database online] available from http://www.huffingtonpost.com/2012/05/02/john-yoo-torture-bush-administration-jose-padilla_n_1471587.html ; Internet; accessed August 14, 2013, 1.
336. Ibid.
337. "Berkeley Law - Faculty Profiles: John Yoo," *The University of California Berkley* [database online] available from http://www.law.berkeley.edu/php-programs/faculty/faculty-Profile.php?facID=235 ; Internet; accessed August 14, 2013, 1.
338. Ibid.

339. "Rick Renzi, Former Congressman, Convicted On 17 Of 32 Counts In Corruption Case," *Huffington Post* [database online] available from http://www.huffingtonpost.com/2013/ 06/11/ rick-renzi-convicted_n_3424403.html ; Internet; accessed August 15, 2013, 1.

340. "Renzi Resigns From All His House Committee Assignments," *Politico Live* [database online] available from http://www.politico.com/blogs/thecrypt/0407/Renzi_resigns_from _all_his_House_committee_assignments.html; accessed August 15, 2013, 1.

341. "Indicted Rep. Rick Renzi Will Not Resign From Congress," *Fox News* [database online] available from http://www.foxnews.com/story/2008/02/25/indicted-rep-rick-renzi-will-not-resign-from-congress/ ; Internet; accessed August 15, 2013, 1.

342. "Arizona Rep. Rick Renzi Pleads Not Guilty in Land Deal Fraud Case," *Fox News* [database online] available from http://www.foxnews.com/story/0,2933,334891,00.html ; Internet; accessed August 15, 2013, 1.

343. U.S. District Court District of Arizona, *United States v. Richard G. Renzi Et Al. (CR 08-0212-TUC-DCB)*, *Fox News* [database online] available from http://www.foxnews.com/ projects/pdf/renzi_indictment.pdf ; Internet; accessed August 15, 2013.

344. "Indicted Rep. Rick Renzi Will Not Resign From Congress," *Fox News* [database online] available from http://www.foxnews.com/story/2008/02/25/indicted-rep-rick-renzi-will-not-resign-from-congress/ ; Internet; accessed August 15, 2013, 1.

345. Ibid.

346. "Rick Renzi, Former Congressman, Convicted On 17 of 32 Counts In Corruption Case," *Huffington Post* [database online] available from http://www.huffingtonpost.com/2013/06/11/ rick-renzi-convicted_n_3424403.html ; Internet; accessed August 15, 2013, 1.

347. U.S. District Court District of Arizona, *United States v. Richard G. Renzi, James W. Sandlin and Andrew Beardall, Fox News* [database online] available from http:// www.foxnews.com/projects/pdf/renzi_indictment.pdf ; Internet; accessed August 15, 2013.

348. "Rick Renzi Trial: Former US Rep. Renzi Convicted On 17 of 32 Counts," *ABC* [database online] available from http://www.abc15.com/dpp/news/region_central_southern_az/tuc-son/rick-renzi-trial-jury-has-verdict-in-trial-of-former-rep-renzi ; Internet; accessed August 15, 2013, 1.

349. Ibid., 1.

350. Ibid.

351. Paul Blake. "Ex-Rep. Rick Renzi Sentenced To Three Years in Prison," *The Washington Post* [database online] available from http://www.washingtonpost.com/blogs/post-politics/wp/ 2013/10/28/ex-rep-rick-renzi-sentenced-to-three-years-in-prison/; Internet; accessed November 25, 2013, 1.

352. "Rep. John Doolittle," *Govtrack.us* [database online] available from http:// www.govtrack.us/congress/members/john_doolittle/400113 ; Internet; accessed August 15, 2013, 1.

353. "California Rep. John Doolittle Announces Retirement Amid Investigation," *Fox News* [database online] available from http://www.foxnews.com/story/2008/01/10/california-rep-john-doolittle-announces-retirement-amid-investigation/ January 10, 2008, accessed August 15, 2013, 1.

354. Ibid.

355. Erica Warner, "Doolittle Linked To 2 Bribery Scandals," *USA Today* [database online] available from http://usatoday30.usatoday.com/news/washington/2007-07-06-858095226_x .htm ; Internet; accessed August 15, 2013, 1.

356. "FBI Raided Virginia Home of Rep. John Doolittle," *Fox News* [database online] available from http://www.foxnews.com/story/2007/04/18/fbi-raided-virginia-home-rep-john-doo-little/ ; Internet; accessed August 15, 2013, 1.

357. Ibid.

358. Gus Thomson, "Ex-Congressman John Doolittle Steps Into New Lobbying Role," *Auburn Journal* [database online] available from http://www.auburnjournal.com/article/ex-con-gressman-john-doolittle-steps-new-lobbying-role ; Internet; accessed August 15, 2013, 1.

359. "Congressman Resigns After Bribery Plea," *CNN* [database online] available from http:/ /www.cnn.com/2005/POLITICS/11/28/cunningham/ ; Internet; accessed August 17, 2013, 1.

360. Sharon Chen, "Randy 'Duke' Cunningham Released From Prison," *Fox 5 San Diego* [database online] available from http://fox5sandiego.com/2013/06/04/former-san-diego-congressman-randy-duke-cunningham-released-from-prison/#axzz2cK3YvDA0;   Internet;   accessed August 17, 2013, 1.

361. "Congressman Resigns After Bribery Plea," *CNN* [database online] available from http://www.cnn.com/2005/POLITICS/11/28/cunningham/ ; Internet; accessed August 17, 2013, 1.

362. "Ex-Congressman Begins Prison Sentence," *NBC News* [database online] available from http://www.nbcnews.com/id/11655893/print/1/displaymode/1098 ; Internet; accessed August 2013, 1.

363. "Congressman Resigns After Bribery Plea," *CNN* [database online] available from http://www.cnn.com/2005/POLITICS/11/28/cunningham/ ; Internet; accessed August 17, 2013, 1.

364. "Congressman Resigns After Bribery Plea," *CNN* [database online] available from http://www.cnn.com/2005/POLITICS/11/28/cunningham/ ; Internet; accessed August 17, 2013, 1.

365. Ibid.

366. "Ex-Congressman Begins Prison Sentence," *NBC News* [database online] available from http://www.nbcnews.com/id/11655893/print/1/displaymode/1098 ; Internet; accessed August 2013, 1.

367. Ibid.

368. "Congressman Resigns After Bribery Plea," *CNN* [database online] available from http://www.cnn.com/2005/POLITICS/11/28/cunningham/ ; Internet; accessed August 17, 2013, 1.

369. Ibid.

370. John Wilkens, "'Duke' Cunningham A Free Man Today," *U-T San Diego* [database online] available from http://www.utsandiego.com/news/2013/Jun/04/duke-cunningham-free-man-today/ ; Internet; accessed August 17, 2013, 1.

371. "Ga. Congresswoman Scuffles With Capitol Police," *NBC News* [database online] available from http://www.nbcnews.com/id/12070031/ns/politics/t/ga-congresswoman-scuffles-capitol-police/#.Ug67YhafemE; Internet; accessed August 16, 2013, 1.

372. Congresswoman Cynthia McKinney, "Cynthia Ann McKinney," allthingscynthiamckinney.com [database online] available from http://archives.allthingscynthiamckinney.com/mckinney.house.gov/bio.htm ; Internet; accessed August16, 2013, 1.

373. "Ga. Congresswoman Scuffles With Capitol Police," *NBC News* [database online] available from http://www.nbcnews.com/id/12070031/ns/politics/t/ga-congresswoman-scuffles-capitol-police/#.Ug67YhafemE ; Internet; accessed August 16, 2013, 1.

374. Ibid.

375. "Ga. Congresswoman Scuffles With Capitol Police," *NBC News* [database online] available from http://www.nbcnews.com/id/12070031/ns/politics/t/ga-congresswoman-scuffles-capitol-police/#.Ug67YhafemE ; Internet; accessed August 16, 2013, 1.

376. Oren Dorell, "McKinney Apologizes For Incident With Cop," *USA Today* [database online] available from http://usatoday30.usatoday.com/news/washington/2006-04-06-mckinney_x.htm ; Internet; accessed August 16, 2013, 1.

377. "Ga. Congresswoman Scuffles With Capitol Police," *NBC News* [database online] available from http://www.nbcnews.com/id/12070031/ns/politics/t/ga-congresswoman-scuffles-capitol-police/#.Ug67YhafemE ; Internet; accessed August 16, 2013, 1.

378. "Georgia Rep. McKinney Blames Media for Losing Primary Runoff Election," *Fox News* [database online] available from http://www.foxnews.com/story/2006/08/09/georgia-rep-mckinney-blames-media-for-losing-primary-runoff-election/ ; Internet; accessed August 16, 2013, 1.

379. Ibid.

380. Matthew Cardinale, "Cynthia McKinney Running For US House on Green Party Ticket," *Atlanta Progressive News* [database online] available from http://www.atlantaprogressivenews.com/interspire/news/2012/04/02/cynthia-mckinney-running-for-us-house-on-green-party-ticket.html ; Internet; accessed August 16, 2013, 1.

381. "Rooting Out Corruption: A Look Back at the Jefferson Case," *The Federal Bureau of Investigations* [database online] available from http://www.fbi.gov/news/stories/2013/april/a-look-back-at-the-william-j.-jefferson-corruption-case ; Internet; accessed August 17, 2013, 1.

382. Ibid.

383. Ibid.

384. Ibid.

385. Ibid.

386. Peter Overby, "Rep. Jefferson Indicted on Fraud, Bribery Counts," *NPR* [database online] available from http://www.npr.org/templates/story/story.php?storyId=10712500 ; Internet; accessed August 17, 2013, 1.

387. Eric Weiner, "Prosecutors: Congressman Took $400K in Bribes," *NPR* [database online] available from http://www.npr.org/templates/story/story.php?storyId=10712500 ; Internet; accessed August 17, 2013, 1.

388. Cain Burdeau, "Jefferson Overcomes Scandal, Wins Reelection," The Washington Post, http://www.washingtonpost.com/wp-dyn/content/article/2006/12/09/AR2006120900601.html ; Internet; accessed August 17, 2013, 1.

389. "Louisiana Voters Reject Rep. Jefferson," *Los Angeles Times* [database online] available from http://articles.latimes.com/2008/dec/07/nation/na-jefferson7 ; Internet; accessed August 17, 2013, 1.

390. David Stout, "Ex-Louisiana Congressman Sentenced to 13 Years," *The New York Times* [database online] available from http://www.nytimes.com/2009/11/14/us/politics/ 14jefferson.html ; accessed August 17, 2013, 1.

391. Ibid.

392. Ibid.

393. Bruce Albert, "'Substantial' Cooperation in Case Against William Jefferson Cited at Brett Pfeffer Sentence-Reduction Hearing , " *The Time Picayune Greater New Orleans* [database online] available from http://www.nola.com/crime/index.ssf/2009/12substantial_cooperation_in_cas.html; accessed August 17, 2013, 1.

394. Ibid.

395. Ibid.

396. "Janklow Charged With Second-Degree Manslaughter in Crash," *CNN* [database online] available from http://www.cnn.com/2003/ALLPOLITICS/08/29/janklow.charged/ ; Internet; accessed August 18, 2013, 1.

397. Ibid.

398. Ibid.

399. Ibid.

400. "Bill Janklow, Former S.D. Governor and Congressman, Dies,' *USA Today* [database online] available from http://usatoday30.usatoday.com/news/washington/story/2012-01-12/obit-bill-janklow/52517922/1 ; Internet; accessed August 18, 2013, 1.

401. Ibid.

402. "Bill Janklow, Former S.D. Governor and Congressman, Dies,' *USA Today* [database online] available from http://usatoday30.usatoday.com/news/washington/story/2012-01-12/obit-bill-janklow/52517922/1 ; Internet; accessed August 18, 2013, 1.

403. Ibid.

404. "Torricelli Apologizes For Ethics 'Lapses,'" CNN [database online] available from http://archives.cnn.com/2002/ALLPOLITICS/07/30/torrecelli.ethics/index.html; Internet; accessed August 19, 2013, 1.

405. Ibid.

406. "Torricelli Apologizes For Ethics 'Lapses,'" *CNN* [database online] available from http://archives.cnn.com/2002/ALLPOLITICS/07/30/torrecelli.ethics/index.html; Internet; accessed August 19, 2013, 1.

407. United States. Senate. U.S. Select Committee on Ethics, "Gifts," *United States Senate* [database online] available from http://www.ethics.senate.gov/public/index.cfm/gifts ; Internet; accessed August 19, 2013, 1.

408. Ibid.

409. Ibid.

410. Ibid.

411. "Torricelli Apologizes For Ethics 'Lapses,'" *CNN* [database online] available from http://archives.cnn.com/2002/ALLPOLITICS/07/30/torrecelli.ethics/index.html; Internet; accessed August 19, 2013, 1.

412. Ibid.
413. Ibid.
414. Ibid.
415. "Ethics Committee Faults Torricelli on Gift Violations," *The New York Times* [database online] available from http://www.nytimes.com/2002/07/31/nyregion/ethics-committee-faults-torricelli-on-gift-violations.html?pagewanted=all&src=pm ; Internet; accessed August 19, 2013, 1.
416. "Torricelli Apologizes For Ethics 'Lapses,'" *CNN* [database online] available from http://archives.cnn.com/2002/ALLPOLITICS/07/30/torrecelli.ethics/index.html; Internet; accessed August 19, 2013, 1.
417. Ibid.
418. Ibid.
419. Ibid.
420. Ibid.
421. Ibid.
422. Ibid.
423. "Frank Lautenberg Dead: New Jersey Senator Dies At 89," *Huffington Post* [database online] available from http://www.huffingtonpost.com/2013/06/03/frank-lautenberg-dead-dies_n_3377916.html ; Internet; accessed August 19, 2013, 1.
424. Adam Clymer, "Frank Lautenberg, New Jersey Senator in His 5th Term, Dies at 89," *The New York Times* [database online] available from http://www.nytimes.com/2013/06/04/nyregion/ frank-lautenberg-new-jersey-senator.html?pagewanted=all&_r=0 ; Internet; accessed August 19, 2013, 1.
425. "Ohio Rep. Traficant Indicted," *ABC News* [database online] available from http://abcnews.go.com/Politics/story?id=121699&page=1 ; Internet; accessed August 20, 2013, 1.
426. Ted Barrett, "Panel Will Investigate Traficant, Lawmakers Say," *CNN.com* [database online] available from http://europe.cnn.com/2002/ALLPOLITICS/04/17/traficant.ethics/ ; Internet; accessed August 20, 2013, 1.
427. Ted Barrett, "Panel Will Investigate Traficant, Lawmakers Say," *CNN.com* [database online] available from http://europe.cnn.com/2002/ALLPOLITICS/04/17/traficant.ethics/ ; Internet; accessed August 20, 2013, 1.
428. "Ohio Rep. Traficant Indicted," *ABC News* [database online] available from http://abcnews.go.com/Politics/story?id=121699&page=1 ; Internet; accessed August 20, 2013, 1.
429. Ibid.
430. Ibid.
431. Ibid.
432. "Ohio Rep. Traficant Indicted," *ABC News* [database online] available from http://abcnews.go.com/Politics/story?id=121699&page=1 ; Internet; accessed August 20, 2013, 1.
433. "Traficant Guilty of Bribery, Racketeering," *CNN* [database online] available from http://archives.cnn.com/2002/LAW/04/11/traficant.trial/ ; accessed August 20, 2013, 1.
434. Ibid.
435. Tom Squitieri, "Traficant Expelled After Final Jabs in House," *USA Today* [database online] available from http://usatoday30.usatoday.com/news/washington/legislative/house/2002-07-24-traficant_x.htm ; Internet; accessed August 20, 2013, 1.
436. Tom Squitieri, "Traficant Expelled After Final Jabs in House," *USA Today* [database online] available from http://usatoday30.usatoday.com/news/washington/legislative/house/2002-07-24-traficant_x.htm ; Internet; accessed August 20, 2013, 1.
437. "Traficant Sentenced to Eight Years in Prison," *Fox News* [database online] available from http://www.foxnews.com/story/0,2933,59129,00.html ; Internet; accessed August 20, 2013, 1.
438. Mary Jordan, Traficant Completes Sentence for Bribery," *The Washington Post* [database online] available from http://articles.washingtonpost.com/2009-09-03/news/36826530_1_traficant-second-house-member-ohio-democrat ; Internet; accessed August 20, 2013, 1.
439. Ibid.

440. "Traficant To Run As Independent For Old House Seat," *Fox News* [database online] available from http://www.foxnews.com/politics/2010/05/03/traficant-run-independent-old-house-seat/ ; Internet; accessed August 20, 2013, 1.

441. Meghann Barr, "Jim Traficant, Ex-Congressman And Convicted Felon, Will Be On The Ballot Again In November," *Huffington Post* [database online] available from http://www.huffingtonpost.com/2010/09/01/jim-traficant-convicted-felon-congress-man_n_702710.html ; Internet; accessed August 20, 2013, 1.

442. "Ohio Ex-Rep Traficant Loses New Bid for Congress," *Fox News* [database online] available from http://www.foxnews.com/politics/2010/11/02/ohio-ex-rep-traficant-loses-new-bid-congress/ ; Internet; accessed August 20, 2013, 1.

443. "James Traficant Fast Facts," *CNN* [database online] available from http://www.cnn.com/2013/03/25/us/james-traficant-fast-facts ; Internet; accessed August 20, 2013, 1.

Chapter Four

Conclusion

Each day of our lives, we are faced with making a plethora of decisions in our personal and professional lives. Throughout our lives, our integrity and ethical code is tested! We must choose between that which is right and wrong. Every human being must decide whether to do that which is good or that which is inherently evil. We are inundated with decisions that challenge our character and call into question our personal and professional ethics. Whenever we engage in that which is just and morally upright, we add to the quality of our lives. Likewise, every time a human being behaves in an unethical and corrupt manner, the quality of their personal and professional life diminishes. Moreover, our influence in the lives of others either encourages them to engage in ethical behavior or unethical behavior. Hence, we can either positively or negatively affect the lives of those they encounter. As such, a healthy ethical code is necessary to safeguard against crossing boundaries that are detrimental to one's self, family, friends, colleagues and career.

The sex based and non-sex based political scandals represented in this study identifies consequences associated with yielding to temporary gratification (i.e., money, greed, sex, power, etc.) rather than reason. This research demonstrates how the absence of good ethical judgment on the part of elected officials or political officials impact their lives, the lives of their families and the lives of others associated with them (staff and colleagues). The presence of lapses in judgment on the part of government officials or public servants are demonstrated in a series of sexually oriented scandals and non-sexually based scandals that span from 2000-2011. The actions of political officials highlights their inability to recognize the dangers associated with their personal weaknesses and proclivities toward certain urges or desires.

All of the officials in this research demonstrate an inability to control their (1) sexual desire, (2) greed, and (3) desire to wield power and authority.

Chapter Two of this study discusses sex based political scandals involving elected or appointed officials. Some of the inappropriate or unethical sexually oriented behavior exhibited by elected officials like Tom Ganley, Samuel B. Kent, John Edwards, Vito Fossella, and David Vitter were indicted on criminal charges. They were found guilty in a court of law and sentenced to prison for their unscrupulous and illegal behavior. Brian Doyle, former press secretary for the U.S. Department of Homeland Security, was charged with using a computer to seduce a minor. He was also charged with disseminating inappropriate images to a child. Doyle was convicted in a court of law and sentenced to 5 years in prison and ten years probation. Additionally, Doyle was required to register as a sex offender, a consequence of his inappropriate sexual activities because of his depraved sexually oriented behavior.

Although, all sexually based political scandals are explosive in nature. Occasionally, a sex scandal erupts in an extraordinarily explosive manner. This is precisely what occurred in the "D.C. Madam Scandal." Deborah Jeane Palfrey, known as the D.C. Madam, apparently could not come to terms with being sentenced to prison for running an elite prostitution business which serviced members of Congress, highly ranked military officials, and highly ranked political appointees to various department and agencies. Palfrey committed suicide in response to being convicted of running a prostitution ring and sentenced to four (4) months in jail. Thus, the sex-based scandals treated in this research serve as a series of cautionary tales about what can happen when people, especially persons entrusted with power and authority, exercise poor judgment and their behavior is exposed to the public by the media.

Chapter Three identifies the consequences associated with a variety of unethical and illegal non-sex based activities perpetrated by government officials. The behavior exhibited by public servants included selling government documents for financial gain, failure to disclose income and property, theft, using campaign funds, tax evasion, and failure to disclose property and income. A number of political officials not only engaged in unethical behavior, they participated in illegal activities as well. Among the illegal acts committed included: bribery, conspiracy, misuse of campaign funds, tax evasion, soliciting or paying for sex, etc. Former congressional representatives Randy Cunningham, William J. Jefferson, Jim Traficant and the former mayor of Detroit Kwame Kilpatrick were indicted and convicted on bribery charges. A few key government officials were indicted on conspiracy charges. Former United States Representatives including Tom Lay, Bob Ney, Dusty Foggo, Jim Traficant, and Randy Cunningham were among those charged with conspiring against the government. Former Congressmen Jim Traficant and

Randy Cunningham were charged with tax evasion. The consequences identified in Chapter 3 were linked to misuse or abuse of power, as well as greed.

All of the scandals captured in the pages of this study capture the reality of what can happen when human beings have developed a faulty ethical code. The unethical behaviors displayed in Chapter Two and Chapter Three paint a picture of how quickly one decision can change a person's life forever. Good decisions can lead to a bright future full of promise and hope. However, a poor decision can lead a person down a path that spirals out of control. Moreover, poor decisions tend to have a ripple effect. An individual's decision to engage in unethical, inappropriate, corrupt and illegal behavior not only damages the perpetrator, unethical or corrupt behavior has a way of casting a shadow of suspicion on others associated with the individual who has demonstrated poor character. The inappropriate or unethical behavior of a husband reflects negatively on his wife. Likewise, illegal activities carried out on the part of a wife reflects poorly on her husband. Unethical behavior on the part of parents reflect poorly on the family, including children. Similarly, the demonstration of a lack of integrity on the part of children raises questions about the parents. When we elect political officials to legislative bodies and executive branches locally, statewide and nationally, there is an expectation they will abide by the laws they enact. When political leaders and appointed leaders fail to adhere to the very laws they create, it damages the public's ability to trust government officials. The demonstration of diminished character damages the way citizens and constituents view political leaders in general.

I am by no means suggesting there is a human being alive who possess "perfect" character, nor am I suggesting there exists individuals who are void of weaknesses and failures. Although the sex based and non-sex based scandals covered in this research highlight the fallibility of human beings, possessing integrity does not require perfection. It has been said character is who we are when no one is looking. If the statement is true, the true measure of a man /woman's character is represented by both the things he/she does and that which he/she refrains from when no one is looking. A person's character is also reflected in the way one responds when their errors in judgment are exposed. Whether the individual assumes responsibility or plays the "victim" or the blame game speaks volumes about his/her character. This research reflects both responses. In many instances, professional and political careers were salvageable when public servants acknowledged and assumed responsibility for their mistakes. For example, Eric Massa never assumed full responsibility for inappropriately touching his male staffers. When given the opportunity to speak to the media, he argued his inappropriate touching or groping was meant as a joke. Likewise, Anthony Weiner, a former U.S. Representative who became infamous for sexting, reemerged as a mayoral candidate during the summer of 2013 after resigning from Congress in 2011.

He appeared to have rebounded from his sexting scandal and was the Democratic Party's favorite in the New York City mayoral primary election when new allegations surfaced that he continued sexting after he resigned from Congress and entered a rehabilitation center for treatment for a sex addiction. In his first sex scandal, Weiner initially maintained that his computer had been hacked before acknowledging he sent the images himself. Following the revelation of another sexting scandal, the former congressional representative and NYC mayoral candidate was urged to end his mayoral bid. True to form, Weiner with his wife at his side refused to withdraw from the mayoral race. When he addressed the media about the new allegations, he told the media "I said that other texts and photos were likely to come out, and today they have."[1]

Unlike Massa and Weiner, Congressman Vito Fossella seemed genuinely remorseful after being arrested for driving under the influence when he apologized to his family, his constituents and the public. Fossella told the public, driving under the influence was a mistake he would not repeat. His avowal to refrain from drinking and driving was short lived. Fossella was arrested on two additional occasions for driving while intoxicated. In a second drinking and driving case in 2008, he was convicted and served 5 days in jail after causing the death of three people. After causing the death of three people, Fossella had to come face-to-face with his drinking problem. Consequently, Congressman Fossella announced his intention to retire at the end of the 110th Congress.[2] It is unclear as to whether his retirement announcement was simply a political ploy or whether he was encouraged to continue serving in Congress by his colleagues and constituents. Despite driving under the influence repeatedly and causing the death of three people, Representative Fossella continues as a member of the 113th Congress.

As we teach and train students for the careers of their choice, it is imperative they receive an education and training in both the field they have selected as well as ethical training related to issues, problems and pitfalls they might come face to face with as professionals. As educators, we must find a way to teach that which is appropriate to engage. We must also spend time teaching and dialogue with students about the darkness or evils associated with the career path they have chosen to study. If we do not address the less than attractive aspects associated with the career path they choose, we inevitably send them out ill prepared for the realities they are likely to face. Withholding the unflattering truth about career paths and professions may be tantamount to sending them out as sheep to be slaughtered. I am by no means suggesting every student will succumb to the pitfalls of his/her chosen profession. I am suggesting as preventive measure students, employees and the public will be better served by engaging in honest conversations about ethical dilemmas, corrupt behavior and illegal activities that have the propensity to taint, dismantle and destroy everything one has accomplished in life. It is my belief sex based and non-sex based scandals can be utilized as tools to demonstrate what happens when one yields to temporarily gratifying behaviors that prompt one to make poor decisions or a series of choices that produce devastating consequences.

Finally, it is essential that every individual know their personal and professional weaknesses in order to critically evaluate their proclivity towards certain inappropriate, unethical and illegal behavior. Some people have an inclination that drives or propels them toward inappropriate sexually based behaviors such as extramarital affairs, sexually harassing behavior, and soliciting sex. Some engage in sexual acts in exchange for money with prostitutes. A few "heterosexual" male political officials were exposed for seeking sexual relationships with homosexual men despite being married to heterosexual women.

Not every weakness or predisposition is sexual in nature. A number of political officials like Janet Rehnquist, Jim Traficant, Jack Abramoff, Julie MacDonald and Lurita Alexis Doan demonstrated an inability to properly utilize the power and authority with which they had been professionally entrusted. Some elected and appointed officials like former judge G. Thomas Porteous, former United States Representative Jesse Jackson, Jr., Congressman Charles B. Rangel, and the former mayor of Detroit Kwame Kilpatrick demonstrated a tendency toward money or greed.

At the end of the day, every human being is flawed. Nevertheless, every individual is the "steward" of his/her character or integrity. Thus, everyone is responsible for his or her decisions. When one demonstrates a lapse in judgment, an honorable man or woman assumes responsibility for their actions. In cases when the ethical lapses or inappropriate behavior of government officials was exposed, those who readily admitted their mistakes and asked for forgiveness emerged with their career intact. Conversely, political scandals involving public servants who failed to assume responsibility for their actions were either forced to resign or retired early in order to avoid being terminated from their positions.

Ultimately, the sex oriented and non-sex based political scandals from 2000-2011 serve as a lens through which students, leaders and the public can evaluate their weaknesses or potentially destructive tendencies (i.e., lying, cheating, dishonesty, procrastination, etc.) and the consequences associated with succumbing to temporary desires and the consequences they tend to yield. Therefore, these scandals provide an opportunity for people to see elements of themselves in the lives and careers of various elected and appointed officials. Thus, it is crucial that people learn from the mistakes of officials who capitulated to the culture by engaging in inappropriate, unethical or illegal behavior. Their political career, sometimes even their family life, were tainted or ruined of their own doing. In conclusion, it is imperative to view these political scandals as blaring examples of what happens when people fail to identify the negative tendencies or predispositions that entice them to participate in unethical and illegal behavior. The scandals also serve as a reminder that when one fails to yield to reason and give in to their impulse(s), there is a hefty price to be paid. Hence, one should ask themselves questions like: (1) What predisposition or proclivity do I possess that has the ability to damage or destroy my academic or professional career?, (3) What predisposition or proclivity do I possess that has the ability to damage or destroy my personal life?, (4) What predisposition or proclivity do I possess that has the ability to damage or destroy my personal life?, (5) Do I have a tendency to gravitate toward inappropriate sexual behavior, infidelity, bribery, or greed?, (6) Do I have a tendency that gravitates toward misusing power?, (7) What is the condition of my character?, (8) How does my weakness impact my life, (9) How does my weakness affect and influence others?, (10) Am I satisfied with the current state of my character and integrity?, (11) Is my weakness or proclivity leading me toward a path of self-destruction?, and (12) What steps or tools can I employ to curtail the results of my weakness? It is the author's belief that every reasonable man or woman desire to preserve their relationships, careers, livelihood and legacy. As such, it is critical that one remember the choices he/she makes in inevitably sets in motion a series of consequences he/she cannot control. I am reminded of a scene in the motion picture *The Counselor* that debuted in autumn 2013. After entering into a supposed "one-time" scheme with a drug cartel, the counselor is left to come to terms with the consequences of his actions, which lead to his fiancé Laura being kidnapped and murdered. After realizing she has disappeared, the counselor has a telephone conversation with a member of the cartel named Jefe. In a failed attempt, the counselor tries to exchange his life for that of his beloved fiancé. The scene that captures the conversation between Jefe who represents the cartel and the counselor offers insight about an individual's choices and the ripple effect it has on those associated with us. Jefe urges the counselor to accept the reality of the consequences of his decision to participate in the drug scheme. The cartel member tells the counselor, "I would urge you to see the truth of your situation." Jefe continues saying, "It is not for me to say what you should have done. Or not done. I only know that the world in which you seek to undo your mistakes is not the world in which they were made. You are at a cross in the road, and here you think to choose. But here there is no choosing. There is only accepting. The choosing was done long ago."[3] Eventually, the counselor receives a package that confirms the truth about what has happened to Laura, his love interest, played by Penelope Cruz. Laura was murdered because of his decision to participate in the drug scheme. In closing, no one can foresee the consequences that will be assigned to their deeds. However, the sex based scandals, non-sex based scandals and the film *The Counselor* points to the reality there is a hefty price to be paid for unethical and illegal behavior.

NOTES

1. Jonathan Lemire, "I Have Forgiven Him: Huma Abedin Defends Embattled Husband Anthony Weiner As Pressure Mounts To Quit New York Mayoral Race," *National Post* [database online] available from http://www.nationalpost.com/m/wp/news/world/blog.html?b=news.nationalpost.com/2013/07/24/i-have-forgiven-him-huma-abedin-defends-embattled-husband-anthony-weiner-as-pressure-mounts-to-quit-new-york-mayoral-race ; Internet; accessed July 31, 2013, 1.

2. Jen Chung, "Fossella's Plea Partly Prompted By Ball Player's Death," *Gothamist* [database online] available from http://gothamist.com/2009/04/14/ fossellas_plea_partly _prompted_by b.php ; Internet; accessed December 10, 2011, 1.

3. *The Counselor*, dir. by Ridley Scott (Twentieth Century Fox, 2013).

Bibliography

BOOKS

Aristotle. Rackham, Harris. *The Nicomachean Ethics. Great Britain: Worsdworth Editions, Ltd., 1996.*

Felice, William. *How Do I Save My Honor?* Maryland: Rowman and Littlefield Publishers, Inc., 2009.

Fleishman, Joel. "Self-Interest and Political Integrity." Joel Fleishman, Lance Liebman, and Mark Moore, eds., *Public Duties: The Moral Obligation of Government Officials.* Cambridge: Harvard University Press, 1981.

Kant, Immanuel. "Good Will, Duty, and the Categorical Imperative." in Christina Hoff Sommers, ed., *Right and Wrong: Basic Readings in Ethics.* San Diego: Harcourt Brace Jovanovich Publishers, 1986.

Key, V. O. Key. *Public Opinion and Democracy.* New York: Alfred Knopf, 1961.

Lippman, Walter. *The Phantom Public.* New York: Harcourt Brace, 1925.

Lowell, A. Lawrence. *Public Opinion and Popular Government.* New York: Longmans Green and Company, 1930.

Mill, John Stuart. Oskar Piest ed. *Utilitarianism.* Indianapolis: The Bobbs-Merrill Company, Inc., 1957.

Oxford Dictionaries [database online] available from http://www.oxforddictionaries.com/us/definition/american_english/waterboarding; Internet; accessed August 28, 2013.

Smart, J. J. C. "Utilitarianism" in *Right and Wrong: Basic Readings in Ethics*, ed. Christina Hoff Sommers. San Diego: Harcourt Brace Jovanovich, 1986.

ARTICLES

Rice, Dan and Craig Dreilinger. "Rights and Wrongs of Ethics Training." *Training and Development Journal.* May 1990; Internet; accessed July 15, 2013.

PERIODICALS

Wilson, Francis. "Concepts of Public Opinion." *The American Political Science Review.* Vol. 27, no. 3 (June 1933): 371-372.

PUBLIC OPINION POLLS

"Trust in Government." *Gallup Poll* [database online] available from www.gallup.com/ poll/ 5392/trust-government.aspx; Internet; accessed November 10, 2013.

NEWS ARTICLES WITH AUTHORS

Adams, Cindy. "Kerik Now Out, Gave Tips In Jail." *The New York Times* [database online] available from http://www.nytimes.com/2009/11/06/nyregion/06kerik.html?_r=0; Internet; accessed August 14, 2013.

Albert, Bruce. "'Substantial' Cooperation in Case Against William Jefferson Cited at Brett Pfeffer Sentence-Reduction Hearing." *The Time Picayune Greater New Orleans* [database online] available from http://www.nola.com/crime/index.ssf/2009/12 substantial_cooperation_in_cas.html; accessed August 17, 2013.

Andrews, Edmund L. "Ex-Deputy of Interior Dept. Pleads Guilty." *The New York Times* [database online] available fromhttp://www.nytimes.com/2007/03/23/washington/23cnd-giles.html; Internet; accessed August 6, 2013.

Arena, Kelli and Terry Frieden. "Former CIA No. 3 Indicted For Steering Contracts to Friend." *CNN.com* [database online] available from http://www.cnn.com/2007/LAW/02/13/cia.foggo/; Internet; accessed August 7, 2013.

Babcock, Charles R. and Renae Merle. "U.S. Accuses Pair of Rigging Iraq Contracts." *The Washington Post [database online] available from* http://www.washingtonpost.com/wp-dyn/content/article/2005/11/17/AR2005111701879.html; Internet; accessed August 26, 2013.

Baker, Peter and James V. Grimaldi. "Rove Aide Linked To Abramoff Resigns." *The Washington Post* [database online] available from http://www.washingtonpost.com/wp-dyn/content/article/2006/10/06/AR2006100600965.html; Internet; accessed August 6, 2013.

Baldas, Tresa. "Kwame Kilpatrick's Wife Evicted From Texas Home." *NewsTalk WCHB News* [database online] available from http://wchbnewsdetroit.com/2808214/kwame-kilpatricks-wife-evicted-from-texas-home/; Internet; accessed August 24, 2013.

Barakat, Matthew. "Kyle 'Dusty' Foggo, Former CIA #3, Gets More Than 3 Years In Prison." *Huffington Post* [database online] available http://www.huffingtonpost.com/2009/02/26/kyle-dusty-foggo-former-c_n_170240.html; Internet; accessed August 7, 2013.

Barbaro, Michael Matt Flegeheimer and Ashley Parker. "Weiner Resigns in Chaotic Final Scene." *The New York Times* [database online] available from http://www.nytimes.com/2011/06/17/nyregion/anthony-d-weiner-tells-friends-he-will-resign.html?pagewanted=all&_r=0; Internet; accessed December 14, 2011.

Barr, Meghann. "Jim Traficant, Ex-Congressman And Convicted Felon, Will Be On The Ballot Again In November." *Huffington Post* [database online] available from http://www.huffingtonpost.com/2010/09/01/jim-traficant-convicted-felon-congressman_n_702710.html; Internet; accessed August 20, 2013.

Barrett, Devlin. "NY Congressman Admits Child From Affair." *Fox News* [database online] available from http://www.foxnews.com/wires/2008May08/0,4670,CongressmanAffair,00.html; Internet; accessed December 15, 2011.

Barrett, Ted. "Panel Will Investigate Traficant, Lawmakers Say." *CNN.com* [database online] http://europe.cnn.com/2002/ALLPOLITICS/04/17/traficant.ethics/; Internet; accessed August 20, 2013.

Beekman, Daniel. "Former NYPD Commissioner Bernard Kerik To Be Released From Federal Prison Tuesday: Report." *Daily News* [database online] available from http://www.nydailynews.com/new-york/ex-top-bernard-kerik-released-prison-report-article-1.1356153; Internet; accessed August 14, 2013.

Bradshaw, Kit and Tyler Treadway, "Rep. Tim Mahoney's Wife File for Divorce, Seeks Assets." *TCPALM* [database online] available from http://www.tcpalm.com/news/2008/oct/20/mahoney/; Internet; accessed December 14, 2011.

Bresnahan, John. "FEC Fines John Ensign's family $54,000." *Politico* [database online] available from http://www.politico.com/story/2013/05/fec-fines-ensign-family-54000-91575.html; Internet; accessed July 12, 2013.

Bresnahan, John and Josh Kraushaar. "Hoyer Knew of Massa Allegations." *Politico* [database online] available from http://www.politico.com/news/stories/0310/33864.html; Internet; accessed December 12, 2011.

Bresnahan, John and Glenn Thrush. "Rep. Eric Massa To Resign." *Politico* [database online] available from http://politico.com/news/stories/0320/34001.html; Internet; accessed December 14, 2011.

Bruce, Mary. "Obama Says GOP Candidates Are Wrong, Waterboarding is 'Torture.'" *ABC News* [database online] available from http://abcnews.go.com/blogs/politics/2011/11/obama-says-gop-candidates-are-wrong-waterboarding-is-torture/; Internet; accessed August 28, 2013.

Buettner, Russ. "Bernard Kerik's Double Affair Laid Bare." *Daily News* [database online] available from http://www.nydailynews.com/news/bernard-kerik-double-affair-laid-bare-article-1.340899; Internet; accessed August 14, 2013.

Burdeau, Cain. "Jefferson Overcomes Scandal, Wins Reelection." *The Washington Post [database online] available* http://www.washingtonpost.com/wp-dyn/content/article/2006/12/09/AR2006120900601.html; Internet; accessed August 17, 2013.

Byrne, John. "Anti-gay Congressman David Dreier, Said to be Gay, 'Lived With Male Chief of Staff.'" *The Raw Story* [database online] available from http://www.rawstory.com/exclusives/byrne/david_dreier_outed_brad_smith_gay_920.htm; Internet; accessed July 2013.

Capehart, Johnathan. "Censured Charles Rangel Can't Help Himself." *The Washington Post* [database online] available from http:/www.washingtonpost.com/blogs/post-partisan/wp/2013/04/25/censured-charles-rangel-cant-help-himself/; Internet; accessed August 6, 2013.

Cardinale, Matthew. "Cynthia McKinney Running For US House on Green Party Ticket." *Atlanta Progressive News* [database online] available from http://www.atlantaprogressivenews.com/interspire/news/2012/04/02/cynthia-mckinney-running-for-us-house-on-green-party-ticket.html; Internet; accessed August 16, 2013.

Chapman, Mary. "Former Mayor of Detroit Guilty in Corruption Case." *The New York Times* [database online] available from http://www.nytimes.com/2013/03/12/us/kwame-kilpatrick-ex-mayor-of-detroit-convicted-in-corruption-case.html?_r=0; Internet; accessed August 24, 2013.

Chen, Sharon. "Randy 'Duke' Cunningham Released From Prison." *Fox 5 San Diego* [database online] available from http://fox5sandiego.com/2013/06/04/former-san-diego-congressman-randy-duke-cunningham-released-from-prison/#axzz2cK3YvDA0; Internet; accessed August 17, 2013.

Chen, Joyce. "Anthony Weiner is The Latest Politician To Don Notorious 'Sex ScandalFace." *Zimbio* [database online] available from http://www.zimbio.com/Huma+Abedin/articles/ajw9rblwLK1/Anthony+Weiner+latest;Internet; accessed December 14, 2011.

Chen, Joyce. "Anthony Weiner is Latest Politician To Don Notorious 'Sex Scandal Face." *Zimbio* [database online] available from http://www.zimbio.com/Huma+Abedin/articles/ajw9rblwLKq/Anthony+Weiner; Internet; accessed December 14, 2011.

Chung, Jen. "Fossella's Plea Partly Prompted By Ball Player's Death." *Gothamist* [database online] available from http://gothamist.com/2009/04/14/fossellas_plea_partly_prompted_by_b.php; Internet; accessed December 10, 2011.

Clark, Champ. "INSIDE STORY: Gary Condit After Chandra Levy Case." *People* [database online] available from http://www.people.com/people/article/0,,20264057,00.html; Internet; accessed July 22, 2013.

Clymer, Adam. "Frank Lautenberg, New Jersey Senator in His 5th Term, Dies at 89." *The New York Times* [database online] available from http://www.nytimes.com/2013/06/04/ nyregion/ frank-lautenberg-new-jersey-senator.html?pagewanted=all&_r=0; Internet; accessed August 19, 2013.

Cook, Theresa and Gina Sunseri, "Not Guilty Plea in Judges Sex Abuse Case." *ABC News* [database online] available from http://www.abcnews.go.com/TheLaw/FedCrimes/story?id=5716176&page=1; Internet; accessed July, 10, 2013.

Cook, Theresa and Gina Sunseri. "Federal Judge Indicted in Sex Abuse Case." *ABC News* [database online] available from://abcnews.go.com/TheLawFedCrimes/story?id=5681319& page=1; Internet; accessed July, 10, 2011.

Condon, Stephanie. "David Wu Announces Resignation Amid Sex Scandal." *CBS News* [database online] available from http://www.cbsnews.com/2101-503544_16220083560.html ?tag+contentMain;contentBoo; Internet; accessed December 14, 2011.

Crabtree, Susan and Jordan Fabian. "Massa Scandal Expodes." *The Hill* [database online] available from http://thehill.com/homenews/house/85829-massa-scandal-explodes- ?tmpl=component; Internet; accessed December 14, 2011.

Cratty, Carol and Tom Cohen. "Jesse Jackson Jr., Wife Plead Guilty to Charges Involving Campaign Funds," *CNN* [database online] available from http://www.cnn.com/2013/02/20/ politics/jackson-plea-deal; Internet; accessed August 21, 2013.

Daly, Michael. "Scott Broadwell Proves to Be a Class Act in the Wake of His Wife's Affair." *The Daily Beast* [database online] available from http://www.thedailybeast.com/articles/ 2012/11/21/scott-broadwell-proves-to-be-a-class-act-in-the-wake-of-his-wife-s-affair.html; Internet; accessed July 22, 2013.

Davey, Monica. "For a Soaring Political Career, Uncertain Turns." *The New York Times* [database online] available from http://www.nytimes.com/2012/07/12/us/for-a-soaring-political- career-uncertain-turns.html?pagewanted=all&_r=0; Internet; accessed August 22, 2013.

Davey, Monica. "Jesse Jackson Jr. Resigns, Facing Illness and Inquiry." *The New York Times* [database online] available from http://www.nytimes.com/2012/11/22/us/jackson-jr-to-re- sign-house-seat.html; Internet; accessed August 21, 2013.

Dillon, Nancy. "Ex-CIA Director David Petraeus Apologizes for Affair in First Public Speech Since Resignation." *Daily News* [database online] available from http:// www.nydailynews.com/news/politics/petraeus-apologize-affair-speech-resigning-article- 1.1299224#ixzz2ZocoYUue; Internet; accessed July 22, 2013.

Dorell, Oren. "McKinney Apologizes For Incident With Cop." *USA Today* [database online] available from http://usatoday30.usatoday.com/news/washington/2006-04-06-mckin- ney_x.htm; Internet; accessed August 16, 2013.

Dorning, Anne-Marie. "Running To Rehab." *ABC News* [database online] available from http:// abcnews.go.com/Politics/story?id=2518173&page=1; Internet; accessed July 17, 2013.

Drier, Peter. "HUD Secretary Alphonso Jackson's Resignation." *Huffington Post* [database online] available from http://www.huffingtonpost.com/peter-dreier/hud-secretary-alphonso- ja_b_94787.html; Internet; accessed August 7, 2013.

Eggen, Dan and Carol D. Leonnig. "Jackson Resigns as HUD Secretary." *The Washington Post* [database online] available from http://articles.washingtonpost.com/2008-04-01/politics/ 36878302_1_jackson-dan-bartlett-hud-contractors; Internet; accessed August 7, 2013.

Eggen, Dan and Charles R. Babcock. "Official Quits; FBI Probes Role in Defense Contracts." *The Washington Post* [database online] available from http://www.expose-the-war-profit- eers.org/archive/media/2006/20060509.htm; Internet; accessed August 7, 2013.

Eggen, Dan and Carol D. Leonnig. "Jackson Resigns as HUD Secretary." *The Washington Post* [database online] available from http://articles.washingtonpost.com/2008-04-01/politics/ 36878302_1_jackson-dan-bartlett-hud-contractors; Internet; accessed August 7, 2013.

Eggen, Dan and R. Jeffrey Smith, "FBI Agents Allege Abuse of Detainees at Guantanamo Bay." *The Washington Post* [database online] available from http:// www.washingtonpost.com/wp-dyn/articles/A14936-2004Dec20.html; Internet; accessed August 28, 2013.

Evans, Bob. "Judge G. Thomas Porteous Faces Impeachment Trial In Congress." *Huffington Post* [database online] available from http://www.huffingtonpost.com/2010/09/13/judge-g- thomas-porteous-impeachment-trial_n_715336.html; Intenet; accessed August 6, 2013.

Fabian, Jordan. "Charles Rangel at IRS Hearing: "Wrong to Abuse the Tax System." *ABC News* [database online] available from http://abcnews.go.com/ABC_Univision/Politics/con- gressman-charlie-rangel-wrong-abuse-tax-system/story?id=19201621; Internet; accessed August 6, 2013.

Friedman, Dan Friedman. "Rep. Charles Rangel Will Run For Reelection In 2014 — For Now." New York Daily News [database online] available from http://www .nydailynews.com/news/politics/rep-charles-rangel-run- reelection-2014-article-1.1407246; Internet; accessed August 15, 2013.

Glanz, James. "Former U.S. Official in Iraq to Plead Guilty to Corruption." *The New York Times* [database online] available from http://www.nytimes.com/2006/02/01/international/middleeast/01cnd-reconstruct.html?_r=0; Internet; accessed August 26, 2013.

Goldman, Russell. "Senator's Wife Finds Herself at Center of Storm." *ABC News* [database online] available from http://abcnews.go.com/Politics/story?id=3538964&page=1# .UebtoxafemE; Internet; accessed July 12, 2013.

Gray, Madison, S. James Snyder and M.J. Stephen. "Sinful Stateman: Kwame Kilpatrick." *TIME* [database online] available from http://www.time.com/time/specials/2007/ article/0,28804,1721111_1721210_1721124,00.html; Internet; accessed August 24, 2013.

Gray, Steven Gray. "Jesse Jackson Jr.: The Trouble with Being Candidate 5." *TIME* [database online] available from http://www.time.com/time/politics/ article/0,8599,1866058,00.html; Internet; accessed August 22, 2013.

Greiner, Andrew. "Jesse's Girl?" *NBC Chicago* [database online] available from http://www.nbcchicago.com/blogs/ward-room/Jesse-Jackson-Responds-to-New-Allegations-103457694.html; Internet; accessed August 22, 2013.

Greiner, Andrew. "Jesse Jackson Jr. Wins Reelection From Mayo Clinic." *NBC Chicago* [database online] available from http://www.nbcchicago.com/blogs/ward-room/Jesse-Jackson-Jr-Wins-Reelection--175717941.html; Internet; accessed August 21, 2013.

Grimaldi, James V. "Ex-Official Linked to Abramoff Pleads Guilty." *The Washington Post* [database online] available from http://www.washingtonpost.com/wp-dyn/content/article/2008/04/22/AR2008042202430.html; Internet; accessed August 6, 2013.

Grimaldi, James V. and Carol D. Leonnig. "Former Aide to Ex-Congressman Ney Pleads Guilty in Abramoff Case." *The Washington Post* [database online] available from http:/www.washingtonpost.com/wp-dyn/content/article/2007/02/26/AR2007022601631.html; Internet; accessed August 6, 2013.

Fitzgerald, Jim. "Bernie Kerik Sentenced To Four Years In Prison." *Huffington Post* [database online] available from http://www.huffingtonpost.com/2010/02/18/bernie-keriks-jail-sent-en_0_n_467097.html; accessed August 14, 2013.

Florin, Hector. "Mahoney's Florida District Has Sex Scandal Deja Vu." *TIME* [database online] available from http://www.time.com/time/printout/0,88161851084,00.html; Internet; accessed December 14, 2011.

Harris, Gardiner. "Ex-Head of F.D.A. or Wife Sold Stock in Regulated Area." *The New York Times* [database online] available from http://www.nytimes.com/2005/10/27/ politics/27fda.html?_r=0; Internet; accessed August 8,2013.

Harrow Jr., Robert and Scott Higham. "Doan Ends Her Stormy Tenure as GSA Chief." *The Washington Post* [database online] available from http://www.washingtonpost.com/wp-dyn/content/article/2008/04/30/AR2008043001271.html; Internet; accessed August 6, 2013.

Hersh, Seymour. "Annals of National Security: Who Lied To Whom?" *The New Yorker Magazine* [database online] available from http://www.newyorker.com/archive 2003/03/31/030331fa_fact1; Internet; accessed August 27, 2013.

Hill, James, Teri Whitcraft, Nadine Schubailat and Lauren Sher. "John Edwards Made Sex Tape, Abortion Plea, Aide Says." *ABC News* [database online] available from http://abcnews.go.com/2020/John_Edwards_Scandal/john-edwards-made-sex-tape-abortion-plea-aide says; Internet; accessed December 14, 2011.

Horwitz, Sari, Scott Higham, and Sylvia Moreno, "Who Killed Chandra Levy." *The Washington Post* [database online] available from http://www.washingtonpost.com/wp-srv/metro/specials/chandra/ch10_1.html; accessed July 22, 2013.

Hsu, Spencer S. "Aide Sentenced in Abramoff Scandal." *The Washington Post* [database online] available from http://www.washingtonpost.com/wp-dyn/content/article/2010/11/22/AR2010112207038.html; Internet; accessed 6, 2013.

Jackson, Jill. "Charlie Rangel: List of Charges," *CBS News* [database online] available from http://www.cbsnews.com/8301-503544_162-20012179-503544.html; Internet; accessed August 6, 2013.

Johnson, Carrie. "No Grand Jury for Gonzales." *The Washington Post* [database online] available from http://www.washingtonpost.com/wp-dyn/content/article/2008/09/28/AR20080 92801057.html; Internet; accessed August 20, 2013.

Johnson, Kevin and Susan Page. "Clinton Adviser Probed About Removing Classified Terror Memos." *USA Today* [database online] available from http://usatoday30.usatoday.com/news/washington/2004-07-19-berger-probe_x.htm?POE=NEWISVA; Internet; accessed August 8, 2013.

Johnston, David. "Ex-C.I.A. Official Admits Corruption," *The New York Times* [database online] available from http://www.nytimes.com/2008/09/30/washington/30inquire.html?_r=0; Internet; accessed August 7, 2013.

Jordan, Mary. "Traficant Completes Sentence for Bribery." *The Washington Post* [database online] available from http://articles.washingtonpost.com/2009-09-03/news/36826530 _1_traficant-second-house-member-ohio-democrat; Internet; accessed August 20, 2013.

Kane, Paul. "Rep. Charlie Rangel Found Guilty of 11 Ethics Violations." *The Washington Post* [database online] available from http://www.washingtonpost.com/wp-dyn/content/article/2010/11/16/AR2010111604000.html; Internet; accessed August 6, 2013.

Karl, Jonathan and George Cooper. "Chief Justice's Daughter To Resign Government Post." *CNN* [database online] available from http://www.cnn.com/2003/ALLPOLITICS/03/04/janet.rehnquist/; Internet; accessed August 15, 2013.

Kay, Katy. "Profile: Gary Condit." *BBC News* [database online] available from http://news.bbc.co.uk/2/hi/americas/1447661.stm; Internet; accessed July 22, 2013.

Kornblut, Anne. "Third Journalist Was Paid to Promote Bush Policies." *The New York Times* [database online] available from http://www.nytimes.com/2005/01/29/politics/29column.html; Internet; accessed August 24, 2013.

Kravitz, Derek. "Another Ex-Abramoff Aide Charged." *The Washington Post* [database online] available from http://voices.washingtonpost.com/washingtonpostinvestigations/2009/01/ exabramoff_aide_charged.html; Internet; accessed August 6, 2013.

Kurtz, Howard. "Writer Backing Bush Plan Had Gotten Federal Contract." *The Washington Post* [database online] available from http://www.washingtonpost.com/wp-dyn/articles/A36545-2005Jan25.html; Internet; accessed August 24, 2013.

Kurtz, Howard. "Gen. John Allen, Caught Up in David Petraeus Scandal, Is Bypassing NATO Post and Retiring." *The Daily Beast* [database online] available from http://www.thedailybeast.com/articles/2013/02/19/gen-john-allen-caught-up-in-david-petraeus-scandal-is-bypassing-nato-post-and-retiring.html; Internet; accessed July 22, 2013.

Lemire, Jonathan. "I Have Forgiven Him: Huma Abedin Defends Embattled Husband Anthony Weiner As Pressure Mounts To Quit New York Mayoral Race." *National Post* [database online] available from http://www.nationalpost.com/m/wp/news/world/blog.html?b=news.nationalpost.com/2013/07/24/i-have-forgiven-him-huma-abedin-defends-embattled-husband-anthony-weiner-as-pressure-mounts-to-quit-new-york-mayoral-race; Internet; accessed July 31, 2013.

Leonning, Carol D. and Amy Goldstein, "Libby Found Guilty in CIA Leak Case." *The Washington Post* [database online] available from http://www.washingtonpost.com/wp-dyn/content/article/2007/03/06/AR2007030600648.html; Internet; accessed August 5, 2013.

Leonnig, Carol D. and Paul Kane. "Rep. Charles Rangel Broke Ethics Rules, House Panel Finds." *The Washington Post* [database online] available from http://www.washingtonpost.com/wpdyn/content/article/2010/07/22/AR2010072204704.html; Internet; accessed August 6, 2013.

Leonnig, Carol. "HUD Chief Accused of Retaliation," *The Washington Post* [database online] available from http://articles.washingtonpost.com/2008-02-04/news/36892229_1_carl-greene-jackson-authority; Internet; accessed August 7, 2013.

Lewis, Neil A. "Libby Guilty of Lying in C.I.A. Leak Case." *New York Times* [database online] available from http://www.nytimes.com/2007/03/07/washington/07libby.html ?pagewanted=all&_r=0; Internet; accessed August 5, 2013.

Lofflin, John. "John Ensign Returns to Veterinary Practice." U.S. Department of Veterans Affairs [database online] available from http://veterinarynews.dvm360.com/ dvm/

Law+and+Ethics/John-Ensign-returns-to-veterinary-practice/ArticleStandard/ Article/detail/ 781653; Internet; accessed July 12, 2013.

Lutz, B. J. "Alderman Sandi Jackson Resigns." *NBC Chicago* [database online] available from http://www.nbcchicago.com/blogs/ward-room/chicago-alderman-sandi-jackson-resign-186527151.html; Internet; accessed August 21, 2013.

McArdle, John. "Craig Arrested, Pleads Guilty Following Incident in Airport Restroom," *Roll Call* [database online] available from http://www.rollcall.com/news/-19763-1.html; Internet; accessed December 15, 2011.

McCarty, James and Mark Naymik. "Tom Ganley Blames Opponent, Democrats After Second-Woman Accuses Him of Sexual Misconduct." *Cleveland.com* [database online] available from http://blog.cleveland.com/metro//print.html; Internet; accessed December 14, 2011.

McCarthy, Katie. "Gary Condit's Son: Dad Got a 'Bad Deal', Didn't Deserve What Happened." *ABC News* [database online] available from http://abcnews.go.com/blogs/politics/ 2010/11/gary-condits-son-dad-got-a-bad-deal-didnt-deserve-what-happened/; Internet; accessed July 22, 2013.

Meland, Marius. "Lay Points Finger At Fastow For Enron Collapse." *Law 360* [database online] available from http://www.law360.com/articles/6261/lay-points-finger-at-fastow-for-enron-collapse; Internet; accessed August 14, 2013.

Michaels, Scott. "Federal Judge Probed on Harassment Allegations." *ABC News* [database online] available from http://abcnews.go.com/TheLaw/story?id=3996717&page=1; Internet; accessed June 10, 2011.

Milbank, Dana. "During National Character Counts Week, Bush Stumps for Philanderer." *The Washington Post* [database online] available from http://www.washingtonpost.com/ wp-dyn/content/article/2006/10/19/AR2006101901621.html;Internet; accessed July 20, 2013.

Miller, S.A. "Scandal-stained Rangel Quits Post." *New York Post* [database online] available from http://www.nypost.com/p/news/national/just_don_o4LUuhrmDip5pcpADAecPK; Internet; accessed August 6, 2013.

Miller, S.A. "Impeached Judge Samuel B. Kent Tenders His Resignation." *The Washington Times* [database online] available from http://www.washingtontimes.com/ news/2009/jun/ 27/impeached-judge-tenders-his-resignation; Internet; accessed July 10, 2011.

Montgomery, David . "The Sex Scandal From Outer Space." *The Washington Post* [database online] available from http://www.washingtonpost.com/wp-dyn/articles/ A6778-2004Jun25_2.html; Internet; accessed July 18, 2013.

Montopoli, Brian. "GOP Congressman Christopher Lee Resigns Over Craigslist Scandal." *CBS News* [database online] available from http://www.cbsnews.com2012-503544_162-20031264.html; Internet; accessed December 14, 2011.

Montopoli, Brian. "GOP Congressman Christopher Lee Resigns Over Craigslist Scandal." *CBS News* [database online] available from http://www.cbsnews.com/ 2101-503544_162-20031264.html; Internet; accessed December 14, 2011.

Morrison, Jane. "Senate Missteps No Longer Dog Veterinarian John Ensign." *Las Vegas Review Journal* [database online] available from http://www.reviewjournal.com/jane-ann-morrison/senate-missteps-no-longer-dog-veterinarian-john-ensign; Internet; accessed July 12, 2013.

Murphy, Patricia. "Senate Removes Judge G. Thomas Porteous, Jr. Following Impeachment Trial." *Politics Daily* [database online] available from http://www.politicsdaily.com/2010/ 12/08/senate-impeaches-judge-thomas-porteous-removes- him-from-office/; Internet; accessed August 6, 2013.

Ngo, Emily. "Huma Abedin to Join Husband Anthony Weiner's Campaign for NYC Mayor." *Huffington Post* (New York) [database online] available from www.huffingtonpost.com/ 2013/06/17/huma-albedin-to-join-husband-anthony-weiner's-campaign-for-nyc-myor_n_3451562; Internet; accessed July 8, 2013.

O'Connor, Maureen. "Married GOP Congressman Sent Sexy Pictures to Craigslist Babe." *Gawker* [database online] available from http:gawker.com/5755071/married-gop-congressman-sent-secy-pictures-to-craigslist-babe; Internet; accessed December 18, 2011.

O'Connor, Maureen. "Congressman Chris Lee Resigns Following Gawker Revelation." *Gawker* [database online] available from http://gawker.com/575677/craiglist-congressman-re-signs; Internet; accessed December 14, 2011.

O'Keefe, Ed. "The Rise and Fall of Jesse Jackson Jr." *The Washington Post* [database online] available from http://www.washingtonpost.com/blogs/the-fix/wp/2013/02/20/the-rise-and-fall-of-jesse-jackson-jr/; Internet; accessed August 22, 2013.

Olsen, Lise. "Details Emerge in Judge Kent Scandal." *Houston Chronicle* [database online] available from http://www.chron.com/news/houston-texas/article/Details-emerge-in-judge-Kent-scandal; Internet; accessed December 14, 2011.

Oppel, Jr. Richard. "Employees' Retirement Plan Is a Victim as Enron Tumbles." *The New York Times* [database online] available from http://www.nytimes.com/2001/11/22/business/employees-retirement-plan-is-a-victim-as-enron-tumbles.html; accessed August 14, 2013.

Overby, Peter. "Rep. Jefferson Indicted on Fraud, Bribery Counts." *National Public Radio* [database online] available from http://www.npr.org/templates/story/story.php?storyId=10712500; Internet; accessed August 17, 2013.

Palmeri, Tara and Josh Saul. "Weiner Flips Out In Defeat." *New York Post* [database online] available from http://nypost.com/2013/09/11/sext-gal-crashes-weiners-party/; Internet; accessed September 25, 2013.

Partington, Richard. "The Enron Cast: Where Are They Now?" *Financial News* [database online] available from http://www.efinancialnews.com/story/2011-12-01/enron-ten-years-on-where-they-are-now?ea9c8a2de0ee111045601ab04d673622; Internet; accessed August 14, 2013.

Pear, Robert. "Inquiries on Gun and Ousters Focus on Health Dept. Official." *New York Times* [database online] available from http://www.nytimes.com/2002/11/13/ politics/13REHN.html;Internet; accessed August 15, 2013.

Perel, David. "John Edwards Hiding in the Bathroom." *Newsweek* [database online] available from htttp://2010.newsweek.com/top-10/sex-scandal-details/john-edwards-hiding-in-the-bathroom; Internet; accessed December 14, 2011.

Pergram, Chad. "Indiana Rep. Mark Souder Resigns After Affair With Staffer." *Fox News* [database online] available from http://www.foxnews.com/politics/2010/05/18; Internet; accessed December 10, 2011.

Peterson, Kim. "Real Cost of US War With Iraq: $1.7 Trillion." *MSN Money* [database online] available from http://money.msn.com/now/post.aspx?post=c6dd9699-4865-4242-852e-0773529464fc%20; Internet; accessed August 27, 2013.

Phillip, Abby. "Weiner Falls Hard in Latest Poll." *ABC News* [database online] available from http://abcnews.go.com/m/blogEntry?   id=19808987& ref=https%3A%2F%2Fwww.google.com%2F; Internet; accessed July 31, 2013.

Pope, Charles and Janie Har. "Rep. David Wu Announces He Will Resign After Accusations of Sexual Misconduct." *The Oregonian* [database online] available from http://www.oregonlive.com/politics/index.ssf/2011/07/rep_david_wu_resigns.html; Internet; accessed December 14, 2013.

Pope, Charles. "Sources: Young Woman Accuses Oregon Rep. David Wu of Aggressive, Unwanted Sexual Encounter." *The Oregonian* [database online] available from http://www.oregonlive.com/politics/index.ssf/2011/07/rep_david_wu_accussed_of_aggres.html; Internet; accessed December 14, 2013.

Risen, James and Eric Lichtbau. "Bush Lets U.S. Spy on Callers Without Courts." *The New York Times* [database online] available from http://www.nytimes.com/2005/12/16/politics/16program.html?pagewanted=all&_r=0; Internet; accessed August 28, 2013.

Rogers, Phil. "Sandi Jackson Pleads Guilty To Tax Fraud." *NBC Chicago* [database online] available from http://www.nbcchicago.com/blogs/ward-room/Sandi-Jackson-Jesse-Jackson-Jr-Plea-192091691.html; Internet; February 20, 2013.

Ross, Brian and Richard Esposito. "Foggo Out at CIA." *ABC News* [database online] available from http://abcnews.go.com/US/Investigation/story?id=1938864&page=1;Internet; accessed August 7, 2013.

Rudin, Ken. "Sanford The Latest In A Series Of Political Sex Scandals." *NPR* [database online] available from http://www.npr.org/blogs/politicaljunkie/2009/06/sanford_just_the _latest_sex_sc.html; Internet; accessed July 20, 2013.

Ruggeri, Amanda. "Sex Scandal Fails Florida Democrat in Former Mark Foley District." *U.S. News and World Report* [database online] available from http://www.usnews.com/news/campaign-2008/articles/2008/11/04/ sex-scandal- fells-florida-democrat-in-former-mark-foley-district; Internet; accessed December 17, 2011.

Russel, Chris. "Woman Sues Ohio Candidate for Congress Alleging Harassment." *The Columbus Dispatch* [database online] available from www.dispatch.com/content/stories/local/2010/10/01/woman-sues-ohio-candidate-alleges-groping.html; Internet; accessed December 15, 2011.

Rutenberg, Jim and Scott Shane. "Libby Pays Fine; Judge Poses Probation Query." *The New York Times* [database online] available from http://www.nytimes.com/2007/07/06/washington/06libby.html?_r=1&oref=slogin; Internet; accessed August 5, 2013.

Sarvay, Scott. "Tracy Jackson Resigns From Congressional Staff." *Indiana News Center* [database online] available from http://www.indiananewscenter.com/news/local/ 94293449.html; Internet; accessed December 12, 2010.

Saul, Michael Howard. "Weiner Drops To Fourth In Poll." *Wall Street Journal* [database online] available from http://online.wsj.com/article SB10001424127887324354704578636532483079010?mg=reno64-wsj,%20July%2030,%202013.html?dsk=y; Internet; accessed July 31, 2013.

Savage, Charlie. "No Charges for Ex-Head of Housing Under Bush." *New York Times* [database online] available from http://www.nytimes.com/2010/05/04/ us/politics/04jackson.html?_r=0; Internet; accessed August 7, 2013.

Savage, Charlie and James Risen. "Federal Judge Finds N.S.A. Wiretaps Were Illegal." *The New York Times* [database online] available from http://www.nytimes.com/2010/04/01/us/01nsa.html; Internet; accessed August 28, 2013.

Schmidt, Richard B. "Ex-GOP Lobbyist Abramoff Sentenced to 4 Years in Prison." *Los Angeles Times* [database online] available from http://articles.latimes.com/ 2008/sep/05/nation/na-abramoff5; Internet; accessed August 6, 2013.

Schmidt, Susan and James V. Grimaldi. "Abramoff Pleads Guilty to 3 Counts." *The Washington Post* [database online] available from http://www.washingtonpost.com/wp-dyn/content/article/2006/01/03/AR2006010300474.html; Internet; accessed August 6, 2013.

Schmidt, Susan. "Republican With Links to Abramoff Is Sentenced." *The Washington Post* [database online] available from http://www.washingtonpost.com/wp-dyn/content/ article/2007/12/14/AR2007121402008.html; Internet; accessed August 6, 2013.

Schmidt, Susan. "Official in Abramoff Case Sentenced to 18 Months." *The Washington Post* [database online] available from http://www.washingtonpost.com/wp-dyn/content/ article/2006/10/27/AR2006102700486.html; Internet; accessed August 6, 2013.

Schouten, Fredreka. "Ex-Rep. Jesse Jackson Jr. Gets 30 Months in Prison." *USA Today* [database online] available from http://www.usatday.com/story/news/politics/2013/08/14/ jesse-jackson-sentenced-sandi-jackson-misusing-campaign-funds/2650453/; Internet; accessed August 22, 2013.

Schwartz, Rhonda, Brian Ross and Chris Francescani. "Edwards Admits Sexual Affair; Lied as Presidential Candidate." *ABC News* [database online] available fromhttp://abcnews.go.com/Blotter/story?id=5441195; Internet; accessed June 15, 2013.

Schwartz, Emma, Rhonda Schwartz and Vic Walter." Congressman's $121,000 Payoff to Alleged Mistress." *ABC News* [database online] available from http://www.abcnews.go.com/Blotter/Politics/story?id=5997043&page=1; Internet; accessed December 14, 2011.

Schwartz, Emma. "Rep. Mahoney Takes 'Full Responsibility' But Doesn't Admit Affair." *ABC News* [database online] available from http://abcnews.go.com/Blotter/Politics/story?id=6030518&page=1; Internet; accessed December 13, 2011.

Schwartz, Emma. "Pelosi Calls for Investigation Into Mahoney." *ABC News* [database online] available from http://abcnews.go.com/Blotter/story?id=6025230&page=1#.UeSRSBafemE; Internet; accessed December 20, 2011.

Schwartz, Emma. "FBI Reported to Begin Probe of Florida Congressman." *ABC News* [databaseonline] available from http://abcnews.go.com/Blotter/Politics/story?id=6034123& page=1; Internet; accessed December 20, 2011.

Schwartz, Emma. "Did Mahoney Help Second Alleged Mistress Win Federal Grant?." *ABC News* [database online] available from http://abcnews.go.com/Blotter/ story?id=6040580& page=1; Internet; accessed December14, 2011.

Schwartz, Emma and Vic Walter. "Congressman Mahoney Admits to Multiple Affairs." *ABC News* [database online] available from http:// abcnews.go.com/Blotter/ Politics/story?id=6058992&page=1; Internet; accessed December 20, 2011.

Schteir, Rachel. "Former Bush Aide Charged in Felony Theft." *Slate Magazine* [database online] available from http://www.slate.com/articles/news_and_politics/this_just_in/2006/ 03/former_bush_aide_charged_in_felony_theft.html;Internet; accessed August 8, 2013.

Sealey, Geraldine. "Condit Affair: The Latest D.C. Sex Scandal." *ABC News* [database online] available from http://abcnews.go.com/Politics/story?id=121497&page=2; Internet; accessed July 22, 2013.

Serrano, Richard A., Ralph Vartabedian and Sam Howe Verhovek. "Outrage, Questions Persist on Firing of U.S. Attorneys." *The Seattle Times* [database online] available from http:// seattletimes.com/html/nationworld/2003613762_attorneys12.html; Internet; accessed August 20, 2013.

Shakir, Faiz. "23 Administration Officials Involved in Plame Affair." *ThinkProgress* [database online] available from http://thinkprogress.org/report/leak-scandal/; Internet; accessed August 5, 2013.

Shear, Michael D. and Chris L. Jenkins. "Va. Legislator Ends Bid for 3rd Term." *The Washington Post* [database online] available from http://www.washingtonpost.com/wp-dyn/articles/ A47194-2004Aug30.html; Internet; accessed July 20, 2013.

Sheehy, Gail and Judy Bachrach. "Don't Ask... Don't Email." *Vanity Fair* [database online] available from http://www.vanityfair.com/politics/features/2007/01/foley200701; Internet; accessed July 15, 2011.

Shenon, Philip. "Ney Is Sentenced to 30 Months in Prison." *The New York Times* [database online] available from http://www.nytimes.com/2007/01/19/washington/19cnd-ney.html; Internet; accessed August 6, 2013.

Skiba, Katherine. "Both Jacksons Get Prison Terms; He'll Serve First." *Chicago Tribune* [database online] available from http://articles.chicagotribune.com/2013-08-14/news/ chi-jesse-jackson-jr-sentence-20130814_1_both-jacksons-sandi-jackson-jackson-jr; Internet; accessed August 22, 2013.

Smith, R. Jeffrey. "In New Memoir, Bush Makes Clear He Approved Use of Waterboarding." *The Washington Post* [database online] available from http://www.washingtonpost.com/ wp-dyn/content/article/2010/11/03/AR2010110308082.html?hpid=topnews; Internet; accessed August 28, 2013.

Smith, Jeffrey. "Tom DeLay, Former U.S. House Leader, Sentenced to 3 Years in Prison." *The Washington Post* [database online] available from http://www.washingtonpost.com/wp-dyn/ content/article/2011/01/10/AR2011011000557.html; Internet; January 10, 2011.

Smith, Jeffrey and Christopher Lee, "DeLay Booked in Houston on Money-Laundering, Conspiracy Charges." *The Washington Post* [database online] available from http:// www.washingtonpost.com/wp-dyn/content/article/2005/10/20/ AR2005102000248.html; Internet; accessed August 6, 2013.

Squiteri, Tom. "Traficant Expelled After Final Jabs in House." *USA Today* [database online] available from http://usatoday30.usatoday.com/news/washington/legislative/house/2002-07-24-traficant_x.htm; Internet; accessed August 20, 2013.

Standora, Leo, David Saltonstall and Kenneth R. Bazinet, "Kerik Bows Out: Nanny Flap Ruins Ex-N.Y.C. Top Cop's Bid To Head Homeland Security." *Daily News* [database online] available from http://www.nydailynews.com/news/kerik-bows-nanny-flap-ruins-ex-n-y-top-bid-head-homeland-security-article-1.340785; Internet; accessed August 14, 2013.

Stanley, Paul. "David Wu Faced Pressure to Resign After Sex Scandal." *Christian Post* [database online] available from http://www.christianpost.com/news/david-wu-faced-pressure-to-resign-after-sex-scandal; Internet; accessed December 14, 2011.

Stanley, Paul. "Democrat Congressman David Wu Embroiled in Sex Scandal." *Christian Post* [database online] available from http://www.christianpost.com/ news/congressman-david-wu-at-center-of-dc-scandal; Internet; accessed December 14, 2011.

Stanley, Paul. "David Wu Faced Pressure to Resign After Sex Scandal." *Christian Post* [database online] available from http://www.christianpost.com/news/david-wu-faced-pressure-to-resign-after-sex-scandal; Internet; accessed December 14, 2011.

Stern, Marcus. "Disgraced Senior CIA Official Heads to Prison Still Claiming He's a Patriot." *ProPublica* [database online] available from http://www.propublica.org/article/ disgraced-senior-cia-official-heads-to-prison-still-claiming-hes-a-patriot; Internet; accessed August 7, 2013.

Steer, Jen. "Auto Dealer Tom Ganley Indicted on Sex, Kidnapping Charges." *News Net* [database online] available from http:www/newsnet5.com/ dpp/news/local_news/ cleveland_metro/auto-dealer-tom-ganley-indicted-on-sex-kidnapping-charges; Internet; accessed December 15, 2011.

Stout, David. "Ex-Louisiana Congressman Sentenced to 13 Years." *The New York Times* [database online] available from http://www.nytimes.com/2009/11/14/us/politics/14jefferson.html; accessed August 17, 2013.

Stride, Megan. "Abramoff Lobbyist Sentenced To 20 Months." *Law 360* [database online] available from http://www.law360.com/articles/225511/abramoff-lobbyist-sentenced-to-20-months; Internet; accessed August 7, 2013.

Stritof, Sherri and Bob Stritof. "John and Elizabeth Edwards Marriage Profile." *About Marriage* [database online] available from http://marriage.about.com/od/celebritymarriages/p/ johnedwards.htm; Internet; accessed July 12, 2013.

Thomson, Gus. "Ex-Congressman John Doolittle Steps Into New Lobbying Role." *Auburn Journal* [database online] available from http://www.auburnjournal.com/article/ex-congressman-john-doolittle-steps-new-lobbying-role; Internet; accessed August 15, 2013.

Toppo, Greg. "Education Dept. Paid Commentator to Promote Law." *USA Today* [database online] available from http://usatoday30.usatoday.com/news/washington/2005-01-06-williams-whitehouse_x.htm; Internet; accessed August 24, 2013.

Turner, Trish. "Ensign Affair Referred o DOJ & FEC - - Torrid Affair Detailed." *Fox News* [database online] available from http://politics.blogs.foxnews.com/2011/05/12/ ensign-affair-referred-doj-fec-torrid-affair-detailed; Internet; accessed July 12, 2013.

Turner, Trish. "Watchdog Group Calls For Ethics Review of Fossella." *Fox News* [database online] available from http://www.foxnews.com/story/0,2933,356632,00.html; Internet; accessed December 14, 2013.

U.S. Congress. House of Representatives Government Reform Committee. "Staff Report"[database online] available from http://oversight-archive.waxman.house.gov/abramoff/docs/abramoff.pdf; Internet; accessed August 6, 2013.

United States Congress. Senate. U.S. Select Committee on Ethics. "Gifts." United States Senate [database online] available from http://www.ethics.senate.gov/public/index.cfm/gifts; Internet; accessed August 19, 2013.

Warner, Erica. "Doolittle Linked To 2 Bribery Scandals." *USA Today* [database online] available from http://usatoday30.usatoday.com/news/washington/2007-07-06-858095226_x.htm; Internet; accessed August 15, 2013.

Walter, Vic and Justin Rood. "No State Charges In Foley Case." *ABC News* [database online] available from http://abcnews.go.com/Blotter/story?id=5840934&page=1; Internet; accessed December 10, 2011.

Walter, Vic and Krista Kjellman. "DHS Official Makes Plea Deal In Online Sex Scandal." *ABC News [database online] available from* http://abcnews.go.com/ blogs/headlines/2006/09/dhs_official_ma/; Internet; accessed December 15, 2011.

Waterhouse, Mike. "Criminal Charges Dropped Against Tom Ganley After Alleged Victim Won't Continue With Trial." *News Net* [database online] available from http://www.newsnet5.com/dpp/news/local_news/cleveland_metro/criminal-charges-dropped-against-tom-ganley-after-alleged-victim-wont-continue-with-trial; Internet; accessed July 10, 2013.

Way, Jo Anne. "Sex Scandal Photos: Laura Fay and Vito Fossella Affair Exposed." *The National Ledger* [database online] available from http://www.nationalledger.com/pop-culture-news/sex-scandal-photos-laura-fay--109931.stml; Internet; accessed December 14, 2011.

Weiner, Eric. "Prosecutors: Congressman Took $400K in Bribes." *National Public Radio* [database online] available from http://www.npr.org/templates/story/story.php?storyId= 10712500; Internet; accessed August 17, 2013.

Weiner, Rachel. "Jesse Jackson Jr. Undergoing Treatment for Bipolar Disorder." *The Washington Post* [database online] available from http://www.washingtonpost.com/ blogs/the-fix/post/jesse-jackson-jr-undergoing-treatment-for-bipolar-disorder/2012/08/13/e2dabca6-e575-11e1-8741-940e3f6dbf48_blog.html; Internet; accessed August 21, 2013.

Wilkens, John. "'Duke' Cunningham A Free Man Today." *U-T San Diego* [database online] available from http://www.utsandiego.com/news/2013/Jun/04/duke-cunningham-free-mantoday/; Internet; accessed August 17, 2013.

Williamson, Elizabeth. "Interior Dept. Official Facing Scrutiny Resigns." *The Washington Post* [database online] available from http://www.washingtonpost.com/wp-dyn/content/article/2007/05/01/AR2007050101920.html; Internet; accessed August 7, 2013.

Willhoit, Dana. "5 Years in Prison For Porn E-Mails." *The Ledger* [database online] available from http://www.theledger.com; Internet; accessed December 15, 2011.

Wing, Nick. "Tom Ganley Accused of Sexually Assaulting Woman He Met At Tea Party Rally," *Huffington Post* [database online] available from http://www.huffingtonpost.com/2010/10/01/tom-ganley-sexual-assualt_n_746858.html?v; Internet; accessed December 14, 2011.

Woods, Ashley. "Kwame Kilpatrick 28-Year Prison Sentence For Corruption Is Long, But Not 'Extreme': Experts." *Huffington Post* [database online] available fromhttp://www.huffingtonpost.com/2013/10/11/kwame- kilpatrick-sentence-jail-corruption_ n_4080 171.html; Internet; accessed October 13, 2013.

Zagorin, Adam. "Why Were These U.S. Attorneys Fired?," *TIME* [database online] available from http://www.time.com/time/nation/article/0,8599,1597085,00.html; Internet; accessed August 20, 2013.

ARTICLES WITHOUT AN AUTHOR

"A Guide To The Abramoff and DeLay Investigations." *The New York Times* [database online] available from http://graphics8.nytimes.com/packages/pdf/politics/04cnd-marsh3.pdf; Internet; accessed August 6, 2013.

"A Guide to the Memos on Torture." *The New York Times* [database online] available from http://www.nytimes.com/ref/international/24MEMO-GUIDE.html; Internet; accessed August 14, 2013.

"A Look At Those Involved In The Enron Scandal." *USA Today* [database online] available from http://usatoday30.usatoday.com/money/industries/energy/2005-12-28-enron-participants_x.htm; Internet; accessed August 14, 2013.

"About David Vitter." U.S. Senate [database online] available from http://www.vitter.senate.gov/ about-david; Internet; accessed July 16, 2013.

"About the Office of the Commissioner." United States Health and Human Services, The Food and Drug Administration [database online] available from http://www.fda.gov/ AboutFDA/CentersOffices/oc/default.htm; Internet; accessed August 8, 2013.

"ACLU Backs Sen. Craig, Argues Sex in Public Bathroom Stalls is Private." *Fox News* [database online] available from http://www.foxnews.com/story/0,2933,323094,00.html #ixzz2ZKQ9NRFP and http://www.foxnews.com/story/0,2933,323094,00.html; Internet; accessed December 14, 2013.

"Anthony Weiner to Seek Treatment." *Huffington Post* [database online] available from www.huffingtonpost.com/2011/06/11/anthony-weiner-treatment_n_875422.html; Internet; accessed July 8, 2013.

"Arizona Rep. Rick Renzi Pleads Not Guilty in Land Deal Fraud Case." *Fox News* [database online] available from http://www.foxnews.com/story/0,2933,334891,00.html; Internet; accessed August 15, 2013.

"Berger to Pay $50,000 Fine for Taking Papers." *The New York Times* [database online] available from http://www.nytimes.com/2005/09/08/politics/08wire-berger.html?_r=0; Internet; accessed August 2013.

"Berkeley Law - Faculty Profiles: John Yoo," The University of California Berkley [database online] available from http://www.law.berkeley.edu/php-programs/facultyfacultyProfile.php?facID=235; Internet; accessed August 14, 2013.

"Bush Attorney General Pick is Alberto Gonzales." *CNN.com* [database online] available from http://www.cnn.com/2004/ALLPOLITICS/11/10/bush.cabinet/; Internet; accessed August 20, 2013.

"Bill Janklow, Former S.D. Governor and Congressman, Dies." *USA Today* [database online] available from http://usatoday30.usatoday.com/news/washington/story/2012-01-12/obit-bill-janklow/52517922/1; Internet; accessed August 18, 2013.

"Bush Advisor Claude Allen Arrested for Shoplifting Scam." YouTube [database online] available from http://www.youtube.com/watch?v=CamqKMLa-pk; Internet; accessed August 8, 2013.

"Bush Attorney General Pick is Alberto Gonzales." *CNN* [database online] available from http://www.cnn.com/2004/ALLPOLITICS/11/10/bush.cabinet/; Internet; accessed August 20, 2013.

"Bush and Iraq: Follow the Yellow Cake Road." *TIME* [database online] available from http://www.time.com/time/world/article/0,8599,463779,00.html; Internet; accessedAugust 27, 2013.

"Bush Says He Signed NSA Wiretap Order." *CNN* [database online] available from http://www.cnn.com/2005/POLITICS/12/17/bush.nsa/; Internet; accessed August 28, 2013.

"California: Court Throws Out Suit Against Bush Lawyer." *The New York Times* [database online] available from http://www.nytimes.com/2012/05/03/us/politics/ lawsuit-against-john-yoo-is-thrown-out.html; Internet; accessed August 14, 2013.

"California Rep. John Doolittle Announces Retirement Amid Investigation." *Fox News* [database online] available from http://www.foxnews.com/story/2008/01/10/ california-rep-john-doolittle-announces-retirement-amid-investigation/,January 10, 2008, accessed August 15, 2013.

"Chandra Levy Murder Case Gets Fresh Look In Closed Door Meetings." *Huffington Post* [database online] available from http://www.huffingtonpost.com/2013/01/24/chandralevy-murder-case-meetings_n_2542007.html; Internet; accessed July 22, 2013.

"Chandra Levy's Remains Found in D.C. Park." *CNN* [database online] available from http://archives.cnn.com/2002/US/05/22/levy.body/; Internet; accessed July 2013.

"Chandra Levy's Parents Have Doubts That Convicted Killer Ingmar Guandique Murdered Their Daughter." *Huffington Post* [database online] available from http://www.huffingtonpost.com/2013/04/20/chandra-levy-killer-ingmar-guandique-murder_n_3104657.html; Internet; accessed July 22, 2013.

"Claude Alexander Allen, III In Court." YouTube [database online] available from http://www.youtube.com/watch?v=7yWZVk6jC94; Internet; accessed August 8, 2013.

"Clinton Adviser Berger Cops Plea." *CBS News* [database online] available from http://www.cbsnews.com/2100-250_162-684458.html; Internet; accessed August 8, 2013.

Collins, Dan. "3rd Columnist On Bush Payroll." *CBS News* [database online] available from http://www.cbsnews.com/2100-250_162-669432.html; Internet; accessed August 24, 2013.

"Congressman Apologizes For Affair in TV Ad." *NBC News* [database online] available from http://www.nbcnews.com/id/15132240/ns/politics/t/ congressman-apologizes-affair-tv-ad/; Internet; accessed July 20, 2013.

"Congress Censures Charlie Rangel." *ABC News* [database online] available from http://abcnews.go.com/Politics/video/congress-censures-charlie-rangel-12299325; Internet; accessed August 6, 2013.

"Congressman Quits In Disgrace." *ABC News* [database online] available from http://abcnews.go.com/WNT/video?id=2509590; Internet; accessed July 17, 2013.

"Congressman Resigns After Bribery Plea." *CNN* [database online] available from http://www.cnn.com/2005/POLITICS/11/28/cunningham/; Internet; accessed August 17, 2013.

"Congressman's $121,000 Payoff to Alleged Mistress." *ABC News* [database online] available from http://abcnews.go.com/Blotter/story?id=5997043&page=1; Internet; accessed December 14, 2011.

"Craig Decides to Stay on as GOP Senator." *ABC News* [database online] available from http://abcnews.go.com/blogs/politics/2007/10/judge-craigs-gu/; Internet; accessed December 5, 2011.

"Craigslist Congressman Resigns." *CNN News* [database online] available from http://www.cnn.com/video/data/2.0/video/bestoftv/2011/02/09/exp.jk.christopher.lee.resigns.chh.html; Internet; accessed July 9, 2013.

"Cynthia Ann McKinney." allthingscynthiamckinney.com [database online] available from http://archives.allthingscynthiamckinney.com/mckinney.house.gov/bio.htm; Internet; accessed August16, 2013.

"David Petraeus Apologizes for Career-Ending Affair With Biographer Paula Broadwell." *CBS News* [database online] available from http:// www.cbsnews.com/8301-201_162-57576484/david-petraeus-apologizes-for-career-ending-affair-with-biographer-paula-broadwell/; Internet; accessed July 22, 2013.

"David Petraeus Affair Began After He Left Army: Former Spokesman." *Huffington Post* [database online] available from http://www.huffingtonpost.com/2012/11/12/david-petraeus-affair_n_2116790.html; Internet; accessed July 22, 2013.

"DHS Official Accused Of Sending Porn To A Minor." *ABC News* [database online] available from http://abcnews.go.com/US/story?id=1806674; Internet; accessed December 15, 2011.

"Don Sherwood Tries To Shake Scandal in Pennsylvania." Fox News [database online] available from http://www.foxnews.com/story/0,2933,199050,00.html; Internet; accessed July 20, 2013.

"Draft GAO Report Criticizes Former HHS Inspector General Rehnquist." Kaiser Health News[database online] available from http://www.kaiserhealthnews.org/daily-reports/2003/june/06/dr00018130.aspx; Internet; accessed August 15, 2013.

"Embattled Interior Official Julie MacDonald Resigns In Wake of Inspector General Report." Environmental News Network [database online] available from http://www.enn.com/press_releases/1945; Internet; accessed August 7, 2013.

"Embattled FDA Chief Lester Crawford Resigns." *NBC News* [database online] available from http://www.nbcnews.com/id/9455426/ns/health-health_care/t/embattled-fda-chief-lester-crawford-resigns/#.UgVXKBafemE; Internet; accessed August 8, 2013.

"Enron Founder Ken Lay Dies of Heart Disease." *NBC News* [database online] available from http://www.nbcnews.com/id/13715925/ns/business-corporate_scandals/t/enron-founder-ken-lay-dies-heart-disease/#.UgvWShafemE; Internet; accessed August 14, 2013.

"Environmental Activist Federici Pleads Guilty to Tax Evasion in Abramoff Probe." *Fox News* [database online] available from http://www.foxnews.com/story/2007/06/08/ environmental-activist-federici-pleads-guilty-to-tax-evasion-in-abramoff-probe/; Internet; accessed August 6, 2013.

"Ethics Committee Faults Torricelli on Gift Violations." *The New York Times* [database online] available from http://www.nytimes.com/2002/07/31/nyregion/ethics-committee-faults-torricelli-on-gift-violations.html?pagewanted=all&src=pm; Internet; accessed August 19, 2013.

"Ethics Panel Urges Probe Ensign." *ABC News* [database online] available from http://abcnews.go.com/Politics/ethics-panel-urges-probe-ensign/storyid=13593947; Internet; accessed December 15, 2011.

"Ex-Aide Gets Probation in Lobbying Scandal." *The New York Times* [database online] available from http://www.nytimes.com/2011/04/08/us/politics/08brfs Washington.html_r=0&gwh=C78F3C581F32158ECE9642589858F0E7; Internet; accessed August 6, 2013.

"Ex-Congressman Begins Prison Sentence." *NBC News* [database online] available from http://www.nbcnews.com/id/11655893/print/1/displaymode/1098; Internet; accessed August 2013.

"Ex-FDA Chief Pleads Guilty to Conflict of Interest." *NBC News* [database online] available from http://www.nbcnews.com/id/15291650/ns/health-health_care/t/ex-fda-chief-pleads-guilty-conflict-interest/; Internet; accessed August 8, 2013.

"Ex-Rep. David Dreier Finds a New Role with Annenberg Group." *Los Angeles Times* [database online] available from http://articles.latimes.com/2013/feb/20/local/la-me-pc-rep-david-dreier-20130220; Internet; accessed July 20, 2013.

"Ex Senator Larry Craig Loses Last Court Battle Over Bathroom Sex Sting." *The Raw Story* [database online] available from http://www.rawstory.com/rs/2013/03/29/ ex-sen-larry-craig-loses-last-court-battle-over-bathroom-sex-sting/; Internet; accessed July 17, 2013.

"Ex-Wife Of GOP Candidate Alleged Sex-Club Forays." CNN [database online] available from http://www.cnn.com/2004/ALLPOLITICS/06/22/ryan.divorce/; Internet; accessed July 18, 2013.

"Ex-White House Aide Arrested in Alleged Refund Scam." CNN.com [database online] available from http://www.cnn.com/2006/US/03/11/claude.allen.arrest/; Internet; accessed August 8, 2013.

"Exclusive: Eric Massa on Glenn Beck." Fox News [database online] available from http://www.foxnews.com/story/0.2933.588685.00.html; Internet; accessed December 14, 2011.

"Family Affair." *New York Post* [database online] available from http://gothamist.com/2008/05/10/vito_fosella.r.php; Internet; accessed December 14, 2011.

"Farewell, Randall Tobias, the Man Who Turned His Wife's Suicide into a Sales Pitch for Prozac." *Information Liberation* [database online] available from http://www.informationliberation.com/?id=21807; Internet; accessed July 16, 2013.

"FBI Raided Virginia Home of Rep. John Doolittle." *Fox News* [database online] available from http://www.foxnews.com/story/2007/04/18/fbi-raided-virginia-home-rep-john-doolittle/; Internet; accessed August 15, 2013.

"Feds Suspend Official Facing Child Sex Charges." *CNN* [database online] available from http://www.cnn.com/2006/LAW/04/05/homeland.arrest/index.html?iref=allsearch; Internet; accessed December 15, 2011.

"Florida Police: Woman Known As DC Madam Commits Suicide in Apparent Hanging." *Fox News* [database online] available from http://www.foxnews.com/story/2008/05/01/ florida-police-woman-known-as-dc-madam-commits-suicide-in-apparent-hanging/; Internet; accessed July 16, 2013.

"Former Abramoff Colleague Kevin Ring Sentenced to 20 Months in Prison for Conspiracy, Honest Services Fraud and Payment of Gratuities Related to Illegal Lobbying Scheme." The United States Department of Justice [database online] available from http://www.justice.gov/opa/pr/2011/October/11-crm-1413.html; Internet; accessed August 6, 2013.

"Former Clinton Aide Pleads Guilty to Taking Classified Docs." *Fox News* [database online] available from http://www.foxnews.com/story/2005/04/03/former-clinton-aide-pleads-guilty-to-taking-classified-docs/; Internet; accessed August 8, 2013.

"Former FDA Chief Crawford Gets Supervised Probation, Fine for Stock Scandal." *Fox News* [database online] available from http://www.foxnews.com/story/2007/02/27/former-fda-chief-crawford-gets-supervised-probation-fine-for-stock-scandal/; Internet; accessed August 2013.

"Former NY Rep. Pleads Guilty to DUI." *Fox News* [database online] available from http://www.foxnews.com/wires/2009Apr13/0,4670,FossellaPlea,00.html; Internet; accessed December 14, 2011.

"Former Rep. Mark Foley Leaves DC In Hurry After E-Mail Scandal." *Fox News* [database online] available from http://www.foxnews.com/story/0,2933,216839,00.html; Internet; accessed December 10, 2011.

"Former U.S. Sen. Larry Craig Addresses University of Idaho Graduates." *Oregon Live* [database online] available from http://www.oregonlive.com/pacific-northwest-news/index.ssf/2013/05/former_us_sen_larry_craig_addr.html; Internet; accessed July 17, 2013.

"Frank Lautenberg Dead: New Jersey Senator Dies At 89." *Huffington Post* [database online] available from http://www.huffingtonpost.com/2013/06/03/frank-lautenberg-dead-dies_n_3377916.html; Internet; accessed August 19, 2013.

"Ga. Congresswoman Scuffles With Capitol Police." *NBC News* [database online] available from http://www.nbcnews.com/id/12070031/ns/politics/t/ga-congresswoman-scuffles-capitol-police/#.Ug67YhafemE; Internet; accessed August 16, 2013.

"Gaithersburg Murder Suspect Appears in Court." *NBC 4 Washington* [database online] available from http://www.nbcwashington.com/news/local/Gaithersburg-Murder-Suspect-Appears-in-Court-209168621.html, May 28, 2013, accessed August 8, 2013. "Georgia Rep. McKinney Blames Media for Losing Primary Runoff Election." *Fox News* [database online] available from http://www.foxnews.com/story/2006/08/09/georgia-rep-mckinney-blames-media-for-losing-primary-runoff-election/;Internet; accessed August 16, 2013.

"Guilty Verdict in Chandra Levy Murder Case." NBC News [database online] available from http://www.nbcnews.com/id/40317461/ns/us_news-_crime_and_courts/t/guilty-verdict-chandra-levy-murder-case/#.Ue1eDhafemE; Internet; accessed July 22, 2013.

"Hannity: Mark Foley Breaks His Silence." *Fox News* [database online] available from http://www.foxnews.com/on-air/hannity/transcript/hannity-mark-foley-breaks-his-silence; Internet; accessed July 10, 2011.

"House Approves Contempt Citations for Miers, Bolten," *Fox News* [database online] available from http://www.foxnews.com/story/2008/02/14/house-approves-contempt-citations-for-miers-bolten/; Internet; accessed August 20, 2013.

"House Leader: Ethics Panel Ends Mass Probe." *Fox News* [database online] available from http://foxnews.com/politics/2010/03/10/ethics-panel-ends-massa-probe-house-leader-says/; Internet; accessed December 12, 2011.

"House Votes For Probe of Foley Email Episode." *CNN* [database online] available from http://www.cnn.com/2006/WORLD/europe/09/29/friday/index.html?iref=allsearch; Internet; accessed December 14, 2013.

"How Vito Lied." *Daily News* [database online] available from http://www.gothamist.com/2008/05/10/vito_fossella_r.php; Internet; accessed December 14, 2011.

"H.Res. 1031." *OpenCongress* [database online] available from http://www.opencongress.org/bill/111-hr1031/text; Internet; accessed August 6, 2013.

"HUD Chief Resigns Amid Ethics Investigations." *CNN Politics.com* [database online] available from http://www.cnn.com/2008/POLITICS/03/31/hud.resignation/; Internet; accessed August 7, 2013.

"Hustler Says It Revealed Senator's Link To Escort Service." CNN [database online] available from http://www.cnn.com/2007/POLITICS/07/10/vitter.madam/ ndex.html?iref=allsearch; Internet; accessed July 13, 2013.

"Indiana Congressman Resigns After Admitting Affair." *CNN* [database online] available from http://news.blogs.cnn.com/2010/05/18/gop-aid-indiana-rep-mark-souder-to   resign/?iref=allsearch; Internet; accessed December 10, 2011.

"Indicted Rep. Rick Renzi Will Not Resign From Congress." *Fox News* [database online] available from http://www.foxnews.com/story/2008/02/25/indicted-rep-rick-renzi-will-not-resign-from-congress/; Internet; accessed August 15, 2013.

"Indictment Shows Six Charges Against Edwards." *The New York Times* [database online] available from http://www.nytimes.com/interactive/ 2011/06/04/us/politics/04edwards-text.html?ref=johnedwards&_r=0; Internet; accessed July 12, 2013.

"Interactive Timeline: Kwame Kilpatrick Corruption Case," *Detroit News* [database online] available from http://www.detroitnews.com/article/99999999/SPECIAL01/130226003; Internet; accessed August 24, 2013.

"Jack Abramoff Urges Ethics Reform In NCSL Speech." *Huffington Post* [database online] available from http://www.huffingtonpost.com/2012/08/09/ jack-abramoff-ethics-reform ncsl_n_1762154.html; Internet; accessed August 6, 2013.

"James Traficant Fast Facts." *CNN* [database online] available from http://www.cnn.com/2013/03/25/us/james-traficant-fast-facts; Internet; accessed August 20, 2013.

"Janet Rehnquist Resigns." *CBS News* [database online] available from http://www.cbsnews.com/ 2100-250_162-542782.html; Internet; accessed August 15, 2013.

"Janklow Charged With Second-Degree Manslaughter in Crash" *CNN* [database online] available from http://www.cnn.com/2003/ALLPOLITICS/08/29/janklow.charged/; Internet; accessed August 18, 2013.

"Jesse Jackson Jr. Investigation: Feds Target Congressman's Finances In New Probe." *Huffington Post* [database online] available from http://www.huffingtonpost.com/ 2012/10/13/jesse-jackson-jr-investig_n_1963714.html; Internet; accessed August 21, 2013.

"John Edwards Looking To Open New Law Firm." *CNN Politics Political Ticker* [database online] available from http://politicalticker.blogs.cnn.com/2013/06/05/john-edwards-looking-to-open-new-law-firm/; Internet; accessed July 12, 2013.

"John Ensigns Affair Prompts Resignation." *ABC News* [database online] available from http:// abcnews.go.com/GMA/video/john-ensigns-affair-prompts-resignation-13595686; Internet; accessed July 12, 2013.

"John Yoo, Former Justice Department Lawyer, Protected From Torture Lawsuit, Rules Appeals Court." *Huffington Post* [database online] available from http:// www.huffingtonpost.com/ 2012/05/02/john-yoo-torture-bush-administration-jose-padilla_n_1471587.html; Internet; accessed August 14, 2013.

"Judge Cops Plea To Elude Sex Crime Trial." *CBS News* [database online] available from http:/ /www.cbsnews.com/stories/2009/02/23/national/main4821904.shtml?tag=mncol;1st; Internet; accessed December 14, 2011.

"Key Players in the CIA Leak Investigation." *The Washington Post* [database online] available from http://www.washingtonpost.com/wp-srv/politics/special/plame/Plame_KeyPlayers .html; Internet; accessed August 5, 2013.

"Louisiana Voters Reject Rep. Jefferson." *Los Angeles Times* [database online] available from http://articles.latimes.com/2008/dec/07/nation/na-jefferson7; Internet; accessed August 17, 2013.

"Lurita Doan Finally Forced Out at GSA." *Politico* [database online] available from http:// www.politico.com/blogs/thecrypt/0408/Lurita_Doan_forced_out_at_GSA.html; Internet; accessed August 6, 2013.

"Memorandum for William J. Haynes II, General Counsel of the Department of Defense." The United States Department of Justice, Office of the Deputy Assistant Attorney General [database online] available from http://www.aclu.org/pdfs/safefree/yoo_army_ torture_memo.pdf; Internet; accessed August 14, 2013.

"Nevada Sen. Ensign Admits Affair." *CNN News* [database online] available from http:// www.cnn.com/2009/POLITICS/06/16/ensign.affair/index.ntml?iref=allsearch; Internet; accessed June 16, 2013.

"New York Congressman Apologizes for Drunk Driving Arrest." *Fox News* [database online] available from http://www.foxnews.com/story/2008/05/02/new-york-congressman-apologizes-for-drunk-driving-arrest/; Internet; accessed on December 11, 2011.

"Ohio Ex-Rep Traficant Loses New Bid for Congress." *Fox News* [database online] available from http://www.foxnews.com/politics/2010/11/02/ohio-ex-rep-traficant-loses-new-bid-congress/; Internet; accessed August 20, 2013.

"Ohio Rep. Traficant Indicted." *ABC News* [database online] available from http://abcnews.go.com/Politics/story?id=121699&page=1; Internet; accessed August 20, 2013.

"Police Close 'DC Madam Investigation, Confirmed She Died By Suicide." *Fox News* [database online] available from http://www.foxnews.com/story/0,2933,445538,00.html; Internet; accessed July 16, 2013.

"Priest Confesses: Had A 'Relationship' With Teenage Mark Foley." *ABC News* [database online] available from http://abcnews.go.com/blogs/headlines/2006/10/ priest_confesse/; Internet; accessed December 12, 2011.

"Prison Term for Fraud in Iraq." *The Los Angeles Times* [database online] available from http:// articles.latimes.com/2007/jan/30/nation/na-contractor30; Internet; accessed August 26, 2013.

"Questions About Souder Affair Surfaced in February." *Indiana News Center* [database online] available from http://www.indiananewscenter.com/news/local/94158474; Internet; accessed December 18, 2011.

"Rare House Censure Ends 2-Year Ordeal for Rangel House Censure Ends 2-Year Ordeal for Rangel House." *Public Broadcast System* [database online] available from http:// www.pbs.org/newshour/bb/politics/july-dec10/rangel_12-02.html; Internet; accessed August 6, 2013.

"Reign of Bush Fish and Wildlife Official Ends in Disgrace." *Environmental News Service* [database online] available from http://www.ens-newswire.com/ens/may2007/2007-05-01-03.asp; Internet; accessed August 7, 2013.

"Rep. Fossella Faces Calls to Resign After Admitting Secret Child." *Fox News* [database online] available from http://www.foxnews.com/story/2008/05/10/rep-fossella-faces-calls-to-resign-after-admitting-secret-child/#ixzz2Z8VenphWhttp://www.foxnews.com/story/0,2933,354869,00.html; Internet; accessed December 14, 2011.

"Rep. Fossella Sentenced to 5 Days for Drunk Driving." *Fox News* [database online] available from http://www.foxnews.com/wires/2008Oct17/0,4670,CongressmanDWI,00.html; Internet; accessed December 14, 2011.

"Rep. Dreier Won't Seek Reelection." *LA Observer* [database online] available from http://www.laobserved.com/archive/2012/02/rep_david_dreier_wont_see.php; Internet; accessed July 20, 2013.

"Rep. John Doolittle." *Govtrack.us* [database online] available from http://www.govtrack.us/congress/ members/john_doolittle/400113; Internet; accessed August 15, 2013.

"Renzi Resigns From All His House Committee Assignments." *Politico Live* [database online] available from http://www.politico.com/blogs/thecrypt/0407/Renzi_resigns_from_all_his_House_committee_assignments.html; accessed August 15, 2013.

"Representative David Dreier To Retire After 32 Years In Congress." *San Bernardino County Sentinel* [database online] available from http://sbsentinel.com/2012/03/representative-david-dreier-to-retire-after-32-years-in-congress/; Internet; accessed July 20, 2013.

"Rick Renzi, Former Congressman, Convicted On 17 Of 32 Counts In Corruption Case." *Huffington Post* [database online] available from http://www.huffingtonpost.com/ 2013/06/11/rick-renzi-convicted_n_3424403.html; Internet; accessed August 15, 2013.

"Rooting Out Corruption: A Look Back at the Jefferson Case." The Federal Bureau of Investigations [database online] available from http://www.fbi.gov/news/stories/2013/april/a-look-back-at-the-william-j.-jefferson-corruption-case; Internet; accessed August 17, 2013.

"Ryan Drops Out Of Senate Race In Illinois." *CNN* [database online] available from http://www.cnn.com/2004/ALLPOLITICS/06/25/il.ryan/; Internet; accessed July 18, 2013.

"Samuel R. "Sandy" Berger." Biography. *The Aspen Institute* [database online] available from http://www.aspeninstitute.org/policy-work/homeland-security/ahsg/members/berger; Internet; accessed August 8, 2013.

"Sandy Berger Fined $50,000 For Taking Documents." *CNN* [database online] available from http://www.cnn.com/2005/POLITICS/09/08/ berger.sentenced/; Internet; accessed August 8, 2013.

"Senate Ends Impeachment of Jailed Judge Following Resignation." *Fox News* [database online] available from http://www.foxnews.com/politics/2009/07/22/senate-ends-impeachment-jailed-judge-following-resignation; Internet; accessed July 10, 2011.

"Senate Ethics Committee Finds Senator Craig Acted Improperly in Airport Sex Sting." *Fox News* [database online] available from http:// www.foxnews.com/story/2008/02/14/ senate-ethics-committee-sen- larry-craig-acted-improperly-in-airport-sex-sting/#ixzz2ZKWxfR00; Internet; accessed July 11, 2013.

"Senate Race Sex Scandal." *The Smoking Gun* [database online] available from http://www.thesmokinggun.com/documents/crime/senate-race-sex-scandal; Internet; accessed December 14, 2011.

"Senator Caught In "D.C. Madam" Scandal." *CBS News* [database online] available from http:/ /www.cbsnews.com/2102-201_162-3037338.html?tag=contentMain;contentBody; Internet; accessed December 14, 2011.

"Senator Tied To Sex Ring allowed To Use Campaign Money For Legal Fees." *Fox News* [database online] available from http://www.foxnews.com/story/0,2933,407743,00.html;Internet; accessed December 14, 2011.

"Senator Larry Craig Resigns." *ABC News* [database online] available from http://abcnews.go.com/US/video?id=3549735; Internet; accessed December 5, 2011.

"Senior Official Linked to Call Girl Ring." *ABC News* [database online] available from http://abcnews.go.com/WNT/video?id=3096548; Internet; accessed July 16, 2013.

"Sixteen-Year-Old Who Worked as Capitol Hill Page Concerned About E-mail Exchange with Congressman." *ABC News* [database online] available from http://abcnews.go.com/blogs/headlines/2006/09/sixteenyearold_/; Internet; accessed July 16, 2013.

"The Enron Trials." *USA Today* [database online] available from http://usatoday30.usatoday.com/money/industries/energy/2006-01-27-charges_x.htm; Internet; accessed August 14, 2013.

"The Petraeus Scandal: What We Know." *CNN* [database online] available from http://www.cnn.com/2012/11/14/us/petraeus-what-we-know; Internet; accessed July 22, 2013.

"The Spoils of War: Billions over Baghdad." *Vanity Fair* [database online] available from http://www.vanityfair.com/politics/features/2007/10/iraq_billions200710; Internet; accessed August 26, 2013.

"This Week Injustice - Edward Schrock." *The Daily Show* [database online] available from http://www.thedailyshow.com/watch/thu-september-16-2004/this-week-injustice---edward-schrock; Internet; accessed July 20, 2013.

"Top Ten Political Scandals: U.S. Attorney Firings – 'Lawyergate.'" *Rolling Stone* [database online] available from http://www.rollingstone.com/politics/pictures/top-ten-political-scandals-20110926/lawyergate-0371211; Internet; accessed August 20, 2013.

"Torricelli Apologizes For Ethics "Lapses."" *CNN* [database online] available from http://archives.cnn.com/2002/ALLPOLITICS/07/30/torrecelli.ethics/index.html; Internet; accessed August 19, 2013.

"Torture Lawyer John Yoo Drafted Legal Rationale For NSA Spying, Protesters Targeting His Talk in SF Tonight." *San Francisco Bay Guardian Online* [database online] available from http://www.sfbg.com/politics/2013/07/10/torture-lawyer-john-yoo-drafted-legal-rationale-nsa-spying-protesters-targeting-; Internet; accessed August 14, 2013.

"Tracy Jackson: Alleged MISTRESS of Rep. Mark Souder." *Huffington Post* [database online] available from http://huffingtonpost.com/2010/05/18/tracy-jackson-mark-souder_n_580144.html; Internet; accessed December 12, 2011.

"Traficant Guilty of Bribery, Racketeering," *CNN* [database online] available from http://archives.cnn.com/2002/LAW/04/11/traficant.trial/; accessed August 20, 2013.

"Traficant Sentenced to Eight Years in Prison." *Fox News* [database online] available from http://www.foxnews.com/story/0,2933,59129,00.html; Internet; accessed August 20, 2013.

"Traficant To Run As Independent For Old House Seat." *Fox News* [database online] available from http://www.foxnews.com/politics/2010/05/03/ traficant-run-independent-old-house-seat/; Internet; accessed August 20, 2013.

"*United States v. Richard G. Renzi Et Al. (CR 08-0212-TUC-DCB)."* *Fox News* [database online] available from http://www.foxnews.com/projects/pdf/renzi_indictment.pdf; Internet; accessed August 15, 2013.

"*United States v. Richard G. Renzi, James W. Sandlin and Andrew Beardall."* *Fox News* [database online] available from http://www.foxnews.com/projects/pdf/renzi _indictment.pdf; Internet; accessed August 15, 2013.

"Update: John Edwards Love Child Scandal!" *National Enquirer* [database online] available from http://www.nationalenquirer.com/celebrity/update-john-edwards-love-child-scandal; Internet; accessed December 14, 2011.

"U.S. Congressman Joe Wilson Biography," Congressman Joe Wilson [database online] available from http://joewilson.house.gov/biography/default.aspx; Internet; accessed November 20, 2013.

"Virginia G.O.P. Congressman Pulls Out of Race." *The New York Times* [database online] available from http://www.nytimes.com/2004/08/31/politics/31virginia.html; Internet; accessed July 20, 2013.

"Vitter Admits Mistake and Takes Full Responsibility." *CNN* [database online] available from http://www.cnn.com/video/#/video/politics/2007/07/10/callebs.vitter.dc.madam.cnn; Internet; accessed July 16, 2013.

"Weiner Admits Tweet." *CNN News* [database online] available from http://www.cnn.com/video/#/video/bestoftv/2011/06/16/exp.sot.weiner.admits.tweet.cnn; Internet; accessed December 18, 2011.

"Weiner Resigns." *CNN News* [database online] available from http://www.cnn.com/video/#/video/bestoftv/2011/06/16/exp.weiner.resigns.com; Internet; accessed December 18, 2011.

"Weiner Featured in Exhibition in New York Museum of Sex." *ABC News* [database online] available from abcnewsgo.com/Health/wirestory/anthony-weiner-featured-museum-sex-exhibit-19603620#unsuphafeme; Internet; July 8, 2013.

"Weiner Should Drop Out, NYC Likely Dem Voters Tell Quinnipiac University Poll; Quinn Leads, With De Blasio, Thompson Tied For Second," Quinnipiac University [database online] available http://www.quinnipiac.edu/institutes-and-centers/polling-institute/new-york-city/release-detail?ReleaseID=1929; Internet; accessed July 31, 2013.

"Weinergate: Congressman Claims 'Facebook Hacked' As Lewd Photo Hits Twitter.'" *Big-Government.com* [database online] available from http://www.biggovernment.com/publius/2011/05/28/weinergate-congressman-claims-facebook-hacked-as-lewd-photo-hits-twitter; Internet; accessed December 18, 2011.

"White House 'Warned Over Iraq Claim.'" *BBC News* [database online] available from http://news.bbc.co.uk/2/hi/americas/3056626.stm; Internet; accessed August 27, 2013.

"Woman Behind Congressman Chris Lee's Craigslist Fallout Speaks Out." *ABC News* [database online] available from http://abcnews.go.com/Politics/congressman-christopher-lees-craigslist-woman-yesha-callahan-speaks/story?id=12890665#.UdwYWBafemE; Internet; accessed December 14, 2011.

"20 Forgotten Bush Scandals." *The Daily Beast* [database online] available from http:www.thedailybeast.com/articles/2009/01/06/forgotten-bush-scandals.html; Internet; accessed August 8, 2013.

FILMS

McCarthy, Cormac. *The Counselor.* Directed by Ridley Scott. Los Angeles: Twentieth Century Fox, 2013.